BETTY'S BARGE

Adventures Afloat
On the Canals of France

BILL HEZLEP

BETTY'S BARGE
Adventures Afloat On the Canals of France

Copyright © 2010 by William L. Hezlep

Front cover photo by Mac Greeley. Rear cover photo by Nancy Greeley. Title page photo by Kerry Berkstresser. Unless otherwise credited, all other photos are by the author. The four sketch maps were drawn by the author.

ISBN: 1453666648
EAN13: 9781453666647

Also by Bill Hezlep
Into the Land of Coconut Dreams
(ISBN: 1-4392-2933-3)

This book is dedicated to:

Betty Berkstresser: Aerospace Engineer, Pilot, World Traveler, Sailor, Navigator, Barge Captain—my cruising companion and best friend, without whom none of this would have happened.

Contents

St. Florentin
Flogny la Chapelle
Kilometers
50
Tanlay
Tonnerre
Chablis
Montbard
Châtel Censoir
CANAL
de BOURGOGNE
les Mines
CANAL
LATERAL
A LA
LOIRE
Beaulon
Pierrefitte sur Loire
Digoin

1. The Beginning

It was time for a change. Our original intent had been to spend a year on my thirty-six foot ketch *Walkabout*. But our year became two, grew to three, slipped into four, and then one morning we realized that we had been living aboard the boat and cruising non-stop for six full years[1]. During six great years of sailing between New England's gray, wave swept coast, the deep blue Caribbean trade wind seas, and the long flat, brown shores of the Gulf of Mexico, thousands of miles had passed under *Walkabout's* keel; without crossing an ocean, sailing to Europe or going around the world–just endless, timeless coastal and island cruising. Now we were back on the Chesapeake Bay, where it all started, restless, ready to move on to a new adventure. If we stayed on the boat, unless we went back to the Caribbean or sailed off to somewhere else, we would end up cruising north in the spring and south in the fall following the seasonal maritime snowbird migration route between New England, the Chesapeake Bay, Miami, the Florida Keys, and The Bahamas–mostly motoring down the Atlantic Intracoastal Waterway, a power boat with two masts and four sails.

Change...where, when and how? We agreed that where was Europe and when was soon, but the how part? A lot of brain cells grew old and feeble thinking about it, and a huge number of words were exchanged talking about it. Betty and I were decent sailors, we'd sailed the Atlantic from Canada to

---

1 For the story of that cruise, see "Into the Land of Coconut Dreams", ISBN: 1-4392-2933-3

Trinidad. Why not just sail *Walkabout* to Europe? We knew
a number of people who had made the Atlantic crossing and,
in a couple of cases...if they could do it, well...we could too.
But–there is always one or two–we once spent a two and a half
day year in near gale conditions and our enthusiasm for small
boat sailing in that sort of weather became and has remained
limited, and I had been through a Typhoon and a northern
Pacific winter storm as crew aboard a very large haze gray
ship and knew exactly how the ocean looks when old King
Neptune is seriously irritated. Shipping *Walkabout* to Europe,
either as deck cargo on a freighter or on one of the dedicated
yacht carriers, was considered. However we would then have
been in Europe aboard a deep draft, two masted, sailboat with
electrical and propane systems that would have to be adapted
to European standards and most of what we wanted to see
was inland and not along the coast. In addition, the cost of
shipping the sailboat was daunting, as, we believed, were the
problems and costs associated with the VAT (the Value Added
Tax) on a boat that the European Union would consider an
imported boat. Except for the sheer adventure of doing it, taking *Walkabout* to Europe didn't make a lot of sense.

During August and the first half of September 1999,
we put *Walkabout* on the hard (up on dry land) in Herrington Harbour North[2] (HHN), a boatyard in Maryland,
for six weeks to do some maintenance. While *Walkabout*
was drying out Betty decided we needed a break from life
on a sailboat, and arranged a boater's vacation. More or less
on the spur of the moment she booked a cruise on a hotel
barge in France; a trip down the Canal lateral a la Garonne

---

2 The Herrington Harbour North marina/boatyard in Tracy's Landing Maryland,
a very good boatyard on the Chesapeake Bay twenty miles south of Annapolis, that
had been our starting point and was still our home base.

from near Toulouse to Castets en Dorthe, where the canal enters the Garonne River.

We flew to Paris on August nineteenth, spent several days sightseeing and eating well—including an excellent dinner at "Willi's Wine Bar" (13 Rue des Petits-Champs), the first of many we would eat in that fine establishment—took the TGV (the high speed train) to Toulouse, where we boarded the *Rosa*, our floating hotel. The week on the *Rosa* was wonderful. Traveling down the Canal Lateral a la Garonne we passed through the heart of the ancient Kingdom of Aquitaine, the domain of Queen Eleanor of Aquitaine who married King Henry II, of England, a marriage which eventually helped cause the one hundred years war, and the attempts by the Plantagenet's of England to assert their sovereignty over most, if not all, of France. The crew of the *Rosa* did their best to educate our minds and palettes in the history, culture, foods, wines and cheeses of southwestern France. Particularly the cheeses, the cheeses were an epiphany; at the age of fifty-six I discovered good cheese. The *Rosa* was a thirty-six meter (one hundred seventeen feet) long former Dutch cargo carrier that had been converted into a comfortable small hotel with accommodations for a crew of three—a captain/chef (a very good cook), an engineer/deck hand and a stewardess/maid—and four double guest cabins, each with an en-suite bath. The canal was interesting and enjoyable, with a lot to see and do, and during the cruise we saw a number of other converted cargo barges, a few working freight barges and a lot of yachts and hire-boats. Some of the converted barges were, like the *Rosa*, small hotels, but many of the smaller ones were privately owned cruising homes. Leaving the *Rosa* at Castets en Dorthe, we went to Bordeaux for two days for a little wine tasting before returning to Paris, the U.S., Herrington Harbour North, *Walkabout*, and the sublime joys of sanding and painting the bottom of a fiberglass boat.

Maintenance done, *Walkabout* launched, we motored out onto the Chesapeake Bay and joined the stream of southbound snowbird cruisers migrating to somewhere warm, chugging down the Atlantic Intracoastal Waterway, a motorboat with two masts and four sails, fulfilling our premonition. But, on this trip south—down the Chesapeake, through the huge port of Hampton Roads, past the sprawling Norfolk Naval Base, through the historic Dismal Swamp Canal, through the great sounds and rivers of North Carolina, past Beaufort, Myrtle Beach, Georgetown, Charleston and Savannah, through the wild and lovely marshes of South Carolina and Georgia, past all the natural wonders and historic sites of the United States' eastern seaboard—all we talked about was our trip on the *Rosa*, the canals of Europe and canal boats and barges.

Down where the winters are warm, at Marathon in the Florida Keys, we parked *Walkabout* at Burdines Waterfront for December and January. The day after Christmas, Betty bought a copy of the Sunday Miami Herald, and that night while reading the travel section she saw an American Airlines ad offering deep last minute discounts on flight, hotel and show packages for people attending the London Boat Show. The package included round-trip airfare, Miami to London (via New York), six nights in a good hotel near the boat show, with full breakfast, and a one week boat show pass for each of us. It was much too good an offer to pass-up; we could learn a lot about canals and canal boating at the boat show and see London too. January eleventh the Keys Shuttle took us to Miami for the flight to New York and on to London. In London, we checked into our hotel and hustled off to Earls Court and the London Boat Show.

4

At the international guests reception room, we presented our passports, were welcomed to London and the show, and were handed our passes and two tickets good for free pints of Guinness at something called the "Long Bar."

I had thought we'd pick up our show passes, go back to the hotel, shower, get lunch in a pub, relax and adjust to the time change. But we were at Earls Court, so why not take just a little peek? And, those free pints of Guinness were calling. We left at the closing bell, exhausted, and were back minutes after the doors opened the next morning. That London Boat Show was the largest, and by far the best, boat show either of us had ever been to. It was a true international show, people from all over Europe, the United States, Canada, Australia, New Zealand, Japan, and any number of other countries were there. All of the European boat builders and marine equipment manufacturers were there, as were many firms from the United States, Canada, and Australia, among others. Supposedly this was the last year that the London boat show would be held at Earls Court, indoors and in the center city; the show was to move to a larger venue outside the city. All of the people at the show—the officials running it, the boat builders, the equipment vendors, and the attendees—seemed to be trying hard to ensure that this show, the last Earls Court show, was a memorable event and for us, it definitely was. Without London the show would still have been a fabulous event and the trip a worthwhile and wonderful experience, but it would have been just another boat show, albeit a really big one. London, one of the world's greatest and most historic cities, was the desert, the frosting on the cake.

Our boat show was devoted, mostly, to research: looking at canal boats, meeting canal boat builders and brokers, learning about hire-boats, and collecting literature and information on everything from costs to the weather and boating seasons, legal requirements, and possible restrictions on canal boat ownership and operation by United States citizens. We bought a dozen books that looked as though they might have interesting information in them along with a copy of every English language magazine that looked like it might be a canal, barging or inland boating magazine. Then, for good measure, we bought a few that were in French, even though neither of us could read them.

One of the boats afloat in the center hall pool was a seriously long narrow boat built of steel by Fox Narrow Boats[3]. Despite its' length, I think fifty-sixty feet, and narrow beam it was not unattractive. On previous trips to the U.K., we had seen narrow boats but had never been aboard one. So we boarded, walked through and found a comfortable saloon forward, followed by a full galley (kitchen), two heads (bath rooms) and three double cabins—although I could not visualize where the fore and aft passageway would be if the berths had been pulled out to full sleeping width (pardon me, I'm just crawling across, need to get to the head you know). Because of the boats narrow beam I had thought that it might be a bit unstable, with a tendency to roll like a log in a pond, but, with straight sides and a flat bottom, it seemed fine, even with a crowd of people aboard it sat firm in the water. A Fox representative spent several hours over the days that we attended the show talking to us about canal boating in the UK, the different types of boats, cruising areas, training and the Royal Yachting Associations testing and certification program, costs (both ownership and hire) and the possibility of a full season charter. I should have bought that man a pint or two at the Long Bar.

---

3 Today (2009): Fox Narrow Boats, Cambridgeshire, (U.K.) +44 (0) 1345-652770, www.foxboats.co.uk.

The center court pool also held a gorgeous Oyster sloop (we were sailors, life is not all research); mast up and fully rigged. I thought it would be great to go aboard and have a good look, so I walked to the gangway and—a velvet rope attended by an extremely well dressed and well groomed gentleman holding a clipboard barred further progress.

> The Gentleman (in a smooth and sophisticated voice): "May I be of assistance sir?"
>
> Me: "May I board and look at the boat?"
>
> The Gentleman (raising the clipboard): "and your name sir?"
>
> Me (thinking he was going to write down my name): "My name is...and I'm from the U.S." (He probably knew that already).
>
> The Gentleman (looking at the clipboard): "I'm sorry sir, but you do not seem to be on today's appointment list, perhaps you have mistaken the date of your appointment?"

OK, end of that conversation, thus relegated to the status of common boater; although I was wearing decent khaki slacks, new deck shoes and socks, I retreated to a boat a bit further down the nautical feeding chain. The Oyster was gorgeous and three years later I boarded a very similar Oyster at the Annapolis boat show...no problem, just get in line with all the other scruffy common boaters and wait for my turn.

Along one edge of the center hall floor was a row of booths occupied by official, quasi-official, and volunteer organizations in some way involved with boating: the Royal Life Saving Service, the Hydrographic Office, the Meteorological Service, the Royal Yachting Association (RYA), etc.

One of the booths belonged to the Dutch Barge Association (DBA)[4]. The DBA seemed to be primarily an organization for owners and wannabe owners of old, generally large, converted Dutch cargo barges or fairly good sized new boats built to resemble Dutch barges. At that point owning a large old barge, or even a large new barge, didn't really seem to be what we had in mind, but we had an interesting and enjoyable twenty minute conversation with one of the members, accepted a membership application form, and picked up a lot of flyers, brochures and other literature. One of the flyers was Tam and Di Murrells.[5] The Murrells—ocean, coastal and inland Master Mariners and RYA Training Instructors—taught, and still teach, a barge driving and handling course in France. The course was taught aboard their twenty-four meter converted Dutch barge *Friesland* and was a five day cruise and learn course aimed at people who were buying large, converted, Dutch barges.

From the DBA, we worked our way, via the Guinness Long Bar (a daily stop), to the area where the canal hire-boat companies had set up shop and spent some time talking to two, Crown Blue Lines[6] and Locaboat Plaisance.[7] On the European canals and rivers, the hire-boat companies operate exactly the way that the sailing charter companies in the Caribbean and

---

4 The Dutch Barge Association is now (2010) called "DBA the Barge Association", on the internet http://www.barges.org, for information e-mail info@barges.org, or call (U.K.) +44 (0) 70000-227434

5 The Murrells still (in 2010) conduct five day training courses for new and future barge drivers; for information call +44 (0) 208 755-1554 (U.K.), or go to http://www.bargehandling.org. Dollar for Pound or Euro, the Murrell's course is, in my opinion, the best introduction to the techniques of, and legal requirements for, operating a large motor barge in Europe. I also think the Murrell's course is one of the best boating courses available anywhere.

6 Current (in 2010) internet address http://www.crownblueline.com

7 Current (in 2010) internet address http://www.locaboat.com

elsewhere operate. You rent (hire or charter) a boat for a specific, defined period, generally one to three weeks, for an out and back trip from one of the companies bases, or for a one way trip between two of the companies bases. In France a boat could be chartered for up to four weeks "sans permis", that is with no boat license, operators permit, or certification of any sort. The hire-boat companies had blanket permits for the canals and areas served by each of their bases and an instructor at each base was supposed to make sure that the charterer knew how to turn on the motor, which end of the boat was the front end and, maybe, a few other useful things. In the U.K. to hire a canal boat and drive it yourself, even if the charter was limited to one week and one canal, a Royal Yachting Association (RYA) Inland Helmsman Certification was mandatory. Obtaining the RYA certificate required a two to three day course involving classroom and practical (on the water and aboard the boat) elements followed by a written test.[8] One to three week charters were the norm, a seasonal charter, at rational cost, was not an option with any of the hire companies. They would gladly rent a boat for multiple weeks at the standard per week cost, but in 2000 they were close to fully booked and had no need to offer extended leases or discounts. Arranging a private, full season, charter also seemed to be out of the question because of operator certification requirements, insurance restrictions, and what seemed to be a host of other nebulous legalities.

The boat show closed the evening of January sixteenth. On the morning of the eighteenth we checked out of our

8 The course includes boat safety, inland navigation rules, steering and boat handling, line handling, locks, docking, bridges, collision avoidance, etc. If you did not hold the Inland Helmsman Certification, some of the hire companies in the U.K. offered the full course and the test at added expense. Fox Narrow Boats taught the course, over a two day weekend, at their base for £120 per person, if you were hiring one of their boats.

hotel, took the train to Heathrow and returned to the real world of New York, the United States, the Florida Keys and a sailboat–minds and memories overloaded and still trying to digest, everything seen, heard and learned. The entire week in London was not spent at the boat show. We went on three "London Walks", guided walking tours, two—in different parts of the city—were evening pub-crawls, visited the Tower of London and St. Katherine's Dock, took a boat tour of the Thames, visited the (Clipper Ship) *Cutty Sark* and toured the Greenwich Observatory. An American boat named *Glen Lyon* that we knew from the Caribbean was in one of the slips at St. Katherine's dock, but no one was onboard.

The flight back was dreadful. It was held for a connecting flight so was late leaving, and completely full. One of the restrooms was out of order and locked. American Airlines had not put sufficient meals aboard for the number of people crammed aboard and the poor flight attendants had to walk the isles asking for volunteers willing to forgo an in-flight meal or two (possibly a few, or half a dozen, extra little bottles of booze or a handful of chocolate bars, or both?). A group of young, collage-age, passengers, apparently returning from one of those "if its' Monday, this must be Bulgaria" tours, were sick. They hacked, coughed, wheezed, gasped and snorted all the way across the Atlantic, when they weren't being sick and stinking up the operating restrooms. The whole group was seated near us and I was sure that we had no hope of escaping whatever they had. Then, our flight was diverted to Chicago, when we landed American Airlines cheerfully told us that they had booked us on a flight to Miami at zero dark thirty the next morning and put us, and a few other luckless people, in a van and sent us off to a wretched airport fringe motel where we were fed a tasteless micro-waved dinner, took a shower and got four hours of semi-sleep before the wakeup call to return to the airport. Two days later we both had full scale cases, in all its' miserable glory, of whatever the kids on the flight from London had been passing around.

2. Education

From Marathon we moved up to Biscayne Bay and Miami before crossing to The Bahamas where research into canal boating in Europe continued: reading the mound of books, magazines and literature collected at the London Boat Show, even the French ones (with a lot of help from a new French-English dictionary), and searching the internet wherever and whenever it was available, looking at boats and barges that were offered for sale. It was clear that more on-site research was necessary–translation: a trip to France and another barge trip sounded like fun. So Betty contacted Tam and Di Murrell and booked a five day course aboard the *Friesland*. Even if we didn't plan to buy a large barge, the course would be fun and we would get our RYA Inland Helmsman Certification and take the test for the "International Certificate of Competence (ICC)".

Back in the United States and headed up the ICW, Betty continued her internet research and decided that since we were going to France for the Murrell's barge driving course anyway, a hire-boat trip on one of the French canals and visits to several boat and barge brokers, would be worthwhile. The traditional look of Locaboat Plaisance's Penichettes appealed to us and Locaboat offered one week, one way, trips on the Yonne River and Nivernais Canal from Joigny to Chitry les Mines. Joigny was not far from Tours sur Marne on the Canal Lateral a la Marne, where our learn to drive a barge course would begin and end and Chitry les Mines was not too far from the Burgundy wine country and was in the general direction of the Saone River towns of St. Jean de Losne and

St. Symphorien sur Saone, both of which had canal boat and barge brokers that we wanted to visit. This was beginning to sound like a plan.

The Locaboat brochure from the London Boat show, almost a magazine, included the contact information for Locaboat's agent in the United States. Our barge driving course would run from the afternoon of September sixth to midday September tenth, so Betty called Locaboat's agent and inquired about a one way trip from Joigny to Chitry les Mines timed to follow the Murrell's course. Five days later we had a fax confirming a Nivernais canal trip, from Chitry les Mines to Joigny, September sixteenth to the twenty-third—backwards and not exactly a follow on to the barge course. The Locaboat agent was also, probably primarily, a general travel agent and she was able to get us a good round-trip flight from New York to Paris, leaving the evening of September fourth and returning the twenty-seventh. September was going to be busy, enjoyable and expensive.

Between arriving at HHN and leaving for France, except for a short sail to Baltimore, boatyard work was the order of the day: sand, paint, polish, varnish and renew some rigging. During the trip to Baltimore, at Maryland Nautical Supply, I found and bought the French waterway cruising guides for the Loire and the Nivernais Region and for Champagne. At the end of August *Walkabout* went on the hard in the boatyard, and we went to my sister's in Philadelphia, for a few days before taking the train to Kennedy airport for the overnight flight to Paris. Arriving at Roissy-Charles de Gaulle airport half awake and a little disorganized, we had one of those strange experiences that just happen if you travel enough. Our flight arrived at a remote gate, walking through the terminal to Customs and Immigration we got a bit confused, made a wrong turn, walked down a long hallway, opened the door at the end and found ourselves outside, on the edge of the ground transportation area. No blaring alarm bells, no tourist card, no Customs or Immigration checks, no passport stamp. Outside and our exit door was a one way door—welcome to France. We took the train to the Gare de l'Est and on to Epernay, arriving in time for lunch.

The afternoon was spent touring the Moet-Chandon Champagne Caves (founded in 1743) and walking through the older part of town looking at the shops and the beautiful homes of some of the wine merchants. I was surprised at how little remained from Epernay's long history. The town dates to at least Roman times, but it sits in the Franco-German Cultural and the Catholic-Protestant Religious frontier zones and has suffered in the frequent wars. Epernay has been rebuilt three times in the last one hundred and fifty years. The town was badly damaged during the Franco-Prussian War, essentially destroyed during World War One and suffered heavy damage during World War Two, but the champagne caves under the town survived nicely. That night we stayed at the "Les Berceaux",[9] an excellent small hotel with a Michelin one star restaurant—well deserved. The next day we were not due in Tours sur Marne to meet Tam and Di Murrell and the couple who would be our fellow students until 4:00 p.m.—plenty of time to tour, and do a little tasting at the Mercier Champagne caves (founded in 1858) and enjoy another good lunch, before catching a taxi for the ten kilometer ride through the beautiful early fall county side of Champagne.

The Murrells welcomed us aboard the *Friesland*, introduced us to George and Maggie Pringle, our fellow students,

---

9 Les Berceaux; phone 03 26 55 28 84, www.lesberceaux.com

gave us a tour of the *Friesland* and popped the cork on a bottle of fine champagne. The *Friesland*'s bilge, below the floor boards, was a well stocked wine cellar and that night at dinner it became very clear that Di was a true gourmet cook; our learn to drive a barge course was going to be a great learning experience.

The *Friesland*, the Murrell's class room and part time home afloat—and our hotel for the duration of our course—was a twenty-four meter (seventy-eight foot) long Dutch "Luxemotor" style self-propelled motor barge. A former commercial cargo carrier built in 1922 and taken out of commercial service in 1987, the *Friesland* had been converted into a very well equipped private canal cruiser. The older Dutch cargo barges frequently converted to hotel barges and privately owned canal cruisers come in a bewildering variety of types ranging from the Aak and the Tjalk, the traditional lee board sailing barges of classic Dutch maritime art, through the Beurtschip, Hagenaar, Klipper, Katwijker, Skutsje, and a bunch more[10], to the Luxemotor. Luxemotors, true motor barges designed for diesel engines, were built between WWI and WWII. Built at first of riveted iron and later of steel, they ranged from fifteen to well over thirty meters in length, depending on intended use. Luxemotors, with their straight stems (bows), cruiser sterns and pronounced sheer line (the curve of the hull between bow and stern) are visually the most attractive of the motor barges, and that visual appeal combined with the fact that as pure motor barges they handle well under power, has made them possibly the most popular barge type for conversion.

---

10 For a detailed discussion of Dutch barge types; see, The Barge Buyer's Handbook, DBA Publications, 2001

Friesland leaving a lock

Class began immediately following an early breakfast the
morning after our arrival. On the water exercises were conducted between Damery on the Marne River and a turning basin
(basin de virement) at Port de Vaudemange on the Canal de
l'Aaisne a la Marne with Tours sur Marne, on the Canal lateral
a la Marne, being the mid-point. This gave us a learning area
of approximately twenty- four linear kilometers that included
the meeting of two canals, the transition from a canal to a
river, thirteen locks and a lot of bridges of various types; all of
the more common situations that would be encountered while
cruising the European waterways. Each day we got underway
after an early breakfast and tied up for lunch. After lunch we
again got underway and tied up just before dinner. During the
morning and afternoon on-the-water learning periods we students took turns driving and line handling–as couples, George
and Maggie worked together, Betty and I worked together–under the very watchful eyes of our instructors. The couple not

driving and line handling, observed from the wheelhouse and tried to absorb the running commentary from the instructor on duty there. During meals we reviewed the situations that had occurred during the day and talked about the inland waterways and general barge stuff.

Friesland was fitted with a powerful bow-thruster;[11] but the students were not permitted to touch it. Many, perhaps most, converted barges don't have bow-thrusters and our instructors wanted us to learn to handle a barge without one. In the Marne River, at Cumieres, Betty was on the wheel and had to turn around in the strong river current. At the bottom of the turn, when the barge didn't seem to be coming around, she very briefly touched the forbidden thruster and Tam promptly slapped her hand. Then he made her turn the barge around a second time. Luckily I didn't have to do it.

Late afternoon, Saturday, September ninth, we were back at Tours sur Marne for a final excellent dinner and a pleasant evening of good wine and good conversation. The next morning Betty, George, Maggie and I took our tests and completed any necessary paperwork, then, after a light lunch and a final glass of wine aboard *Friesland*, it was time to say good-by to Tam and Di Murrell and be on our way. Both of us thought that the Murrell's course was worth every dime, pence, franc and minute; it was an excellent investment. We learned a lot about canals, rivers, locks and boating on the European inland waterways and even though we had been boating for many years—the last six full time—we learned some new and/or improved boat handling tricks and techniques, things that applied to our sailboat equally as much as they did to a canal

---

11 A bow-thruster is a motor and propeller mounted sideways in the bow of a boat and used to push the bow left or right while maneuvering in tight spaces. Thrusters can also be stern mounted.

boat or barge. During the course we also, inevitably, learned a lot about barges, big barges, converted cargo barges, and our thoughts regarding what sort of canal boat we wanted became rather fluid and we found ourselves looking critically and speculatively at the barges we saw.

A short train ride took us to the ancient city of Reims where we visited the Cathedral of Notre-Dame de Reims and paid a much too brief visit to the Tau Palace, arriving barely thirty minutes before it closed. Reims, originally the capital of the Remi tribe of Gauls, is one of the key sites in the history of France. The Cathedral is France's equivalent to England's Westminster Abby and twenty five Kings, beginning in 498 with Clovis King of the Franks, were anointed and crowned here. Unfortunately, we missed all the champagne houses: Pommery, Taittinger, Mumm, Krug, Heidsieck(s), etc. and their caves and tasting rooms (a good reason for a return visit). We spent the night at a tourist hotel a few blocks from the Cathedral, suffered through an unfortunate dinner at a nearby bistro, and took an early morning train to Dijon. If a bistro is smack in the middle of a city's tourist area, has a menu printed in six languages and is full of foreign tourists with children...well, maybe you'd get a better meal somewhere else.

Arriving in Dijon at 8:00 a.m. with no hotel reservation, we walked out of the train station and down the hotel lined Avenue Marechal Foch toward the city center, and inquired about a room at the modern looking Hotel Jura, a Tulip Inn.[12] Despite the early hour there was no problem with a room. Our first appointment with a canal boat/barge broker

---

12 The Golden Tulip Hotels and the Tulip Inns, a Europe wide chain, that like the Ibis Hotels, are almost always clean, reasonably priced and accommodating. In all of our trips to France, we have never made hotel reservations in advance and we have always been able to find something; although we have stayed in a few rather odd places.

was the next afternoon, in the nearby town of St. Jean de Losne. So, once checked in and free of our luggage, it was time for breakfast at a cafe and a day touring Dijon. Most of the morning was spent visiting the Palace of the Dukes of Burgundy and the Fine Arts Museum (Musee de Beaux Arts) which had a fascinating collection of artifacts from the kitchens of the Ducal Palace as well as a fine collection of early Renaissance paintings. The afternoon was spent walking the older parts of the city, looking in the shop windows and at the lovely old half-timber buildings, and visiting the Musee de la Vie bourguignonne (Museum of Life in Burgundy), where the most interesting exhibit was a life-size re-creation of part of an 1850s city street. The museum was followed by several, possibly more than two, samples of Burgundian culture at Le Caveau de la Porte Guillaume, in the Hotel du Nord, an excellent wine bar devoted to the wines of Burgundy. And the day ended with a late and very good dinner, accompanied by more excellent Burgundian culture, at a restaurant recommended by our hotel's receptionist–Le Gril Laure (8, place Saint Benigne): good food, good wine, good atmosphere and reasonable cost. In the morning, before catching the train, there was time for a leisurely cafe breakfast and a walk down to the Port of Dijon where several hotel barges were docked, and one, a converted Luxemotor, was just leaving, headed south down the Canal de Bourgogne to St. Jean de Losne and the Saone River. I wished that we were making the trip by barge and not by train.

The train station in St. Jean de Losne is not in St. Jean de Losne. It's a healthy walk from town or pretty much anywhere, particularly if you are burdened with a bunch of stuff. Betty and I travel light, but this trip was nearly four weeks long and we had, for us, a lot of stuff. We had been advised to take a taxi to our hotel and had been told that the station attendant would call one for us. But, when we arrived, except for a plump well fed cat, we seemed to be the only living, breathing life forms in the station: empty arrival platform, small empty waiting room, closed ticket office, locked restrooms. Thank god I had gone on the train, or the tracks, sort of, whatever, standing in the men's looking down through the facility provided a clear and unobstructed view of the cross ties clicking by under the train. Then Betty heard a faint sound from the closed ticket office. I tried knocking on the window. No response, nothing. Knock again, dead silence. Eventually repeated banging brought a really grumpy old codger to the window who, when he finally understood that all we wanted was a taxi, called the town taxi for us. The taxi, a white van driven by a lady of a certain age, finally arrived and conveyed us to the Auberge de la Marine.[13] Where, a rare occurrence for us, we had reservations. The auberge is technically in the village of Losne, on the south bank of the Saone River, but it is right at the Losne end of the Saone River Bridge and an easy walk to St. Jean de Losne and H_2O, the barge and boat broker we were to visit that afternoon.

After lunch at the Auberge, we walked across the Saone River Bridge into St. Jean de Losne and through the main part of town to the port and the offices of H_2O. H_2Os' size and range of services surprised me. They had been in the canal boat/ barge business for almost twenty years and they were a complete one-stop-shop. In addition to brokering canal boats and barges, they: handled insurance and French vessel registration, operated the largest inland waterways marina in France, had a

13 Hotel-Restaurant Auberge de la Marine, 21170 St. Jean de Losne, France. Phone: 03 80 27 03 27

well stocked chandlery[14] with a used equipment re-sale section, operated maintenance and repair shops that could do everything from minor repairs to a complete barge conversion, and they seemed to be agents for all of the hire-boat companies. Our appointment was with Catherine Rault who handled most of the second hand barge and boat sales at H_2O. Catherine first showed us around the office and chandlery, then gave us a brief view of the marina and the workshops beyond, and introduced us to Charles Gerard, the principal owner. She then spent awhile talking to us about what we had in mind, what type of boat we were interested in, where did we plan to cruise and, delicately, what our budget was. We then looked through H_2O's used boat and barge listing sheets, Catherine handed us the keys to three that interested us, walked us out to the door, pointed out where they were on the docks, and we were on our own.

That afternoon we walked all of the docks in H_2O's marina and looked at eight or nine boats and small barges. When we had looked at the first three we returned to the office, Catherine suggested three more, handed us a new set of keys and off we went. No one accompanied us; no one questioned us or tried to assist us by pointing out the various features of each vessel. It was educate yourself, refine your dreams and sell yourself a boat. In the late afternoon, just before the office closed, we met with Catherine and arranged to return the next morning. On our way back to the Auberge de la Marine, and an excellent dinner, we stopped for an aperitif at a bistro called "L'Amiral"[15] that commanded a nice view over the Saone River. It had been a long day and we had seen a lot

14 A chandlery is a store that sells marine equipment and supplies, a chandler is the person who manages, or runs, a chandlery. The terms are still commonly used in Europe, but not in the U.S.
15 Bistro L'Amiral, 4 Place de la Deliberation, 21170 St. Jean de Losne, France. Phone: 03 80 29 08 06

of boats—converted barges, canal cruisers and former hire-boats—and it was clear that we were paying the most attention to the smaller converted barges.

In the morning, not due at H_2O for more boat looking until 10:00 a.m., there was time for a long exploratory walk around the compact center of St. Jean de Losne–the smallest village in land area in France[16]. Formerly a walled, fortified, military strong point[17], much of the center of town, inside the line of the old walls, is intact with its winding medieval street plan and many houses dating to the fifteenth, sixteenth and seventeenth centuries. Unfortunately, the fortifications were removed in the early years of the nineteenth century, the ancient walls, towers and bastions providing much of the stone used to build the locks and stabilize the banks of the Canal de Bourgogne between the Saone River at St. Jean de Losne and the port of Dijon. The line of the old walls is still evident, revealed by the street names: Allee du Bastion des Chamilles, Rue des Ramparts, Rue du Bastion de Vauxhall, Rue du Chateau, Place des Ramparts, etc. There is a lovely old church, L'eglise St. Jean Baptiste, supposedly one of the most beautiful in France, parts of the church date to the thirteenth century and possibly earlier. There are several good patisseries and boulangeries, a well stocked hardware store, an excellent supermarket, the Supermarche Casino[18], and a large news stand-book store, the "Maison de la Presse". The Maison de la

---

16 St. Jean de Losne has just 36 hectares (.36 square kilometers) of land, and 20 hectares of water.

17 There has been a town or settlement in the area since before the coming of Rome. The Roman military highway from Lyon to Dijon (Roman Castrum Divionenes) and on to Mainz, passed close to the site of St. Jean de Losne and north of the town a long stretch of the old Roman road is still visible.

18 The Casino Supermarkets (Supermarche Casino) are a chain found throughout France; generally they are very good, and some are huge.

Presse carried an astonishing range of newspapers from all over Europe and beyond: the major French and German papers, an Italian paper and one from Spain, the English language edition of the International Herald Tribune, the London Times, the European edition of USA Today, a paper from Turkey, a Turkish edition of a German paper, and an Arabic edition of a French paper. I wondered what the chances were of finding a French daily newspaper, let alone a Turkish one, in a small town on the Ohio River.

Our walk around town took so long that a stop at a cafe for a cafe au lait and, for one of us; a strawberry tart became necessary, which made us late for boat looking at H_2O. However, we still managed to see another half dozen boats and pay second visits to several seen the day before. By the end of the day I was having trouble keeping the boats straight, but we were coming to the conclusion that what we wanted was a barge, a real one, a converted cargo barge, and preferably a Luxemotor.

Our appointment on Thursday was with Bourgogne Marine, a barge broker in St. Symphorien sur Saone, a very small town on the east bank of the Saone four kilometers upstream from St. Jean de Losne, at the junction of the Canal du Rhone au Rhin with the Saone River. The Canal du Rhone au Rhin, which connects the Rhine River to the Saone/Rhone system, is one of the five canal routes between northern Europe and the Mediterranean Sea. All five of the routes connect to the Saone River like a right hand laid on the map of France, thumb to the west. The Saone flows into the Rhone at Lyon and the Rhone reaches the Mediterranean below Arles and between the major seaport of Marseille and the smaller ports west of Marseille. One route, the Canal du Centre—the thumb—meets the Saone at Chalon sur Saone and the other four routes, the Canal de Bourgogne, the Canal de la Marne a la Saone, the Canal des Vosges/

Canal de l'Est, and the Canal du Rhone au Rhin—the fingers—join the Saone near St. Jean de Losne. This central position, the gateway to four of the five canal routes south, explains the little towns outsized importance in the French, and European, inland waterway system and the concentration of boats, barges and marine businesses in the town.

The visit to Bourgogne Marine was something of a disappointment. Our appointment was for 10 a.m. and Betty had called the day before and re-confirmed; but, when we arrived, the one man who appeared to be working in the place seemed surprised to see us. He turned out to be an Englishman who lived on, and was rebuilding, one of the barges at Bourgogne Marine and supported himself by working on other peoples barges. Although there were a lot of barges at Bourgogne Marine, he was able to show us only one, a large and beautifully equipped converted Dutch barge that belonged to an American couple who had left it to be sold. It was lovely, but the asking price was several multiples of our wildest dreams. However, the morning was not a complete waste. Our lone Englishman was friendly and talkative, knew a lot about barges and Dutch barge conversions, and was willing to pass on what he knew...every single bit of it. He walked us around Bourgogne Marine's two mooring basins and pointed out different types of barges and told us what, in his opinion, the strengths and weaknesses of each type were. He also showed us his barge, which he had purchased as a semi-derelict hulk in the Netherlands, completely gutted and largely rebuild.

The four kilometer walk from Bourgogne Marine back to St. Jean de Losne along the levee path (the old barge tow path) on the east side of the Saone was pleasant and pretty.

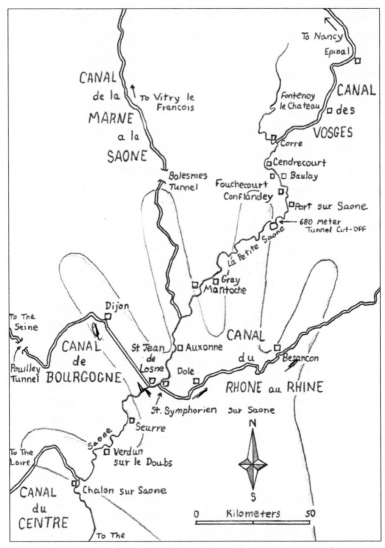

Map 1. Like the fingers of a hand laid on the map of France

Several groups of fishermen had set up shop along the river bank, and there were kids on bicycles and families out for a walk in the clean, crisp, early fall air. There was a lot of boat traffic on the river: a hotel barge headed up-stream, two heavily loaded French Freycinet peniches[19] and a sailboat[20] with its mast lashed on deck headed down-stream, and a flock of hire-boats going in both directions. Back in St. Jean de Losne, lunch was at L'Amiral, which was rapidly becoming our favorite place, even though we had tried very few of the town's restaurants. L'Amiral was a friendly, happy sort of place with a nice atmosphere, reasonable prices, reliable food, and a dog and two cats that politely ignored each other—unless someone was sneaking food to them under the table, in which case they were more than willing to share.

Friday morning was spent at H_2O looking at barges; mostly second or third looks at previously visited barges. Then, after yet another lunch at L'Amiral, it was time to leave St. Jean de Losne and return to Dijon. Our week long trip on a Locaboat Plaisance hire-boat was to begin the next afternoon at Chitry les Mines on the Canal du Nivernais and bus and train schedules dictated a night in Dijon. Neither of us considered that a hardship.

---

19 In 1879, in an attempt to improve the French canal system, the Prime Minister, Charles de Freycinet, had a law passed that standardized the size of the locks on French canals; the gabarit Freycinet (Freycinet gauge) specified that lock chambers should be thirty nine meters long, five and two tenths meters wide and have a depth of water of two and two tenths meters. Many of the older French canals were up-dated to the Freycinet standard and peniches (barges) were quickly built to the maximum size that would fit into the new locks. These barges, the classic bluff bowed French cargo barges still frequently seen on the European inland waterways, became known as Freycinet peniches.

20 The French canal system, from the English Channel ports and the Belgian and German borders to the Mediterranean Sea, is the European equivalent to the Atlantic Intracoastal Waterway in the United States. "Snowbird" yachts moving south in the fall and north in the spring transit the canals, a shorter, safer and pleasanter route than the long and often rough open ocean route across the Bay of Biscay and around Spain.

From Dijon we took a train to Auxerre and transferred to the Yonne Valley local which, very slowly, wound its way south, up the valley to Corbigny. It was another beautiful early fall day and the local, for most of the trip, closely followed the Yonne River and the Canal du Nivernais, stopping at every single marginally significant inhabited place along the way. The trip was an interesting preview of the coming cruise down the canal: brief passing snapshots of picturesque old canal side towns, the canal and its locks, bridges and quays, restaurants, cafes, and the surprisingly rugged and wooded countryside. Our printed train and bus schedule indicated that we'd have an hour and a half wait in Corbigny for the bus to Chitry les Mines, enough time for lunch. The bus part of the schedule was fiction. There was a bus waiting and ready to go when the train arrived. In France the trains, particularly the TGVs, were very punctual; unless one the numerous unions in some way connected to the rail system happened to be on strike, then all bets were off. But out in the more rural parts of France, buses seemed to operate on a schedule that suited local desires and needs—never mind the printed fantasies distributed by the tourist offices. The ride to Chitry les Mines was much shorter than it looked on our map, all of three kilometers, and the bus dropped us right at the Locaboat Plaisance base.

Locaboat had told us to arrive at the base between 3:00 and 6:00 p.m.; by which time our boat would be cleaned, refueled, checked out and ready. It was only 1:00...a bit early. Ted Johnson, an affable, easy going Englishman who was the manager of the Locaboat base (and therefore the de-facto harbormaster for Chitry les Mines) told us to put our luggage in the back office, already filling with luggage from other early arrivers, walk into

Corbigny, have lunch, and see a bit of the town. He also told us
that the boat would have sugar, salt, pepper and a few other basic
condiments on board, but we should stop at a small local market
on the way back and get a few things for dinner and breakfast
plus a couple bottles of wine, some beer or soft drinks—whatever
suited our taste—but not to buy too much, as there were quay-
side restaurants and cafes, and local boulangeries, patisseries and
epiceries in almost every village along the canal.

Returning to Corbigny, we enjoyed a good lunch, visited
the tourist office and learned a little about the town. Prior to
the French Revolution Corbigny, like many of the towns and
small cities of France, was walled and fortified, but only one of
the original fourteen defensive towers, a few bits of the old wall
and none of the five gates remained. Large portions of the wall
and most of the towers were torn down in the first years of the
French Revolution by the revolutionaries, to prevent the towns
being used as a base by counter revolutionary, Royalist, forces.
Then, after the Napoleonic wars, most of the remaining defensive structures became a quarry, a source of construction stone.
However, in Corbigny as in St. Jean de Losne, the street pattern
revealed the location of the old town walls and the central part
of town still had many interesting and attractive old houses
and other buildings. Walking back to the hire-boat base, as
instructed, we picked up a couple bottles of wine, a six-pack
of beer, some juice, coffee, fruit, cheese, a baguette and a few
other groceries. Chartering a hire-boat seemed to require a lot of
walking and general physical effort.

Ted Johnson was busy with a charter group so his young
French assistant, who spoke perfect American English and
apparently several other languages, showed us to our boat,
told us to un-pack, put away our supplies and look around the

boat. He, or Mr. Johnson, would be back soon to check us out, and get us started. Our boat, named *Buffon*[21], was a Locaboat "Classic Penichette 935"[22]. It was nine and three tenths meters long, three and one tenth meters wide, had inside steering, a twenty-seven horse power Yanmar diesel engine, comfortable accommodations for three, uncomfortable accommodations for two more, a complete bath, a small but functional galley, and a comfortable dinette (when it wasn't being used as uncomfortable accommodations for the "two more"). It was a perfect boat for a couple. An hour later, the assistant returned and our check-out began: a tour of the mechanical, electrical and plumbing systems, an engine starting and stopping demonstration, instructions on docking, tying up and basic safety procedures, and then a short four kilometer test drive south, upstream and through several locks, to an old commercial barge dock where we tied up. With a cheerful bon voyage, our instructor stepped ashore and into a waiting van. There were two boats on the dock already, and another two arrived later.

It was 6:00 p.m. and it was apparent why we had been advised to pick up a few things for dinner, there was absolutely nowhere within a reasonable walk to obtain a little drink and/ or sustenance. After dinner we walked up and down the freight dock, looking at the other Penichettes and meeting our fellow voyagers, all of whom, like us, would be leaving in the morning and heading north, downstream, to Joigny. One of the other

---

21 Presumably after Georges-Louis Leclerc de Buffon, the great French scientist and naturalist who laid out the Jardin du Roi in Paris and wrote a monumental thirty six volume history of nature, his Histoire Naturelle. Buffon was born in Montbard in 1707, was appointed to the Academie des Sciences in Paris as a botanist in 1733 at the age of twenty six, was elected to the Academie Francaise in 1752 and died in Paris, while supervising some work being done in the Jardin du Roi.

22 "Penichette", or small peniche (French for barge), is a registered trademark of Locaboat Plaisance. However the term is often used as a generic name for any small barge.

boats was a 935, like ours, and was chartered by an English couple who were reticent and stand-offish to the point of being unfriendly. Another was a large Penichette 1500, fifteen meters long, the largest size permitted for a "sans permis" hire-boat. It was chartered by a group of Americans from California, who had hired a professional captain. We got to know their captain, an Englishman, quite well, but not the Californians. They, like us, were on a one week trip to Joigny and we travelled most of the way with them. The remaining two boats were midsized Penichettes and both had been chartered by a group of Swedes, all of whom seemed to speak English but apparently none of whom spoke French, a trait we shared. The Swedes were on a three week circular trip, from Chitry les Mines to Joigny and then back to Chitry les Mines via several Loire Valley canals, it sounded like a nice trip. The only person in the whole group who could actually speak French was the hired captain on the big penichette. I noted that our boat was the only one that was "sans velos" (without bicycles), everyone else had rented bicycles from Locaboat Plaisance.

In the morning a group of excited people on five penichettes got started early, chugging north down the Canal du Nivernais to Auxerre, the Yonne River and Joigny. The old freight dock at which the trip down the canal actually began was at canal kilometer marker seventy-eight. We traveled north, downstream, through fifty-five locks, to kilometer marker zero, where the canal entered the Yonne River at Auxerre, and then continued thirty-two kilometers further downstream on the Yonne to Joigny, transiting another eleven locks in the process. The entire trip covered only one hundred and ten kilometers but it involved sixty-six locks, an average of one lock every two kilometers, more or less, and for variety, there were seven odd little manual draw bridges spanning the upper canal.

The Canal du Nivernais is one hundred and seventy-four kilometers long, has one hundred and ten locks, and connects the Canal lateral de la Loire at Decize to the Yonne River at Auxerre. From Auxerre, barges can continue down the Yonne Rive to the Seine River and on to Paris and northern Europe. The original justification for building the canal was the need for firewood in Paris. Wood cut over the fall and winter was floated down to Paris from distant forests each spring during high water in the "flottage". The canal linked the forests of the Bazois to the Yonne River, the Seine River and Paris, and it improved the transport of logs from the forests of the Morvan by eliminating the shoals and rapids in the upper Yonne. Work on the canal began in 1784, however disruptions caused by the revolution and the Napoleonic wars slowed construction and the canal took more than sixty years to complete. Once in operation, in addition to supplying firewood to Paris the canal became an important route for freight and passenger barges. The switch to coal, natural gas, oil and electricity for heat and cooking ended the flottage and the coming of the railroad in the mid nineteenth century diminished the canals importance as a freight route and ended passenger traffic. By the 1950s commercial freight traffic had nearly ceased, and today the canal is used almost exclusively by pleasure boaters. Commercial traffic is limited to a few hotel barges and, in the northern most section between Auxerre and Vermenton, the occasional cargo barge.

The locks on the canal, although they had all been upgraded to the Freycinet standard around the turn of the last century, were manually operated and someone on the boat or boats transiting on each cycle of a lock generally helped the lock-keeper with the heavy work of cranking the lock's gates open and closed. For our entire trip that someone always seemed to be me, even when several boats were transiting a lock. Because we were going downstream each lock chamber was full when we entered. We would pull into a lock, go alongside the wall, and drop the bight of a doubled back line over a bollard on the lock wall. I would then step off our boat and help the lock-keeper while Betty managed the line. If the drop (change in water level) in the lock was no more than one to two meters, I would jump back onto the boat and pull our line in and we'd be on our way. If the drop was greater than two meters, Betty would pull in the line, drive the boat out of the lock and, at a suitable spot below the lock she would put the bow of the boat against the bank of the canal, I would climb back aboard and off we'd go. In the Nivernais canal most of the locks had a drop of less than two meters. The eleven locks on the Yonne river were a different thing altogether. They were much larger, deeper, modernized locks intended for large barges. The lock gates and sluices were hydraulic and no one got off the boat. Our relative experience showed and we had no problems with the locks but the same cannot be said of most of the hire-boat crews. It was clear that people hiring boats "sans permis" were under no obligation to have any actual experience with or even to know anything about boats, canals or locks. The captain driving the big Penichette had six or seven passengers on board and as far as I could tell only one, a teenager about thirteen or fourteen, was helping him in any way. He frequently entered locks just behind us and I would help with his lines.

The seven little manually operated draw bridges were all in the first two days of the trip. The bridges had a horizontal clearance just wide enough for a Freycinet barge to pass through and were basically little more than a welded I-beam frame with a steel grate on it, a wood plank driving surface and a simple lifting mechanism. The bridges were intended for local farm equipment and had no bridge tenders. They were a do it yourself operation and boaters were expected to close any bridge they opened. Just upstream from each bridge Betty would put the bow of the *Buffon* up against the canal bank and I would jump ashore, walk up and raise the bridge. Betty would drive the boat through; I would lower the bridge and walk downstream to where she could retrieve me. At the second bridge we noticed that a couple of the boats that had started with us were waiting to follow us through. I had become the draw bridge and lock assistant for the herd.

On that first full day we covered eighteen kilometers, transited twelve locks and passed through four of the seven manual drawbridges. I got a lot of exercise jumping on and off the boat and cranking the lock gates—and those draw bridges—open and closed. The night was spent tied to the quay in the attractive little farming town of Cuzy where we ate dinner at the Hotel du Morvan. The hotel restaurant, lobby and entryway had a collection of interesting old photos of the flottage and nineteenth century life along the canal. The food was basic French country cooking and pretty good. Dinner was accompanied, at the suggestion of our waiter, with a bottle of superb dry white wine produced in Tannay, just a kilometer and a half away across the canal. The next morning we delayed our departure for a couple of hours and walked up to Tannay to visit the source of our evening's excellent wine.

The second day we calmed down and began to get into the rhythm of canal boat life. Each morning one of us would walk to a boulangerie, patisserie or marché (market), whatever was closest to the nights mooring spot, and get a baguette or a small loaf of dark and delicious country bread, some croissants for breakfast and anything else that looked good or was needed. Generally a newspaper was available, the larger towns all had a presse and the smaller towns generally had a tabac[23], which handled a few newspapers and invariably had a copy of the English language edition of the International Herald Tribune. After breakfast we would get under way and move down the canal to a canal side cafe, a town quay or just an attractive spot on the bank, and tie up for lunch—continuing after lunch to the next town that looked like a good overnight stop. The canal was lovely and the week passed much too quickly. Each night was spent in another interesting and attractive old town: Clamecy, where we bought some foies gras and confite de canard at Le Comptoir Eduen, Chatel Censoir, where we walked up to the church of Saint Potentien,[24] Accolay, where we enjoyed a bit much of the fine local wine, and Auxerre, ancient and intriguing. Each day ended early enough for a little walking and exploring and either lunch or dinner was in a local cafe, bistro or restaurant.

Friday afternoon, September twenty-second, entirely too soon, the cruise ended at the Locaboat Plaisance base in the Yonne River town of Joigny: picturesque, old, with a tight, intricate medieval center and an interesting history.[25] After a day

---

23 In Paris and the larger French cities tabacs sell tobacco products, stamps and lottery tickets. Out in the small towns, the local tabac is often much more: the news stand, a small bar/cafe, perhaps even a small market and the place where the delivery truck from a boulangerie in some town down the road drops off bread for sale each morning.

24 Saint Potentien and Saint Savinian were the patron saints and founders of the diocese of Sens. Potentien may have been martyred at Sens in the third or fourth century. The church of Saint Potentien in Chatel Censoir is a lovely old church most of which dates to the fifteenth century but the chapter hall was built in the twelfth century and the chancel in the eleventh.

25 In 1438 the people of Joigny, led by the wine growers and the barrel makers (the coopers), revolted, rose up against their feudal overlord, Count Guy de la Tremoille, and captured his chateau. The apparently not so good Count was shown who was who and was then put in his place or maybe sent off to where he belonged. He was executed, beaten to death by blows from the cooper's mallets.

spent exploring Joigny and visiting Chantier Fluvial de
Migennes, a boat and barge yard in the nearby town of
Migennes, we took the early morning train to Paris. Tam and
Di Murrell had suggested that, time permitting, we should
visit the boat yard and talk to the owner, Jo Parfitt, a marine
engineer from New Zealand. He was an interesting man who
knew a lot about barges and there were usually several for sale
in the yard. Three days in Paris staying at the Timhotel
Le Louvre,[26] being tourists and spending much too much in
restaurants and it was time to bid a temporary adieu to Paris
and France.

H_2O's Office

---

26 Timhotel Le Louvre, 4 rue Croix des Petits-Champs, phone: 01-42-60-34-86—
In the heart of the 1st Arrondissement, across the street from the Louvre and near
the Palais-Royal Metro stop. Like the Tulip Hotels, Timhotels are a good, clean,
moderately priced chain found all over France.

3. Betty Buys Her Barge

Walkabout was right where she had been. We moved aboard and lived for a week, ten feet up, while I serviced the sea cocks, re-packed the stuffing box and put a coat of paint on the bottom. Tuesday, October third *Walkabout* was back afloat and the long fall migration south, down the ICW to Florida, the Florida Keys and The Bahamas began yet again. At forty to sixty miles a day it is a slow and normally very enjoyable trip—one of the world's great boat trips—but this year winter came early, it was cold and our thoughts were elsewhere. November eighth to the thirteenth was spent attending the Seven Seas Cruising Association's annual rendezvous in Melbourne, Florida. The first of December we were in Miami, waiting for a good weather window to make the crossing to the islands. Our window arrived on the eighteenth and we crossed to Bimini, cleared Customs and Immigration, and moved on across the Great Bahamas Bank to the Berry Islands for a week of fishing, shelling and enjoying the company of several boats we knew before continuing to Nassau and the Nassau Harbour Club marina.

All the way down the coast, at every opportunity—libraries, internet cafes and coffee houses, marinas, anywhere that offered access—Betty searched the internet sites of the Dutch Barge Association, H_2O, and several other barge brokers, looking at every small, fifteen to twenty meter long, converted Dutch barge that was listed for sale. Nassau was no exception. At an internet cafe near Prince George Wharf (the cruise ship dock), she found two new and interesting barges on H_2O's web site. That night, over dinner, another trip to France, to see and board those barges was planned. If we bought a barge, at least we wouldn't be paying for as many airline tickets, hotels, trains and restaurant meals. Instead our money could be tossed into a hole in the water. We were used to that and good at it...and the hole in the water would be in France.

The flight from Nassau to Paris was smooth, the Miami-Paris leg, an AA 757, was only half full and I was able to claim three contiguous seats and sleep for seventy-five percent of the trip. From the airport we took the TGV directly to Dijon, by-passing Paris, and then the local on to St. Jean de Losne. Betty had called Catherine Rault at H_2O and told her we were coming and Catherine had made reservations for us at a lovely B&B owned by a friend of hers, Catherine Rassalle, a Belgian who had lived on barges for many years. The B&B was a large and beautiful eighteenth century house, described as a "Maison Bourgeois", behind the levee on the south bank of the Saone River in Losne, just a few doors down from the Auberge de la Marine. When we arrived at the St. Jean de Losne train station we called H_2O, arranged to be there the next day, and they called the town taxi for us. The taxi, the same white van and same driver as the previous September, picked us up and took us to the B&B. After meeting Catherine, we walked to L'Amiral for an early dinner. It was just 5:00 p.m. but already dark[27] and coming from Nassau, it was very cold. Nevertheless, it felt good to be back.

In the morning I walked over to the Supermarche Casino and picked up some croissants, coffee, orange juice, and some other stuff and, on the way back, stopped at the

---

[27] France lies at approximately the same north latitude as Nova Scotia and Newfoundland in Canada; in the winter the days are short, in the summer, long.

presse for a paper. Our B&B was really more of a gite[28]; our room was a very comfortable small apartment with a living room, bedroom, dining area and a small but complete kitchen. We could eat breakfast, lunch and dinner in, if we wanted to. From the living room window there was a spectacular view of the old part of St. Jean de Losne, the Saone River quays, and the entrance to the Canal de Bourgogne. After a leisurely breakfast we wandered slowly over to H_2O, met Catherine, collected the cabin door keys for two modest converted Dutch barges that we had not seen during the previous visit, and started doing what we had come all the way across the Atlantic, in mid-winter, to do...look at barges.

The first of the mornings two barges, named *La Vagabonde*, had an asking price of 320,000 French Francs (in January 2001, $43,000 or €48,780), and was an attractive little eleven meter long iron hulled Tjalk, a sailing barge converted to power. The cute little thing was registered in Belgium, had been built in 1908, possibly as a yacht, and was the smallest Dutch barge we have ever seen. It appeared to be in good condition: it had a new fifty-five horse power Peougeot diesel (with a matching spare still in the shipping crate), wheel steering, and it was heated and insulated. But, I am six feet tall and *La Vagabonde* had been built for midgets, there was no head room. There was nowhere inside that barge where I could come close to standing straight and, although I didn't try one out, the berths looked much too short.

---

28 A "gite" is a furnished house or apartment equipped with linens, kitchen ware, etc. that is generally rented by the week or month. Gites are not B&Bs, breakfast is not included. Formerly gites were predominantly rural, generally farm houses, converted farm outbuildings or free standing homes in small towns. The term is now frequently also applied to furnished and equipped short term rental apartments in cities.

The second of the mornings' barges, named *Crisal*, was another converted Tjalk built in 1908. It was registered in France, had an asking price of 450,000 FF (€68,600), was just under fifteen meters long, had an iron hull, a welded steel superstructure, a sixty-five horse power Perkins diesel (rebuilt in 1998), a diesel cabin heater, good insulation and a nice interior layout. The barge was more than attractive. It was downright pretty, with a nice sheer line, a visually harmonious and well built deck house and jaunty red top sides. But, again, there was that headroom thing, it was better than in *La Vagabonde*, but there was still no where below decks for me to stand fully upright and put my pants on. The toilet compartment was very small with no sink, just a toilet and a tiny stall shower in which I could not stand straight up and could barely turn around. Finally, the barge still had its original tiller steering, a long deck sweeper of a tiller and the helmsperson would, despite a little canvas awning, be exposed to wind and rain.

After a break for lunch, which we ate at our B&B, we returned to H_2O for more barge looking. Lunch was an excellent soup, tomato bisque, part of a baguette and a couple of good cheeses, all of which I had picked up at the Casino during my morning walk. The soup intrigued me. It was far better than any canned or packaged soup that I had ever purchased in the United States, and it came in a brick shaped soft package, not a can. I had seen milk, we used it on our sailboat, in similar packaging, but never soup, or anything else except little drink packs for children. The instructions on the side of the package were also interesting, four small graphic symbols with a short two or three word statement beside each. The first symbol was a curved double headed arrow, one point up, one down, beside which were the words "Agitez la brique". Shake the brick? An excellent term that entered my vocabulary as shaking bricks or just shaking the brick ("how's the job going?", "slow, all I'm doing is shaking bricks").

Back at H$_2$O, we looked at two more barges. The first, named *Gergovie*, was yet another Tjalk. It was French registered, had an asking price of €68,600, was eighteen meters long , had a riveted iron hull and, while it had a few nice features such as a good Saab diesel and a generator, it had a number of draw backs. It was also almost one hundred and twenty years old; it had been built in 1882. Neither of us cared for it at all and its age put it beyond the pale.

The fourth and last barge of the day was a converted iron hulled Dutch Luxemotor built in the Netherlands, at the P.C. Van der Plas Scheepsbouwwerf (Shipyard), in 1927. Named *Nova Cura*, the barge had been built to carry agricultural products on the small canals of northeastern Holland and was listed for sale at 395,000 French Francs (€59,848). Even though the barge had been built in the Netherlands it was on the Small Ships Registry and the hailing port was London. *Nova Cura* had relatively small fuel and water tanks, an old DAF diesel and an electrical system that I could clearly see needed more than a little work. But it had two meters of headroom down the center line of the entire forward cabin area and the aft cabin (the old crew's quarters) was close. The interior had a good layout[29] and, with some work, would be very livable. *Nova Cura* was easily the prettiest of the day's barges and it was a Luxemotor.

---

29 In the bow there was a large storage compartment, next aft was a sleeping cabin with two bunks, followed by a large head (bathroom), a comfortable saloon (main cabin) and the galley (kitchen). Then, up five steps to a wheelhouse that was over the engine space, and down five more steps to a second, larger, sleeping cabin with a comfortably large double berth.

BETTY'S BARGE

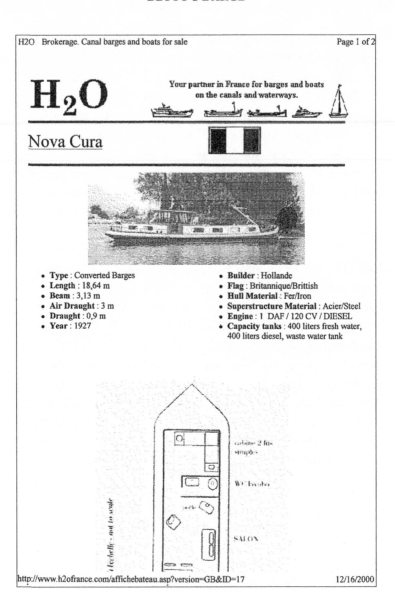

H₂O

Your partner in France for barges and boats
on the canals and waterways.

Nova Cura

- **Type** : Converted Barges
- **Length** : 18,64 m
- **Beam** : 3,13 m
- **Air Draught** : 3 m
- **Draught** : 0,9 m
- **Year** : 1927

- **Builder** : Hollande
- **Flag** : Britannique/Brittish
- **Hull Material** : Fer/Iron
- **Superstructure Material** : Acier/Steel
- **Engine** : 1 DAF / 120 CV / DIESEL
- **Capacity tanks** : 400 liters fresh water, 400 liters diesel, waste water tank

Nova Cura listing sheet, page 1

3. Betty Buys Her Barge

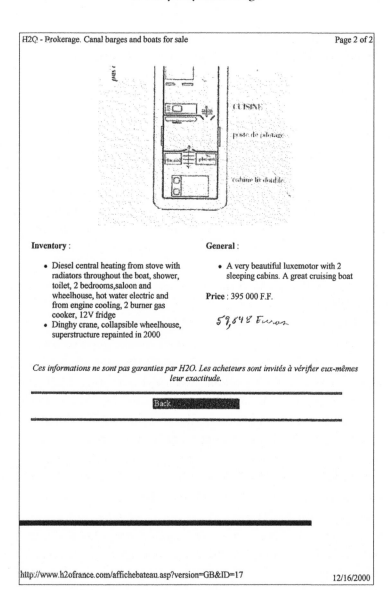

Inventory :

- Diesel central heating from stove with radiators throughout the boat, shower, toilet, 2 bedrooms,saloon and wheelhouse, hot water electric and from engine cooling, 2 burner gas cooker, 12V fridge
- Dinghy crane, collapsible wheelhouse, superstructure repainted in 2000

General :

- A very beautiful luxemotor with 2 sleeping cabins. A great cruising boat

Price : 395 000 F.F.

59,848 Euros

Ces informations ne sont pas garanties par H2O. Les acheteurs sont invités à vérifier eux-mêmes leur exactitude.

Back

Nova Cura listing sheet, page 2

In the fading late afternoon light we returned to the office, spent a half hour talking to Catherine and Charles Gerard about the barges we had seen, and then returned to the B&B for a pleasant evening fixing dinner, enjoying a good bottle of fine Vin de Bourgogne and discussing the four barges at length. After dinner Betty laid out the listing sheets (one or two page information sheets provided by the broker) for the barges and compiled a comparison table, sort of a spread sheet. Friday we checked out another three fifteen to twenty meter long barge conversions, none interesting, and, out of pure curiosity, spent a few minutes looking at a gorgeous and very expensive Linssen®, an eleven meter long Dutch built, steel hulled motor yacht capable of canal and coastal cruising. In the evening Betty added the three new barges to her comparison table.

Saturday morning Betty told Catherine that, rather than look at more small barges, she wanted to take good second looks at *Crisal* and *Nova Cura*. We spent the morning going over both of them, took a long lunch at L'Amiral and talked about them, in detail, and then returned to H_2O, where Betty told Catherine she wanted to make an offer on *Nova Cura*. Charles Gerard[30] was summoned and he, Catherine and Betty discussed the offer. *Nova Cura*'s asking price was 395,000 French Francs (US $56,428 at seven French Francs to the Dollar) and Betty offered 350,000 French Francs (US $50,000), conditional on *Nova Cura* passing both a general survey and an engine survey, both to be carried out to the rigorous French standards. Everything was gone over at length. Was Betty's offer adequate? Would the owner accept it? How long would the process take? Betty would not raise her initial offer and, in

---

30 We learned later that Charles and five family members had brought *Nova Cura* down to St. Jean de Losne from the Netherlands some years earlier.

the end it was accepted "for presentation to the owner." Then, for an hour or so, Betty, Catherine and Charles filled in, signed and stamped forms, H_2O's secretary provided blank forms and ran to and from the copying machine, and I stood around trying to look helpful and providing moral support for Betty. When the paper work was complete—the last form signed, the last notary seal applied, the last copy made—we spent the final half hour before H_2O closed at 5:00 p.m., aboard *Nova Cura*, and then walked to L'Amiral for an aperitif before returning to the B&B, where we fixed a good dinner, contemplated what Betty had just done and dreamed about canal trips to come. The waiting and negotiating could now begin.

Sunday, after a late breakfast and a walk along the Saone and through town, our landlady drove us to the train station and we returned to Paris, the Timhotel Le Louvre, and yet another excellent dinner at Willi's Wine Bar. The barge looking trip that became a buying trip had taken less time than expected, and we had three full days to enjoy Paris before our return flight. The first day was spent visiting the Museum of Humanity and the Maritime Museum, and then walking down the left bank from the Eiffel Tower to the foot bridge by the Louvre. The Paris Maritime Museum is one of the under-appreciated jewels of Paris. It houses some of the finest maritime art and ship models to be found anywhere, and for anyone with even a passing interest in boats, ships and the sea, it's book and gift shop is excellent.

The second day we went to the Place de la Bastille to visit the large marina, the Port de l'Arsenal, located there. The Port de l'Arsenal, a basin at the Seine River end of the Canal St. Martin, separated by a lock from the river, is the largest marina in Paris and, after St Jean de Losne, the second largest inland marina in France. It is a popular place for

livaboard canal boaters to winter over and we went to look at
the numerous converted barges docked there for the winter,
and compare them to Betty's purchase. To our surprise, an
Antigua 44 ketch named *Glen Lyon* that we knew and had
last seen during the London Boat Show the previous winter
was there. I banged on the hull, the companionway hatch
opened, Rod's head popped up and we were invited aboard.
Rod and Sue had sailed over from The Bahamas, spent the
previous winter at St. Katherine's Dock, London, and cruised
northern Europe over the summer and were now wintering
over in Paris before continuing on to the Mediterranean in the
spring. Betty and Sue walked to a local market, picked up a
roasted chicken, a baguette, a couple of good cheeses, a few
salad things and a couple bottles of good wine...lunch. The
rest of the afternoon was spent eating, drinking and talking
about *Glen Lyon's* trip across the Atlantic (Sue, "never again"),
Betty's offer on *Nova Cura* ("Oh well, what the hell, you only
live once"), Paris and the French canals.

Our third and, for this trip, final full day in Paris was
spent taking a "Paris Walks" tour of the older part of the Marais and poking around in the alleys of the Ile de la Cite and
the Ile Saint Louis. Thursday, February 1, 2001, we took the
train to the airport and, via Miami, returned to Nassau, the
Nassau Harbour Club and *Walkabout*.

The first week back aboard *Walkabout* was spent in Nassau, where Betty could access the internet and faxes could be
sent and received. Betty, Catherine and *Nova Cura's* owner,
exchanged large numbers of e-mail messages and faxes. Friday,
February ninth, Betty and *Nova Cura's* owner came to an
agreement on the price for *Nova Cura*, 365,000 French Francs.
A purchase contract was faxed back and forth, funds were
transferred from Betty's bank to H_2O's escrow account and,

pending acceptable general and mechanical surveys, Betty had bought her barge. We owned, almost anyway, two boats—no house, no car...his and her boats. In the dream land that we inhabit the future was winters on the sailboat in the Florida Keys and in the islands, fishing, swimming and enjoying warm weather and clean clear water, while summers would be spent aboard the barge in France, visiting canal side villages and enjoying the good food and wine...particularly the wine.

Port de l'Arsenal, Paris

4. Agitez la Brique - Un

The morning after Betty bought her barge we sailed out of Nassau, planning to spend another month to six weeks in The Bahamas, in places where e-mail and fax service were available, then turn north and try to reach our base at Herrington Harbour by mid-April and fly to France around May first—more or less at the start of the canal season[31]. It was an ambitious plan that almost worked. April third, we left The Bahamas and after a brisk overnight Gulf Stream sail, cleared back into the U.S. at Cape Canaveral. The good e-mail, fax and phone facilities in Cape Canaveral enabled Betty to again communicate freely with H_2O and large numbers of messages and calls were exchanged. The general and mechanical surveys on *Nova Cura* were complete and there were some issues in both surveys that needed to be addressed. Betty, Catherine and *Nova Cura's* owner returned to the bargaining table to decide how much of a survey adjustment would be needed before the sale could finally close. Three days after arriving in Cape Canaveral, after a particularly long phone conversation with Catherine, Betty said she thought everything was settled and she owned a barge.

The morning after the I-own-a-barge call, the journey north to the Chesapeake Bay and Harrington Harbour began. An unusually strong late season cold front forced a

---

31 The pleasure boating season on the canals of France is, roughly, May first through late October. Because France is so far north, in the winter the water in the canals often freezes. To prevent ice damage to the locks, quays and stone banks of the old, historic, canals, many are drained. At St. Jean de Losne the basin that the Marinas are in freezes in the winter and if you are wintering over aboard your barge, you live in the ice.

week long lay-over at the Blue Water Point Marina in Holden Beach, North Carolina. The morning after seeking shelter *Walkabout's* anemometer indicated winds gusting to forty-five knots and the temperature on deck was thirty-five degrees. In Norfolk, Virginia, a second strong late season cold front, one that brought gale conditions to the Chesapeake Bay, forced a second extended lay-over and by the time we were finally able to move up the bay to Herrington Harbor the great May first plan had become the excellent May fifteenth plan. So...sailboats are slow, a trait they share with most canal barges and boats.

Monday, April thirtieth, we reached Herrington Harbour, where *Walkabout* would was hauled out, to patiently and safely await our return and May fourteenth we left Philadelphia on our slightly delayed flight to France. The flight to Paris was almost full, no chance to grab three seats and stretch out and it was an hour and a half late leaving Philadelphia because of problems with the cabin pressurization system. We landed in Paris, at Roissy-Charles de Gaulle, at 10:30 a.m., exactly one and one half hours late. I had reserved a rental car for a week because this trip we were going to be in France for more than five months and had a lot of luggage, and a car would be useful for running around buying the things that would be needed on the barge. Keeping with our hour and a half delay, we got to the Avis desk exactly one and one half hours late— just as they gave the car we had reserved to another couple. Avis was most apologetic, they had no car like the one we had reserved available. They offered us an up-grade, at no additional cost, and we drove out of the airport, around the Paris beltway and down the A6 Motorway toward Dijon, St. Jean de Losne and Betty's barge, in a comfortably large diesel powered Mercedes. Sometimes there are benefits to being late.

The A-6 Motorway south from Paris passes the village of Chablis. A quick exit and a short drive into town—lunch in Chablis, a great start to our canal season. Because of our leisurely lunch in Chablis and a minor discrepancy in our map—the map was sure a road existed and if large quantities of dirt and construction equipment count, it did—we did not arrive in St. Jean de Losne until early evening. We went directly to our B&B, the same wonderful maison bourgeoise that we had stayed in during our January visit. We had booked it for a month because when Betty notified H_2O of our arrival date she had been told that we would not be able to move onto, live aboard, *Nova Cura* until the work called for in the final sales contract—the issues found during the surveys—was finished. The barge would have to be dry docked, and work might still be in progress when we arrived and... umm...it might take a week or so, possibly even...ahh...a bit more, maybe several weeks, to complete. Apparently because the work was specified in, and a part of, the sales contract the barge was in some sort of legal limbo and could not be fully released to Betty until she had accepted, and signed for, the work and, of course, we could not live on it while it was dry docked. After checking into the B&B, we walked across the bridge and had a late dinner at L'Amiral—breakfast in Philadelphia to a late dinner in St. Jean de Losne had been a very long thirty-six hours.

The next morning we slept late, walked into town for a croissant and coffee and then to H_2O. Catherine was not there, Charles was busy with another client and no one in the office really seemed to know what *Nova Curas'* exact status was. H_2O's Harbormaster, Jean-Paul Fortin, said that we needed to speak to Philippe Gerard, Charles' nephew and H_2O's "Chef d'Atelier" (chief technician and manager of H_2O's service and maintenance shops). Philippe would know the exact status of the work being done on *Nova Cura*; unfortunately he had gone to Dijon to pick up a truck load of material for the workshops and would not return until after H_2O had closed for the day. However, Jean-Paul told us that *Nova Cura* was just a short walk away; in front of H_2O's workshops in the basin at the lower end of the Canal de Bourgogne, just inside the lock that separated the canal from the Saone River. I have no idea what Jean-Paul's background was, but he was both H_2O's Harbormaster and the manager of H_2O's large and well stocked chandlery. He knew as much about marine hardware and equipment as anyone that I have ever met. In addition to French, he spoke fair English and had at least a basic grasp of several other languages[32].

Since no definitive information about *Nova Cura* was available, patience and lunch became plan two—walk to the Supermarche Casino, buy more food, wine and beer than a donkey could carry, lug it back to the B&B and fix lunch. After lunch, remembering that fancy rental car, we drove to a spot next to H_2O's marina and walked around the marina, up and down all the docks, looking at all the boats and barges, then drove to the far side of the canal basin to check out *Nova Cura*. Betty's little, relatively speaking, barge was one of the outer most barges in a nest of nine or ten rafted three deep along the bank in front of H_2O's workshops. There was no gangway to, no way to get aboard, the innermost barge of the

---

32 I was impressed by the staff at H_2O, all of the principle people were fluent in at least three languages and I believe that Charles Gerard could speak four or five and at least communicate in several more. Many of the technicians in the workshops were also multilingual. The entire staff was competent and reasonably helpful and accommodating. Although we had a few disagreements with H_2O, they and their marina became our principle operating base for the entire time that Betty owned *Nova Cura*.

three that *Nova Cura* was the outermost of, so we could not go out and look around. We retreated to our car and conducted a driving exploration of the canal basin, the large marina basin and St. Jean de Losne, circling all three.

The general trend of the Saone River as it meanders across the flat land of the Burgundian plain is north-northeast to south-southwest but the section of the river that St. Jean de Losne sits on, for about four kilometers, runs almost east-west. The town sits on a small peninsula, barely a kilometer long and less than that wide, framed by the Saone River to the south, the marina basin (the gare d'eau) to the north and the entrance to the Canal de Bourgogne to the west. The marina basin is approximately three quarters of a kilometer long by one half kilometer wide and is ringed by: the large, impressive H_2O marina, a Crown Blue Line hire-boat base, Ets. Blancart—a second marina with a chandlery and workshops—and the workshops of Atelier Fluvial, a barge building and repair company with a substantial dry dock (cale seche). Ets. Blancart and Atelier Fluvial sit on a narrow finger of fill (manmade land) that separates the marina basin from the Canal de Bourgogne. The canal basin, the first half kilometer of the Canal de Bourgogne, is a section of the canal that is three times the canals normal width. The east side of the basin was taken up by Atelier Fluvial, Ets. Blancart and some land owned by H_2O. The west side was occupied by H_2O's workshops and an odd barge storage facility named "Club Luxemotor". In addition to the marine businesses around the marina and canal basins, there was a canvas and upholstery shop in town, and on the Saone River bank, at the east edge of town, there was a large boat/barge building, repair and maintenance facility named CBV, with a marine railway capable of handling large vessels. The village of Losne lies to the south across the Saone

River and is connected to St. Jean de Losne by the Saone River Bridge. Although St. Jean de Losne and Losne are physically and politically separate entities they are often spoken of as though they were one town. St. Usage, larger than St. Jean de Losne, lies north of the marina basin and the town of le Couvent is west of the Canal de Bourgogne.

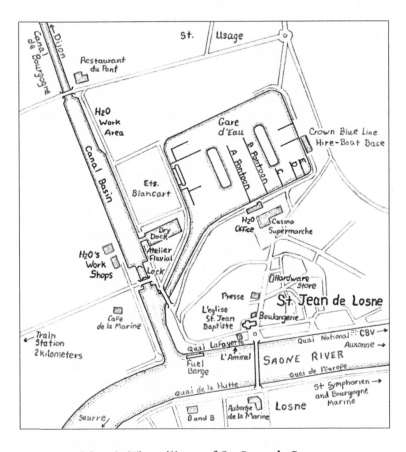

Map 2. The village of St. Jean de Losne

The next morning we were at H_2O early, just before the start of business, and managed to corner both the Gerards: Charles and Philippe. Charles told us that he needed to talk to Betty later in the day about arranging insurance coverage, in her name, for *Nova Cura*, and then hurried off to a scheduled meeting. Philippe, a very large young man who seemed to have a naturally pleasant and sunny disposition, whom we were meeting for the first time, said that he would check on the status of the work being done on *Nova Cura* and would get together with us later. He also said there were several passerelles (boarding plank or gangplank) scattered around in front of H_2O's workshops, and we could grab any one that was not in use and go aboard anytime we wished and do any sort of cleaning or work that we wanted to do. We drove to the workshop area, found a gangplank, and climbed across the two, substantially larger, barges that lay between *Nova Cura* and the quay.

That first close look at *Nova Cura* in the clean, bright sun light of a late spring day was depressing. The little barge seemed smaller and shabbier then we remembered. It was also filthy beyond belief and there was no sign that any of the needed, and agreed to, work had been done. We poked around for awhile and made some interesting discoveries. In the engine room bilge, under the engine, there was a murky black pool of engine oil and water that I did not remember from January. Some equipment—fenders, fire extinguishers, good dock lines and life jackets—that had been on the barge in January and that we had understood would transfer as part of the sale was not there now. We went to the presse for a spiral bound notebook, some graph paper, a ruler, a couple of pens, and some pencils, and then on to the hardware store for the first of a great many tools—a carpenters rule and a measuring tape. Returning to *Nova Cura* in the afternoon, we spent several hours making lists and notes, measuring, sketching and poking into every accessible nook and cranny, before going to the H_2O office for meetings with Charles, to discuss insurance for Betty's barge, and Philippe to find out what was going on with said barge.

Charles explained that the insurance on the barge was still in the name of the previous owner, and if anything happened to the barge there was no guarantee on the insurance because the previous owner had a bill of sale and was no longer the responsible party. Also, when we went to the VNF[33] to pay the annual waterway usage fee[34], they would want proof of insurance in the owner's name. H_2O was an agent for several French insurance firms that handled marine/waterway insurance. Betty told Charles to go ahead and arrange insurance in her name and he replied that in the morning he would contact AXA, the largest and best insurance firm in France. AXA would issue an immediate binder and would then send the policy and an invoice by mail to Betty, care of H_2O.

After a half hour of talking to Philippe we realized that other than scheduling a dry docking and starting the search for some difficult to find parts, nothing had been done. The general and mechanical surveys had been carried out during the week of March nineteenth to the twenty-third. The mechanical survey had been done by a diesel mechanic from CBV. The general survey by Jo Parfitt, a New Zealand born Marine Engineer who owned and ran Chantier Fluvial de

---

33 VNF: Voies Navigables de France, the French inland waterways navigation authority, sometimes referred to simply as la Navigation.

34 All vessels using the French inland waterways pay an annual usage fee, with the cost based on the size of the vessel and the number of days of waterway usage. The fees helped to pay for canal maintenance, lockkeepers salaries and VNF operated moorings.

Migennes, a barge/boatyard at the north end of the Canal de Bourgogne, where the canal met the Yonne River. Jo had been recommended to us by Tam and Di Murrell and we had gotten to know him during our initial barge looking trip. Jo had recommended that CBV do the mechanical survey. Today was Thursday, May seventeenth, nearly two full months since the surveys and not one thing had been done to *Nova Cura*. To be fair to H_2O, the amount and potential cost of the work called for in the two surveys was substantially greater than anyone had expected. H_2O had to wait for the survey reports, relay them to Betty and the owner and then, to keep the sale from falling apart, mediate between the owner and Betty regarding how much of the necessary work he would cover and what Betty was willing to cover and it was a tricky, drawn-out process. A process not aided by the fact that H_2O and the barge were in St. Jean de Losne, while the owner was in Switzerland and Betty was on a sailboat on the U.S. east coast and, at times, both the owner and Betty were hard to get hold of. Additionally, a portion of the delay can be attributed to the fact that *Nova Cura*, although on the small side for a barge, was still a large, heavy iron hulled vessel, essentially a small ship, and an antique one at that. The dry dock had to be scheduled, difficult to obtain parts found, and the work of a dozen different specialists coordinated. Finally, *Nova Cura* was far from the only boat or barge being worked on.

However, it had been over a month since Betty and the owner had agreed on who would cover what, the final sales contract had been signed and money changed bank accounts. It was clear that in French boatyards, as in a few boatyards we have had experience with in the U.S. and in the Caribbean, the squeaky wheel gets the grease. In *Nova Cura's* case, the squeak had arrived and was in residence in St. Jean de Losne.

It was also clear that we were going to need our B&B for the whole month we had booked it for…and perhaps longer. Also there was a great deal of basic work, cleaning, sanding, painting, varnishing, electrical wiring, etc. that needed to be done, work that Betty and I were capable of doing and we were now in a position to put in a lot of long days in the boatyard. Not idyllic canal cruising but, hey, boatyard work on our own barge in a lovely town in Burgundy, just a few miles from the wine country, things could certainly be worse.

Friday, May eighteenth, we put our work clothes on and went to the hardware store and the Casino where we bought a wet/dry shop type vacuum cleaner, a broom, a mop and bucket, scrub brushes, cleaning products, sponges and a couple of hand tools. Thus equipped, on to *Nova Cura* for what was supposed to be a long day of cleaning. There was an electric line running from an outlet on shore to *Nova Cura*. I connected the power cable to the shore-power receptacle on *Nova Cura*, plugged the vacuum cleaner into one of the electric outlets in the main cabin, and then switched on the main shore-power circuit breaker. Instantly the circuit breaker sparked, smoked, and snapped off. OK…well, the shore-power system had been called out as problematic in our survey. Score one for the survey. The shore power system was problematic alright, at least parts of it were, no doubt about that. I carefully disconnected the power cord, and went in search of Philippe. I went over what had happened, Philippe called one of his older and more experienced technicians, a man named "Pierre" and told him to meet me at *Nova Cura* the morning of Wednesday, May twenty-third. May twenty-third? That seemed rather far into the future, why not this afternoon? Well…today was Friday, in another hour it would be lunch time, because of the thirty-five hour work-week, no one worked Friday afternoon, Pierre was

busy, the weekend was coming, Monday Betty and I would
not be available (we had to drive to Migennes to talk to our
surveyor), Pierre had Tuesday off...ah, right, OK, Wednesday
it would be. At least we could wash, sweep, mop and scrub;
back to *Nova Cura*. Uh, there was no hose on the barge and we
had not bought one. By one of the workshops I found several
hoses but not enough to cover the seventy five or a hundred
meters from the nearest water tap to the barge.

Oh well, some days are better than other days and this day
needed improving: back to our B&B, change clothes, into our
rented Mercedes. The Cote d'Or, the celebrated wine country
of Burgundy beckoned. We drove to Nuits St. Georges with
a stop along the way at the Abbaye de Citeaux, an important
and influential site in the history of western Christianity—
both the Cistercian and the Trappist orders trace their origins
to the Abbaye. Unfortunately it was largely destroyed during
the French revolution, the revolution was aimed as much at
the abuses of the clergy, the Catholic Church, as it was at the
King and the Nobility and a great many religious sites were
damaged or destroyed during the early years of the revolution. In Nuits St. Georges we had a good lunch, bought a half
dozen bottles of wine, and visited the village museum. I had
thought that the museum would be devoted primarily to wine
but little was wine specific, most of the collection was local
history from Gallo-Roman through almost current times.
From the museum we drove to Vosne Romanee, mostly to
take a few pictures and to be able to say we had been to the
home of some of the worlds most expensive and, presumably,
best wine.

Saturday was shopping in Dole at the Supermarche Cora,
a store our landlady had told us about. The Supermarche Cora
in Dole was colossal, easily larger than the largest Wal-Mart,

and the quality of the merchandise was far superior to
Wal-Mart's. We bought two shopping cart loads of barge
stuff: towels, bedding, kitchen appliances, pots, pans, cooking
tools, wine glasses, etc. Sunday, we drove to Beaune, toured
the Hotel Dieu, and the Musee du Vin de Bourgogne, and
enjoyed a large and excellent lunch at the Aux Vignes rouges
(Red Book, one couvert). Lunch was partially compensated
for by a walking tour of several sections of the old ramparts.
The day ended with visits to the tasting rooms of a couple of
the famous wine negociants, and the purchase of a half-case of
very good wine. Beaune, probably founded by the Gauls, was
an important Roman and Gallo-Roman wine center and the
seat of the Dukes of Burgundy before they moved to Dijon.
Monday we went to Migennes, talked to Jo Parfitt the survey
and picked up the final drawing of the ultra sound survey of
Nova Cura's old iron hull[35]. Tuesday, after returning the car to
Avis in Dijon, we walked around the downtown area for several hours checking out the shops for things the barge needed—
and bought a rug which the shop promised to deliver to H_2O.
Back in St. Jean de Losne, we walked to the Intermarche in
St. Usage, another large supermarket that in addition to
groceries carried a lot of general merchandise, to see if they
had any good, usable bicycles. Now carless, bicycles—basic
transportation—were a necessity.

Thus passed the time before the appointed coming of
Pierre.

---

35 In France a part of the general survey of any old iron barge is an ultra sound
survey of the hull plates. The plates must have a minimum thickness. If thin places
are found a covering plate is welded over the thin area. If too much of the bottom
is thin, one or more of the bottom plates may be removed and new, steel, plates
welded on. *Nova Cura's* hull thickness was fine but one old covering plate had been
badly welded and a requirement of our survey was that the welds on that plate be
ground down and the plate re-welded.

Wednesday morning I went straight to *Nova Cura* while
Betty went to the hardware store for a twenty-five meter
hose (the first of an eventual three) and the necessary French
snap-on type hose fittings. I got to *Nova Cura* several minutes
before 8:00 a.m., notebook in hand, and found Pierre waiting. Pierre was a short, stocky, Frenchman who appeared to be
of late middle age, he had worked in boat and ship yards for
many years and spoke a little of what he thought was English.
I could understand a lot of what he said, in part because many
technical terms are similar in French and English. For two
hours after my evidently late arrival, Pierre—volt meter and
flashlight in hand, and with me close behind—went over *Nova
Cura's* electrical, plumbing and propane systems. He showed
me a lot of the items that had been found during the general
survey, and he found a few new goodies. During our tour,
Pierre kept shaking his head and mumbling, from which,
over and over, emerged "un problem", "poor", "bad", "kaput",
"mal." It was not encouraging. When Pierre was through, he
said that he would report to Philippe and might get started
on the needed work after lunch.

Briefly. In the 220 volt shore-power system: the shore-
power inlet receptacle, the shore-power circuit box and all the
breakers, the battery charger, at least two of the half dozen
electrical outlets in the barge, and most of the 220 volt wiring
would have to be replaced. When the barge was converted,
much of the wire that had been used in the 220 volt system
was too thin (it looked like household lamp wire), and the
work had been badly done and did not meet French maritime
standards. The existing refrigerator was an older duel voltage
(220-12 volt) model and the wiring connecting the refrigerator to the 220 volt system was too thin and had burned. The
refrigerators 12 volt power connection was also deteriorating

and both connections had to be fully rewired. The propane locker, which held two large propane bottles, was in *Nova Cura's* bow and the long, flexible rubber gas hose linking the propane locker to the galley (the kitchen cook-top was the only gas appliance on the barge) was of a type that had been illegal in France since 1993. One of the three burners on the cook-top leaked gas and the cook-top was an old three burner unit of a type not certified for marine use and it would have to be replaced. The diesel fired cabin heater was "kaput". The fresh water system was archaic, had numerous minor leaks and needed to be gone over carefully. The counter in the galley would have to be extensively rebuilt or replaced. The counter had a nice stainless steel top, was freshly painted and, at first glance did not look too bad. But it was built of non water-proof particle board, sections of which had gotten wet (those fresh water system leaks) and deteriorated. There was more...a lot more. Finally, as he was going ashore, Pierre pointed out some areas of blistering paint on the steel deck house and said "rouille (rust)". Large areas of the deck house would have to be ground down, primed, and repainted. Between our general and mechanical surveys and Pierre's re-survey, it was clear—not possible or probable—that Betty and I would be enjoying St. Jean de Losne and our B&B through at least the end of June, and that we were going to be very busy.

When Pierre returned in the afternoon; Philippe, was with him. Atelier Fluvial had called, *Nova Cura* was to go into the dry dock on Monday, May twenty-eighth. It seemed as though serious work on Betty's barge was about to begin. Pierre went to work immediately after lunch. During the afternoon and the whole of the next day, with a little help from me, he completed and tested the needed work on our 220 volt shore-power system. For all practical purposes, the barge had a new shore-power system. I had been afraid that Pierre would not show up Thursday morning as it was Ascension, a Catholic religious holiday and many banks and some government offices were closed; but there were no great signs of religious fervor at H_2O, or anywhere else in town. At the end of the first afternoon of electrical work, when Pierre left for the day, I walked to the hardware store and spent a large wad of francs on a good tool box, a volt meter, a set of electrical tools (wire cutter, stripper, crimper, etc.), and a few more general hand tools. I was going to be doing most of the work on the 12 and 24 volt DC systems (*Nova Cura* had both)

While Pierre was working on the shore-power system, Betty had been cleaning and thinking about *Nova Cura's* interior. Betty enjoyed and read architectural and interior design books and magazines. Over the years she had bought, rehabbed and redecorated a number of old houses, projects she had thoroughly enjoyed and from which she derived a great deal of satisfaction. She had decided that her barge was her home in France and her next rehab/interior design project, and had begun to conceptualize an interior design and what would be needed to achieve it.

Thursday afternoon Pierre finished what he was doing, and a half hour before the 5:00 p.m. closing bell at the office,[36] we walked over for a scheduled meeting with Philippe. A meeting at which we were to learn what was supposed to be done while *Nova Cura* was in the dry dock and get final word on

---

36 At H_2O the technicians and other workers came in early, took long lunches, left early and did not work Friday afternoons—in 2001, France had a thirty five hour work week. The office and chandlery operated on a different schedule, office hours were 8:00 a.m. to 5:00 p.m. Monday through Friday and a half day on Saturday. The chandlery was officially open every day but Sunday from 8:00 a.m. to 5:00 p.m. However, since the chandlery was run by the harbormaster and his assistant and it doubled as their office, you could generally buy stuff on Sundays

repairs to *Nova Cura's* gearbox, which was slipping in both
forward and reverse, badly in forward, and was one of the
major items that had been called out during CBV's mechanical survey. Philippe estimated ten days in the dry dock and
said that while the barge was in there seven[37] of the major
items from the general hull survey were to be taken care of.
The news on our gearbox was not as good. The gearbox, it
seemed, was a real problem. The DAF 575 diesel, installed in
1972, had been coupled to the existing, much older mechanical gearbox. All of the clutch plates in the gearbox were, to
some degree, burned and would have to be replaced, but new
plates were unavailable. Hand machining a full set of new
plates was out of the question, the cost would be astronomical.
So the barge would be getting a new, hydraulic transmission.
Philippe was looking for one that would work with the DAF,
fit in the available space, and was available at a rational cost—
the survey adjustment on *Nova Cura's* price had included some
funds for the gear box, but not the full cost of a new hydraulic
gear.

---

37 1) the keel cooling pipes would be replaced and protective plates welded to
the hull where the cooling pipes exited and entered, 2) the propeller shaft would
be pulled and inspected, the stern tube replaced and the stuffing box repacked, 3)
the rudder shaft bearings would be replaced, 4) the carrier bearing between the
engine and the stern tube would be replaced, 5) the rudder quadrant would be
realigned, 6) one of the protective doubling plates welded over thin spots in the
hull had defective welds which would be ground out and re-welded, and 7) eight
new magnesium alloy (fresh water) anti-galvanic corrosion anodes would be welded
to the hull. In addition, at our request, the bottom would be cleaned and a new
layer of protective tar, or something, would be applied to the bottom. Old iron
hulled canal barges and boats were traditionally tarred, literally; boiling roofing
tar was brushed onto the hull. Modern practice at H_2O and most other barge and
boat yards is to protect old iron hulls with a black coal tar epoxy. If marine bottom
paint is applied, which is very rare, it goes on over an epoxy base because the copper in the marine paint reacts with the old iron hulls.

When the planned part of the meeting was over, Betty brought up her interior design concept and some work she wanted done. At first Philippe seemed a little confused, confused changed to bemused and then, surprisingly, to active interest. Philippe was the "Chef de Atelier" and he was interested in anything that interested his clients, and might interest future clients—H_2O did a lot of barge interior work, from complete conversions down to new bathrooms. As we were leaving, he told Betty that as soon as *Nova Cura* was out of the dry dock and back in the shop area, work on her interior would begin. We left the meeting and walked to our B&B, via an aperitif at L'Amiral, happy in our ignorance and our inability to see the future.

L'eglise St. Jean-Baptiste
(photo by Warren Berkstresser)

Commercial freight barges on the Quai Lafayette,
the fuel barge is visible astern of them

The canal basin looking north,
Cafe du Pont in the right background
(photo by Berry Barnett)

The Place de la Deliberation & Bistro L'Amiral
(photo by Warren Berkstresser)

5. Agitez la Brique - Deux

Confident that *Nova Cura* would be going into the dry dock in three days and knowing that we would not get much work done while it was in there; Friday, Saturday and Sunday, practically sunrise to sunset, were devoted to cleaning and painting. Betty went to the hardware store and bought an electric sander, sand paper and some paint and painting materials. Then she started repainting the forward sleeping cabin, planning to work her way aft through the entire interior. I tackled the forepeak; starting with cleaning out an amazing amount of trash, dirt and old junk (bits of wood, scraps of old rope, bags of assorted nails, nuts, bolts and pipe fittings, etc.). I discovered that parts of the, possibly original, wooden storage racks were rotten and that our existing aluminum water tanks were in very bad condition. I repaired, sanded and painted the salvageable parts of the storage racks and then sanded and painted the floor boards. I tried—with little success—to stop the numerous small leaks in our water system. Water leaking from one of the old tanks had trickled down a pipe and dripped onto the electric water pump and the electrical connections on the pump were badly corroded. While I was cleaning the pump, one of the connections simply disintegrated. A new water pump was now a critical necessity, and new water tanks, a new accumulator tank (helps regulate the pressure in the water system) and a lot of new plumbing would be a good idea. The to-be-purchased and the work-to-be-done lists were moving in the wrong direction.

The deck (floor) in the primary living area, originally the cargo hold, was large sheets of thick, good quality plywood which were screwed to the iron floor beams.[38] Over the years the floor had been several colors, most recently gray, and it again needed painting. Betty planned to paint the floor Burgundy Red but, before starting, she wanted to take up a couple of the floor panels and see what was underneath. When the first of the floor panels came up and the light of day reached the bilge for the first time in, possibly, decades, a monumental and none too sweet smelling mess was exposed. The ballast[39]—rows of large bricks, some short pieces of railroad track and a few heavy pigs of iron—was nearly awash in an evil witches' brew: years...decades...of dirt, saw dust, grease, old engine oil and trash swimming in rusty bilge water. At least there was no wiring or plumbing down there, it all ran along the sides of the hull up in the cabin, behind the cabinets and paneling. We took up two more floor panels and started cleaning. First a hand pump and a bucket were used to remove ninety-five percent of that fetid water, bucket full after bucket full. Then, section by section, the width of the hull and two ribs worth at a time, the ballast was moved, each piece wiped down with a de-greasing agent, soap and clean water, and then allowed to dry. When a section was free of ballast, any residual water was sponged up, and putty knives and paint scrappers

---

38 Apparently when *Nova Cure* was built the cargo hold had a wood floor to keep whatever was being carried up and out of any bilge water. There were original, thick and strong, iron floor beams spanning the width of the hull and riveted to iron knees and the ribs.

39 Cargo barges converted to pleasure use must be ballasted to stabilize the barge and make it ride level, on or close to its loaded water line. We were lucky *Nova Cura* had moveable ballast. On some barge conversions, cement is simply poured into the old iron hull, over time water gets under the cement and the hull rusts from the inside out.

were used to scrap up the filthy muck. As each section was de-mucked, it was treated with an industrial grease remover and scrubbed with a brush, soap and water. After a cleaned section had dried, a rust remover and a wire brush removed any rust on the hull (surprisingly, there was very little), then a stiff brush and a ballast brick wrapped in a piece of heavy leather were used to rub the thickest, heaviest, nastiest, grease available into the iron of the hull and, as far as possible, into the iron ribs[40]. There were no drain holes in the ribs, so as long as the water level was kept below the height of the ribs we could work on almost isolated sections. When a section was clean, free of rust and well greased, I replaced the, now dry, ballast and work began on the next section.

Monday came, but our move to the dry dock did not. Bilge cleaning continued.

Monday, as seems to be inevitable, was followed by Tuesday; but our move to the dry dock did not happen. Bilge cleaning continued.

Wednesday arrived at the usual time, but there was still no sign that *Nova Cura* was to be moved to the dry dock. The morning passed finishing up the bilge cleaning project. Glad to see the end of that job, we knocked off work and walked to the Cafe du Pont in St. Usage for a long and leisurely lunch. The Cafe du Pont is a nice small cafe beside the bridge that

---

40 The black iron used in the hull plates of old barges is very slightly porous, heavy grease well worked in renders the iron almost water proof, for a few years anyway. In the old shipyards, after rubbing in the grease, they would use a torch to melt it further in and then apply a second layer. I did not go to all that trouble, but on one section I experimented with Betty's hair dryer and on high it seemed to almost work, just needed to be a bit hotter. Modern shipyard practice is to clean the hull with live steam and degreasing solvents, chip or grind off any rust and then apply specially formulated epoxies.

carries the Rue du Canal across the Canal de Bourgogne. Even though the sky was gray and thickly overcast and the day almost uncomfortably cool, we ate at one of the three tables on the cafe's small terrace. A spot from which we could see the canal. As we were finishing our cheese and a bottle of fine white Bourgogne Aligoti, two private barges about *Nova Cura's* size passed, headed up the canal toward Dijon. Almost simultaneously, both of us said we wished that *Nova Cura* was one of those barges, and then we speculated a bit about how long it would be before we would be able to move aboard, let alone actually start cruising.

After lunch we walked back along the canal to where *Nova Cura* was tied up—she hadn't moved—continued around the basin to Atelier Fluvial—nothing was happening at the dry dock—and moved on to H_2O's pontoons, where we spent some time talking about boat and barge projects with two couples we had met, one American and one British. Both couples were living aboard in the marina and working on their boats, the Brits on a small Dutch barge. We were beginning to fit into the boating community in St. Jean de Losne and, at least a little, into the local community as well. The couple who owned and ran the maison de la presse recognized me and, if I was late for the morning paper, would generally save a copy of the International Herald Tribune. The ladies at the Boulangerie that I most often went to also recognized me, and had started trying to get me to ask for what I wanted in French.

One of the couples at the marina told us that the Casino was having a clearance sale on bicycles, so leaving the dock we walked that way. While still on the road around the gare d'eau, an H_2O van roared up, screeched to a halt, and as a cloud of dust and engine exhaust enveloped us, Philippe stuck his head out and yelled "this afternoon! This afternoon!" and charged off—blessing us with a fresh blast of exhaust gases and dust. At the Casino there was indeed a special clearance sale on bicycles and they had one that worked for me, but not one for Betty. Pushing our one new bicycle down the road, we returned to the B&B for a shower, an adult beverage of choice and dinner.

Thursday, May thirty-first, the last day of May 2001, we had been in St. Jean de Losne for sixteen days and still did not know when we would be able to move aboard the barge. I rode the bike into town, picked up the morning's paper and some bread, and then swung past the canal basin. It was very early but the dry dock was flooded, the gate wide open. *Nova Cura* was being pushed away from the large barge she had been tied to; two long lines led from her bow across the basin to Atelier Fluvial, one to each side of the dry dock gate. I rode back to the B&B and told Betty what was happening. There was nothing we could do, so we ate breakfast, read the paper and, with our land ladies help, Betty ordered a washing machine for *Nova Cura* from the But Store in Dole. The But stores are a chain of big box stores found throughout France that sell large and small appliances, televisions and, computers.

Mid morning we walked to the dry dock. *Nova Cura* was in the back behind a much larger barge, looking very small in comparison. Both barges were held in place by dozens of lines. The dry dock gate was closed and water was being pumped out. Along with a small crowd of curious passersby, Betty and I stood and watched as the water dropped and the barges emerged. Held in place by all those lines both barges settled neatly on to pre-positioned steel supports. When most of the water had been pumped out and both barges were resting on their supports, a couple of steel beams were secured to the barges mooring bits and to the edges of the dry dock—insurance against the barge moving or rolling over. By the time the beams were in place, the water had all been pumped out of the dry dock. A group of men then descended into the dry dock and, with a lot of arm waving and pointing, began inspecting both barges. Looked like a good time to go to lunch.

That afternoon, at H_2O's chandlery, I ordered new water tanks and bought a new water pump, an accumulator tank, a rebuild kit for our marine toilet and assorted bits and pieces of plumbing. I also ordered a stylish new marine certified propane cook top for Betty's new kitchen—yes kitchen, not "galley". The former cargo hold was for all intents and purposes, a one bedroom, one bath apartment (or flat), and we took to using the everyday landlubber terms—bedroom, bathroom, living room, and kitchen—when talking about that area, but the aft sleeping cabin, the former crews quarters remained "the aft cabin". It was all perfectly reasonable. The next day our land lady loaned us her car and we drove to the But in Dole, and paid for *Nova Cura's* washing machine, and then to the Supermarche Cora for a bicycle for Betty (assembly required, some things are universal) and another load of barge furnishings: a toaster, a good counter top toaster/broiler oven, a coffee maker, a quilt and some other stuff. Back at the B&B, I assembled Betty's bike and we went for a ride around Losne, St. Jean de Losne and St. Usage, ending up at the dry dock. *Nova Cura's* propeller lay on a wooden pad at the stern of the barge, the propeller shaft was gone, a worker was grinding something under the hull and banging noises came from inside. It was near quitting time, gray, heavily overcast with a few spits of rain and it was cold for June. It was a bright cheerful day to us—work had commenced and things were happening.

Saturday was the start of another three day religious holiday, a double barreled one—Pentecost and Whit Monday—and everyone had warned us that this one, unlike Ascension, was observed, get your cash on Friday because the banks would be closed all three days and the ATMs would run dry. All official offices and many smaller retail stores would be closed for all three days. Except for the brokerage office at H_2O, which would be open Saturday, the only marine businesses that would be open were the H_2O harbormasters office and the Crown Blue Line hire-boat base; both would be open all three days. No boat or barge work, of course, would be done. On Sunday nothing but a few restaurants, the presse (half day), one of the boulangeries (also half day) and the Intermarche in St. Usage would be open. There were four boulangeries and/or patisseries (three were both) between St. Jean de Losne, Losne and St. Usage and they appeared to co-ordinate Sunday and Holiday openings. Both the Intermarche in St. Usage and the Supermarche Casino in St. Jean de Losne had in-house bakeries. The Intermarche seemed to observe no holidays, religious or secular. They were open seven days a week although they did close early on Bastille Day and, I think, Christmas. The Casino was inconsistent, they might be open, they might be closed or they might be open for just part of the day; the only way to know in advance was to read the small Xeroxed notices often taped to the door. The maison de la presse was; apparently, open for at least part of the day, every day.

H_2O owned, or operated, a second protected basin called the "old lock" (ancienne ecluse) located several kilometers down the Saone from St. Jean de Losne, near the town of Le Clos du Roy. We had never been there so Saturday morning we rode down. The basin was full of large—most over twenty five meters long—privately owned converted barges, some of which were very good looking. Sunday we tried to have lunch at the Auberge de la Marine, the best restaurant in town, but because it was a holiday the Auberge was reservations required and they were "complete" (full). So we walked to L'Amiral and enjoyed an excellent lunch of Steak Frites. The owner urged us to try a white wine he had on hand that came from the village of St. Bris de Vineux—between Auxerre and Chablis—and it was excellent. I thought it was almost indistinguishable from good Chablis. During our seasons aboard *Nova Cura* we frequently bought, and enjoyed, St. Bris, unfortunately like many lesser known French wines it is apparently not exported to the United States. Monday, during a ride around town for a little exercise, Betty saw the *S/V Glen Lyon* and our friends Rod and Sue coming down the Saone. We hurried down to the Quai National, upstream from the Saone River Bridge, and helped them tie up. When *Glen Lyon* was secure, we all walked over to L'Amiral and over dinner and too much wine, Betty and I gave them the critical need to know information about St. Jean de Losne, and they told us about their month long trip down through the canals from Paris.

Tuesday morning barge work resumed and it continued until *Nova Cura* was taken out of the dry dock—despite several days of sometimes heavy rain and unseasonably cold temperatures.[41] There was a slightly springy and rather narrow

---

41 On June third the low temperature in St. Jean de Losne was thirty seven degrees! That was degrees Fahrenheit, not degrees Celsius.

Nova Cura in the dry dock

The *Glen Lyon*

plank leading from the edge of the dry dock to the deck of the barge. The men working on *Nova Cura* walked back and forth across that plank all day, sometimes carrying tools or large pieces of barge, but my balance is not very good and I was not about to walk that disaster waiting to happen. There was also a ladder from the floor of the dry dock up to *Nova Cura's* deck. One, and often both of us, would climb aboard several times each day to see what was going on, but we stayed out of the way and the only work either of us did was a little exterior painting. The day before the barge came out of the dry dock we rode nine kilometers to the village of les Maillys where we ate lunch in the "Restaurant Virion". The restaurant was listed in the Red Book with two forks and a Bib Gourmand, one step below a one star restaurant. Our lunch was not worth the price or the bike ride; whoever prepared it lunch was not going to earn them that Michelin star.

On June fourteenth *Nova Cura* was pulled back to H_2O's side of the basin, the raft of barges was shuffled and she was put next to shore and right in front of the carpenter's shop— in the spot previously occupied by the barge belonging to Philippe, the Chef d'Atelier, which he was restoring. Except for the new gearbox, some engine work and some wiring details, all of the items called out in our surveys had been taken care of. In addition: the new water tanks were in and the carpenter had measured for and had started work on Betty's kitchen. After two weeks in the dry dock Betty's antique was again absolutely filthy and most of the day was spent giving it a thorough bath—finishing just in time to help Rod and Sue move *S/V Glen Lyon* from the Saone River quay to a place in the marina on the head of one of H_2O's pontoons. They had to move because the next day, was the start of still another three day holiday weekend, but this one was strictly local. It was the annual Celebration of the Barge Industry and the Blessing of The Fleet. The only businesses closing for the holiday were the marine businesses. The crews of a number of commercial peniches that had moored, sometimes rafted together, along the Saone River quays, had been washing and touching up the paint on their vessels in preparation for the Blessing. On Friday they, along with a number of privately owned converted barges and canal cruisers—but no hire-boats—moved to positions along the Quai National where they moored bow to the quay. Along the shore in front of the barges and boats were children's rides, food vendors, craft vendors and all the other trappings of a small town fair, even a shooting gallery. Saturday was more rain and showers, but there were crowds of people in town for the Fete, no one seemed to mind a little rain. Sunday morning *Glen Lyon* left for the trip down the Saone and the Rhone to the Mediterranean. After seeing them off, we walked over to the Quai National and attended the Mass that was the actual Blessing of the Fleet, it was an impressive, very formal and solemn, High Mass. Late that afternoon when we returned to our B&B, Catherine, our land lady, had some possibly bad news for us. If we were not living on our barge by Saturday the twenty-fourth, we would have to find alternative accommodations as our apartment was booked from June twenty-fifth through August. She had alluded to this problem several weeks earlier, but assuming that we would surely be living aboard *Nova Cura* by late June, neither of us had paid attention.

Monday morning, as soon as H_2O opened, Betty talked to Catherine and Philippe about our possible housing problem. Philippe said he would speak to his men and see what could be done, but no guarantees. Catherine assured Betty she and her friend Catherine (Catherine the Second, our land lady) could easily find a short term rental, they knew everybody. All week Betty and I and H_2O worked steadily. Betty completed painting the floor and started painting the walls in the main living area. I rebuilt our toilet, installed new faucets in the bathroom sink and shower, cleaned out and repaired the shower sump pump (the pump that removes waste shower water) and completed work on the barges 12 volt electrical system. The entire 12 volt switch panel now worked, as did everything controlled through the panel, even the 12 volt side of the refrigerator. H_2O installed and tested our new hydraulic gearbox and the single lever engine control Betty had requested, rewired the refrigerators 220 volt circuit, installed new battery boxes, cables and selector switches in the engine room and the carpenter shop made considerable progress on the new kitchen.

It was not enough. By Wednesday night it was clear that an alternate place to live for at least another week, maybe longer would be necessary. Catherine found us a good gite in St. Usage, clean, well equipped and a short bike ride from *Nova Cura*; but lacking the view and charm of the maison bourgeoise beside the Saone. Saturday morning, June twenty-third, with the help of our land lady and her car, we moved all of the things we had purchased for the barge and most of our clothes and personal belongings from the B&B to the bedroom on the barge. The bedroom (the forward cabin) was clean, repainted and out of the work zone. Then we moved ourselves and a few clothes and essential items to the gite. After the move, Betty and I ate lunch at the Bar/Café de la Navigation on the Quai National and my lunch entrée tasted slightly off, not really bad, just not right. By evening I was violently sick. The next day I felt miserable, had no energy and could not eat, so—assuming I had a bacterial intestinal infection—

I started to take some antibiotics from our sailboats medicine cabinet that we had brought over with us. By Monday morning I felt a good deal better.

Tuesday I felt well enough that I thought I would tackle my next big job on the barge, repainting the deck. *Nova Cura's* deck was original, vintage 1927, iron and at some point in the past had been tarred. Previous owners had removed most of the tar and painted the deck but much of the paint was gone and the remaining patches of tar were a mess. Philippe said to use one of H_2O's power washers on the deck. The high pressure spray would remove almost all of the remaining paint and a lot of the tar. I could then prime the deck with a special water based primer and paint it with a gray non skid paint designed for iron and steel decks. I got the power washer and started work. An hour later I was back at the gite, again very sick. Wednesday I gave up and went to a French doctor in St. Usage. The doctor had worked in the United States and spoke excellent English, flavored with slightly out of date American slang. She told me that I had a viral gastro-enteritis and the antibiotic was making me worse, not better. She gave me three prescriptions and told me to stay in bed until Friday and to do nothing strenuous—boat work or long bike rides—until Monday.

As time passed and our costs mounted the idea that maybe Rod and Sue had had the right idea when they sailed *S/V Glen Lyon* across the Atlantic began creeping unbidden into the deepest recesses of my mind. They had enjoyed a winter in London and another in Paris, and were now on their way to the Mediterranean: to Italy, Greece, Turkey and all the rest. Betty and I were camping in a dark gite built into an eighteenth century farm house in a rural village in Burgundy, and pitch forking our savings into an antique iron floating money

pit. The dream of living on a pretty Dutch barge and slowly
cruising through the lovely French canals seeming to hover,
just out of reach, a chimera in a foggy, slowly receding, some-
day.

Sitting in the gite, I was accomplishing nothing, ignor-
ing the doctor; I went back to work, finished power washing
the deck and started rolling on the primer as soon as it dried.
Betty sanded and started varnishing the interior of the wheelhouse. Also on Saturday, much to our surprise as we had never
seen anyone from H$_2$O's workshops do any weekend work,
Bernard, the head carpenter, arrived and worked until late
afternoon. He put the plywood top on the breakfast bar and
glued the Formica surface on, then he put the stainless steel
top on the new kitchen counter. The stainless steel top was the
only part of the old kitchen counter that had been salvaged. It
was a nice top that covered the whole counter and had a raised
rim and a molded in sink. During my sick week, Pierre had
put the refrigerator in its place in the breakfast bar, run a new
propane hose from the propane locker in the bow to where
the cook top would sit in the breakfast bar, installed Betty's
washing machine under the counter and had put in new water
lines and a new drain. With their tops in place, the breakfast
bar and counter looked almost finished; even with no paint or
trim and with the boards, lead weights and clamps that were
holding the Formica until the glue cured.

The next morning I felt much better, the great gastro
whatever-it-was a thing of the past. After a healthy breakfast, the first in several days, I finished priming the deck and
started rolling on the thick, heavy deck paint while Betty continued her varnishing job. Varnishing was not going well. The
flat plains of the Saone River have been farm country since
before the time of Christ, the Adeui, the largest of the tribes

in Gaul, farmed the plains long before the coming of Julius Caesar, and the spring wheat harvest was in full swing. There were several large grain silos and a combined barge and rail car loading facility nearby. On their way to and from the silos, trucks loaded with grain and tractors towing large trailers and farm equipment made frequent use of a gravel road that ran past H_2O's workshops. Despite the cool damp weather, every passing truck and tractor raised a cloud of dust which, inevitably and happily, settled on Betty's varnish. Dust and thick gray deck paint appeared to be more compatible than dust and varnish.

Monday and Tuesday, the second and third of July, were red letter days.

Monday when we got to *Nova Cura* Bernard and Pierre were both working. Bernard had removed all the weights and clamps from the top of the breakfast bar, used a hand router to trim the Formica, and was installing hardwood trim and Pierre had installed the new cook top, connected its propane line and electrical wiring (which he demonstrated by repeatedly lighting first one burner and then the other). While Bernard installed drawer runners and Pierre connected the plumbing under the kitchen counter, Betty and I went back to our more prosaic jobs; painting and varnishing. When we, all of us—Betty, Bernard, Pierre and I—got back from lunch, Jean-Paul, the Harbormaster, was waiting and *Nova Cura's* engine was running.

With Jean-Paul issuing instructions, *Nova Cura* was extricated from the nest of barges in front of H_2O's workshops. For the first time since our arrival in St. Jean de Losne, Betty's barge was under way under its' own power. We left the canal basin and locked through to the Saone River, our first lock aboard *Nova Cura*. Once out in the river, Betty—for the very first time—took the wheel of her barge. She drove us up river for a couple of kilometers, turned around and came back down, testing the steering and the single lever engine control. Jean-Paul then took over and drove us into the Marina; to a spot on one of H$_2$O's pontoons. Jean-Paul and Bernard left. Pierre, before he too left, showed us (again) that the cook top worked, that the refrigerator was on and cooling down, and that there was running water in the kitchen sink. I connected the shore-power, which worked exactly the way it should, hooked up our hose and topped up our new water tanks, and then we spent the rest of the afternoon cleaning the barge before heading over to L'Amiral for a celebratory dinner.

Tuesday we paid our bill at the gite and moved aboard. *Nova Cura* was still in St. Jean de Losne, still tied to one of H$_2$O's pontoons, and some minor work still needed to be done before she could actually leave and cruise up a canal to some-where—to anywhere. The next day was the fourth of July, Independence Day, and we had a new beginning to celebrate. We were living aboard at last, and living comfortably on a barge that could finally, actually move.

6. To the Roof of the World

Several of the people in the marina and at H_2O had told us that Bastille Day in St. Jean de Losne was an event worth waiting for. Bastille Day was July fourteenth, ten days away, more than enough time to complete the work that still needed to be done, buy the things we still needed, plan our first trip and prepare for departure. The Monday after Bastille Day became our target...Departure Day. Betty and I did a little additional desultory and unenthusiastic sanding and painting and I installed 12 volt electrical outlets in the wheelhouse and aft cabin. Bernard, the carpenter, completed the drawers, trim and other final details on the breakfast bar and the kitchen counter. Pierre made a few adjustments in the plumbing and fixed a small leak that appeared the second or third time Betty ran the washing machine. And H_2O's work on *Nova Cura* was done, at least for the 2001 season.

The weather did not cooperate; it stayed gray, cloudy, cold, windy and damp. The daily forecast in the International Herald Tribune kept calling for abnormally cold, windy and rainy weather, and it was right with depressing consistency. On one particularly raw day we took the train to Dijon and bought bedding for the aft cabin, some more kitchen equipment, a toilet paper holder, and a few of life's other necessities. Returning from Dijon, as soon as the trains doors opened I ran to the hardware store, and got there just before they locked the doors—the days last customer bought a small fifteen hundred watt electric heater. That night the temperature in the cabin dropped to fifty-five degrees and the brand new electric heater came out of its box.

The VNF, like the Coast Guard in the United States, has a little list of things that all pleasure craft need to have on board. When Betty made her initial offer on *Nova Cura*, there were life jackets, fenders, dock lines, fire extinguishers, etc. on board and we assumed that all of that equipment transferred with the barge. However, between January and the merry month of May, mostly it had sort of gone away...just disappeared. The missing things had not been specifically itemized in the sales contract, so that buying what was needed was the only option. Several thousand francs past across the counters at the hardware store and the chandleries in exchange for: a spot light, four life jackets, six large fenders, dock lines, four fire extinguishers ("extincteur" in French, another great word), a French flag and a flag of Burgundy, a two kilo hammer, four steel mooring stakes, an ax[42] and some miscellaneous equipment like galvanized shackles.

The Bastille Day Holiday was cool, gray and windy, with rain for a little variety. Despite the weather, all the trappings of a small town fair were set up along the quays: children's rides, food and wine stands, and the ever popular shooting gallery. Friday afternoon—partly cloudy but no rain—there was a great small town parade with floats, tractors, fire engines, the police band, the queen of this and the princess of

---

42 When barges are moored to a canal bank, a common practice, mooring stakes are often driven into the ground back from the bank to provide a place to attach the barges mooring lines. The stakes we used were eighty centimeters long (approximately two and one half feet) and had a steel ring, for the mooring line, in one end and a sharp point on the other. The two kilo hammer (about four and one half pounds) was to drive the stakes into the ground. We made frequent use of our hammer and stakes. The ax was to cut mooring lines in an emergency. For example, if one of the lines securing the barge in a lock caught or jammed as the water in the lock was dropping. We never needed the ax, but we saw (after the event) a hireboat that needed, and didn't have one. Shoddy construction saved them, a cleat tore out of the deck.

that. On Saturday the fourteenth, Bastille Day, rain, alternating between light, heavy and torrential, fell for most of the day. In spite of the rain a market was set up on the main street through town (the Rue Monge/Rue de la Liberte, different ends of the same rather short street). We put on our rain jackets, joined a crowd of soggy Frenchman, and walked through the market; buying some good sausage, including one made from duck confit that I absolutely loved (and never found again), and an outstanding cheese, a well aged Comte.[43] The village markets were one of the things we came to love about canal cruising in France. In the markets food shopping was a constant adventure. Move twenty kilometers down a canal and the local produce, sausage, cheese, even wine, all the products-of-the-land, changed. Even the large grocery stores reflected local products. The fresh produce, cheese and wine at the Casino in St. Jean de Losne differed noticeably from what was available at the ATAC Supermarche in Migennes, at the other end of the Canal de Bourgogne.

Our planned departure day—cold, windy and rainy of course—arrived and we did not depart. But we did walk through the rain to the VNF office and, for €215.00, purchase a thirty day canal usage permit, which entitled us to thirty days of actual navigation (movement) on the canals and the days did not need to be contiguous (an annual, for the full year, permit would have been €334.00). We took *Nova Cura's* old permit, a copy of the bill of sale and our insurance

---

43 Comte is an alpine or Swiss type cheese, from the Jura. Most Comte is aged for three to nine months and is very good but it is not the same as a properly and skillfully aged two, or three, year old Comte. Just as a good three month old farm house Cheddar is a pale and anemic cousin to a two, or three, or four year old Cheddar. Incidentally, really good alpine or Swiss type cheese has very few holes in it and, if there are any they are small. The presence of numerous large holes in a "Swiss" cheese is a mark of a cheap factory made cheese.

papers to the VNF office and asked for "un annuel Permis s'il vous plait" (for 2001). The VNF agent winced, and with no possibly embarrassing questions about little matters like an address that changed from document to document, sold us our permit—fractured French from the barbarians at the office window to the rescue. Tuesday the weather did not improve, I changed the engine oil, the oil filter and the fuel filter and we did laundry. Wednesday we paid our bill at H_2O and, without help, left the marina, drove out into the Saone River and spent an hour just driving up and down, trying things out. Then we went alongside the fuel barge and bought two hundred liters of diesel, before returning to the marina. Actually leaving was proving difficult. It was the middle of July, mid-summer; we were wearing blue jeans and heavy shirts and had the cabin heater going most mornings. How did all those wine grapes ever ripen? Maybe there is no summer in Burgundy?

Thursday was another unappealing canal travel day. Betty and I had been reading French Lessons, the new book by Peter Mayle,[44] and were intrigued by the Bresse chickens. Bresse chickens are the only chickens in the world with an AOC, an appellation d'origine controlee, and possibly the only chickens in the world with true blue feet. A day trip by train to Bourg en Bresse for a lunch of blue footed AOC fowl in cream sauce with an appetizer of frog legs (following Peter Mayle's suggestion) seemed like a great way to spend a cold damp day. We ate our frogs and fowl at Le Francais, a large, ornate and comfortable restaurant on the main street (No. 7, Ave. Alsace-Lorraine, Bourg en Bresse) and it was indeed very good. Lunch was accompanied, on the recommendation of our waiter, by a Macon Ige (a white Burgundy) which was also very good, and

---

44 French Lessons, Adventures with Knife, Fork and Corkscrew, by Peter Mayle, copyright 2001, ISBN: 0-375-40590-9, published by Alfred A. Knopf.

is another wine that does not seem to be available across the Atlantic. The strawberry tart that one of us insisted would be the perfect ending to a great lunch was fabulous.

We had been trying to decide which way to go, if we ever actually left St. Jean de Losne. Do we go south down the Saone to the wine country, northeast, to Epernay, Champagne and on to Paris, or somewhere else? Charles Gerard answered the question for us. He told us that, because of rapid suburban development in the area around Dijon, and resultant problems with the water supply, the high section of the Canal de Bourgogne—between Plombieres les Dijon, just above Dijon, and Montbard—was often closed for part of the season. So much water from the canal's reservoirs was being diverted to the Dijon urban area that there was not enough to operate the canal for the full season, and recently, in some drier than average years the high section had not opened at all. This year, because of the unusually cool and wet conditions—the conditions we had been complaining about—the canal was open clear through from the Saone River at St. Jean de Losne to its junction with the Yonne River at Migennes. Charles recommended that, if we wanted to do the Canal de Bourgogne, the canal he considered to be the most picturesque and interesting of all the canals, this was the year to do it. Sounded like a fine idea, especially since the entrance to the Canal de Bourgogne was right around the corner and we didn't even have to turn around. *Nova Cura* was already pointed in the right direction.

Friday, July 20, 2001, two months and five days after our arrival, and five days later than planned, *Nova Cura* left St. Jean de Losne.

Departure morning we were up at sunrise. As soon as things in town began to open, I went to the presse for the paper, to the boulangerie for a baguette and then to the Casino for a few things. When I got back, Betty had the engine running, the shore-power cord disconnected and onboard, and all but two of our dock lines off. The Captain was standing in the wheelhouse, ready to go. I undid the last two lines, stepped aboard, and with no fuss or commotion Betty's barge slipped quietly out of the gare d'eau, away from H_2O, into the Saone River and out of St. Jean de Losne. Jean-Paul, the Harbormaster, was on one of the docks helping a yacht cast off. He waved as we passed. At 8:00 a.m. when the locks opened and the lockkeeper cycled Canal de Bourgogne lock (ecluse) number seventy-six south of the dividing pond[45] for the first time that day, the first inbound (off the river, into the canal) vessel was *Nova Cura*. Even the weather cooperated, for the first time in what seemed like weeks the sun was shining—just a few small, puffy, white fair weather cumulous clouds in a blue and almost clear sky.

Construction of the Canal de Bourgogne, linking the Yonne River, the Seine River and Paris to the Saone River, the Rhone River and the Mediterranean Sea, began under King Louis XVI. Construction began at Migennes, on the Yonne River and worked south toward Tonnerre. Several years later digging also began at St. Jean de Losne, working north toward Dijon, the walls and fortifications of St. Jean de Losne serving as a quarry for the stone used in building the canal. Because of financial problems, construction difficulties and the French Revolution progress was slow. The first barges from St. Jean de Losne, the Rhone and the Mediterranean Sea reached Dijon in 1808, and it was the winter of 1832-33 before a barge from

---

45 In a canal, a pond is the space, or navigable pool of water, between two locks. If a canal crosses a range of hills or crosses the divide between two watersheds, the dividing pond is the summit pond, the highest elevation on the canal and the point from which the canal goes downhill in both directions.

Paris made it through to Dijon. The canal, river portal to river portal, is two hundred forty-two kilometers long and has one hundred ninety-one locks[46], an average of one lock every one and a quarter kilometers. There are one hundred fifteen locks in the northern, Yonne/Seine watershed, which drains to the Atlantic Ocean, and seventy-six in the southern, Saone/Rhone watershed, draining to the Mediterranean Sea. Lock numbers on both sides of the watershed begin at the dividing pond at Pouilly en Auxois and the numbers increase as the canal descends to the river portals. Rather oddly, the kilometer marker numbers run the other way, decreasing from the summit pond to each river portal. The canal assumed its current appearance in the last decade of the nineteenth century and the first decade of the twentieth century when the locks were modernized to the Freycinet standard and a number of locks were eliminated. Prior to the completion of the Main-Donau Kanal (the canal that links the Rhine River to the Danube River), the Canal de Bourgogne reached the highest elevation—three hundred seventy-eight meters (one thousand two hundred twenty-eight feet) above sea level—of any canal in Europe[47]. Nineteenth century barge men supposedly called Pouilly en Auxois and the dividing pond at the canals summit the Roof of the World.

---

46 Various published sources give different numbers, ranging from 187 to 209, for the number of locks on the Canal de Bourgogne. The figures given here came from *Nova Cura's* annual log books (the primary source for this narrative) and from the chart kit we used: <u>Waterways Guide Vol. 3: Bourgogne & Franche-Comte</u>, by Editions du Breil, 11400 Castelnaudary, France, pages 68-94.

47 The Canal de Bourgogne would reach an elevation more than fifty meters higher if the summit pond were on, rather than under, the divide between the watersheds of the Seine/Yonne and the Rhone/Saone at Pouilly en Auxois; but, the dividing pond is, in large part, a tunnel three and three-tenths kilometers long.

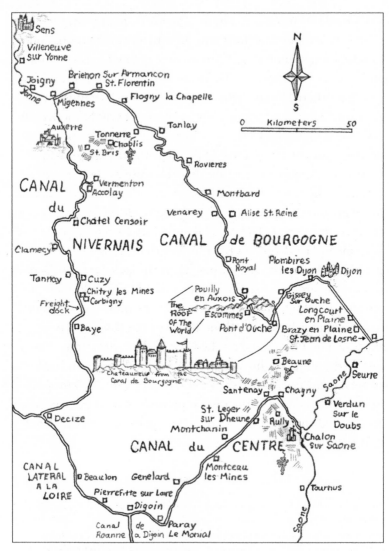

Map 3. The Burgundy and Nivernais Canals

Our first day of actual canal travel was characterized by
caution—six slow kilometers and only three locks before stopping for lunch at an unoccupied dock beside a grain silo, and
then just seven kilometers and five more locks before stopping
for the day just above lock sixty-nine, at Longecourt en Plaine.
Day one ended with a pair of happy bargees taking a bicycle
ride around Longecourt en Plaine and enjoying dinner in the
attractive little town. Day two on the canal, confidence in
ourselves and in *Nova Cura* increasing, we managing fourteen
locks and sixteen kilometers and moved up to the port de
plaisance in Dijon. Between St. Jean de Losne and the outer
reaches of Dijon, the canal passed through the flat farm land of
the Burgundian Plain. A rural landscape of small towns, grain
silos, fields of wheat, soy beans and corn, and grazing cattle.
At Longvic, several kilometers outside Dijon, the landscape
transitioned from rural to industrial and the bleak wastelands
of modern industry—parking lots, chain link fences, massive
warehouses, the sheet metal sheds of unidentifiable dinghy,
smoky gray factories—hemmed the canal closely. Between
locks fifty-seven and fifty-six we passed the depressing port de
commerce. A few cargo barges, survivors of a once great fleet,
were moored along ageing quays covered with loading facilities and heaps of gravel, sand, concrete blocks, lime, timber,
and the other bulk cargos carried by the barges lucky enough
to still be working. Past lock fifty-six our view from the canal
became less industrial and more urban residential. Arriving at
the marina, we tied up in a spot that was clearly marked as reserved for Hotel Barges. The Harbormaster came over, greeted
us in English, and told us to stay where we were for the night,
but to move to another spot (which he pointed out) in the
morning because several hotel barges would be arriving.

At a civilized hour in the morning, well after breakfast, with the harbormaster directing and assisting, we moved *Nova Cura*. Less than an hour later the first hotel barge arrived and tied up in our overnight parking spot. The port de plaisance in Dijon was a loop of water off the canal that had been the original commercial port for Dijon, the former cargo handling area around the port had been made into an inviting and attractive park. From the park's main entrance it was just two short blocks up Rue de l'Hopital to the line of the old walls (of which very little was left), and the center city's restaurants, museums, tourist sites and shopping. Across the street from the main entrance to the park, I found a small boulangourie-epicerie (a combination bakery and market) which, in addition to baguettes, offered one of the major requirements of civilized life. A rack of newspapers stood by the door and slot three, from the top, held the International Herald Tribune... English edition.

On the way to Dijon, we had known exactly where we were and what to expect just ahead, thanks to our chart kit of the Canal de Bourgogne. For the Burgundy canal, the scale was 1:50,000 or two centimeters per kilometer. Each lock, bridge and kilometer marker was clearly shown. The length of all but the smallest ponds (the pool of water between two locks) was given in meters. The name and number of each lock, the type of lock (manual or automatic) and the rise/fall of the water in the lock (in meters) was also given. In addition the charts showed navigation hazards such as shoals and ruins, the towns and roads along the canal and anything that might be of interest to passing boaters: marinas, boatyards, restaurants, shopping, fuel, train stations, post offices, places of historical interest, etc. Each chart page was accompanied by a page of text and photos arranged in three columns: French,

English and German; and reading across the columns, seeing the same phrases and terms in both French and English, contributed to our ability to read any paper work pertaining to *Nova Cura* and the signs, headlines, menus and schedules that surrounded us every day. The charts were well designed, attractive, easy to read, and seemed to be very accurate. We used chart kits from the same publisher on all of the canals we travelled and, generally, they were all good.

I had a portable, battery powered, e-mail device[48], that first morning in Dijon, when I checked for e-mail on the pay phone at the harbormaster's office, there was one from Mac and Nancy Greeley, sailing friends from the Chesapeake Bay and The Bahamas.

> "We're in Europe for our son's wedding, have a rental car and will be driving through the St. Jean de Losne area in a few days."
> "Excellent, by all means stop and spend a night on the barge, but we have moved up to the marina in Dijon."
> "We would love to, we'll arrive Wednesday."
> "We're looking forward to it."

It was Sunday morning; we had three days to enjoy Dijon and, more important, go shopping. *Nova Cura* was livable and even fairly comfortable, but still lacking a lot of

---

48 PocketMail©, essentially an elaborate electronic organizer powered by three AA batteries, with a two and one half by six inch LCD screen, a full qwerty key pad, a very rudimentary word processor, a calendar, an address book and a built in acoustic coupler. All packaged in a clam shell case that slipped neatly into a pocket and opened to six inches by seven inches. It worked very well although at three hundred bits per second, it was painfully slow.

necessary household items: enough knives, forks and spoons for four people to actually eat a civilized meal, a can opener that worked, some stools for the breakfast bar and a good chair or two, so that more than two people could sit down at the same time. Monday was small item shopping in the inner city, an excellent lunch at the Bistro des Halles (73 Rue Auxonne) and a visit to an archeological dig at a construction site that had uncovered Roman ruins. Tuesday, in the morning we took a taxi to a store recommended by the harbormaster, "Troc de Isle", where we bought three new mattresses (a double for the aft cabin and twins for the bedroom). The mattresses were purchased conditional on delivery to the barge that day—no problem, Betty and I got a free ride back to the port in the delivery truck...perched on our mattresses. The harbormaster told us to set our old mattresses beside the marina's trash bin. Twenty minutes later, while we were eating a quick lunch aboard, a beat-up old truck pulled up and two ragged, dark skinned men took all three mattresses.

After lunch, another long taxi ride, this time to the suburb of Quetigny, where the big box furniture stores were located. At one store, we bought a pair of nice stainless steel and molded teak stools for the breakfast bar and, at the store immediately next door, we bought a chair. Make that a CHAIR. Betty likes good design and she was in her modern Euro Style period. The store and the chair were Roche Bobois. The chair really was a superb piece of furniture: fine leather on a well made hardwood frame, good looking and very comfortable. Again, purchase was conditional on same day delivery. Again, no problem, at 6:00 p.m. when the store closed, the chair would be delivered. Betty, the bar stools and I took a taxi back to the marina. A half hour later, well before 6:00 p.m., the chair arrived. Still well before 6:00 p.m., a very satisfied Betty was sitting in *Nova Cura's* saloon in what was probably the single most expensive chair on any barge in Europe. But *Nova Cura* was ready for guests.

Betty and THE CHAIR

Wednesday morning was cleaning, laundry, filling the water tanks again (the washing machine used a lot of water), and a provisioning expedition to a nearby Supermarche. Mac and Nancy arrived in time for a late lunch and a walk around the Palace of the Dukes of Burgundy and part of the old center city before we all went to dinner at Le Gril Laure, the restaurant we had dinner in on our first visit to Dijon and had already returned to once. The food, wine and atmosphere were again very enjoyable.

Mac and Nancy could stay only one night and Betty wanted them to have at least a short barge ride, in the morning, leaving their car at the marina, they rode up the canal

with us for five kilometers and five locks, to Plombieres les
Dijon where we tied up at a small, clean, well built marina
with free power and water. On the quay a sign called the
facility a "halte nautique[49]" and said that it was provided by
the VNF. After lunch, Mac and Nancy took a taxi back to Dijon
and their rental car. Betty and I decided to stay parked for the
night, and went for an afternoon bike ride during which we
found a butcher shop (boucherie) that was selling fresh rabbit
(lapin). That night dinner was Lapin a la Dijonnaise. Served
with a bottle of fine Burgundy, a simple salad, part of a fresh
Baguette and a good cheese, it was a great dinner. We had
caught the chimera and life was good on *Nova Cura*.

Between St. Jean de Losne and Dijon the Canal de Bourgogne is an almost straight man made canal. From Dijon to
Pont d'Ouche the canal is the canalized River Ouche. Above
Pont d'Ouche the canal is again man made but it is far from
straight. Past Plombieres les Dijon the suburbs of Dijon thin
and disappear, open country returns and the space between
the locks decreases as the canal gradient increases. This side
of Dijon, unlike the flat rich farm land between Dijon and St.
Jean de Losne, is hilly, rocky and mostly forested with narrow steep valleys holding thin ribbons of pasture and crops,
small old stone villages, fortified farms and chateaus, and what
seems like an excessive number of churches. The often large
churches hint at a formerly more populous countryside. Since

---

49 A halte nautique, literally "boat stop", was generally a free pontoon (floating
dock), or a quay, that might, or might not, have (also free) water and/or electricity, but almost never had toilets or a harbormaster. A port de plaisance, generally
found in larger cities or towns, was larger, had better facilities, almost always had a
harbormaster and was rarely free. There were also privately owned, fee for service,
"marinas" (such as H$_2$O's) which were usually the most expensive and had by far
the best facilities. And then there were free standing "base nautiques", most of
which were hire-boat company operating bases. Having said the preceding; there
was a degree of overlap and inconsistency in the way the various names were used.

leaving St. Jean de Losne the weather had steadily improved: warm sunny days, crisp cool nights, and no rain—beautiful conditions for canal cruising. Plombieres les Dijon to Fleurey sur Ouche, and on to Gissey sur Ouche, were short easy eight to ten kilometer and eight to ten lock days: start late, move slowly, stop early and enjoy the beautiful country side.

Gissey sur Ouche had a Sunday market that the harbormaster in Dijon claimed was an excellent place to get good country sausage, dry cured ham, and fresh fruits and vegetables, and the Chateau Barbirey was just a short bicycle ride from town. According to our Michelin Green Guide, the Gardens of Barbirey (les Jardins de Barbirey) were spectacular and should not be missed. Arriving in Gissey at mid-day, we put the bicycles ashore and rode to the Chateau de Barbirey. There was not much left of the original medieval castle, it had largely been replaced in the sixteenth century by a more modern manor house which had, in turn, been rebuilt in the eighteenth century. But most of the sixteenth and seventeenth century out-buildings were intact and open and the gardens were spectacular. The gardens flowed down a long slope from the manor house to the canal in a series of terraces. Upper most, directly behind the manor house, was an herb and flower garden. Next was a formal, almost ridged, eighteenth century garden with broad straight gravel walks, hedges, low stone walls, small fountains and numerous statutes. Below the formal garden a large area of neatly mowed lawn merged gradually and artistically into a very carefully laid out "natural" landscape of woods, paths, and a little brook fed by an (I think) artificial spring. Hidden clearings with benches and small pavilions, well shielded by trees, provided opportunities for a gentleman and a lady to linger in discrete privacy.

The harbor master in Dijon knew his markets, the Sunday morning market in Gissey was excellent. We picked up several good cheeses, a tasty air dried venison sausage, and some fresh fruit—and I learned that a kilo of Mirabelles, delicious little cherry sized plums that I was very fond of,[50] is too many Mirabelles. A kilo, two and two-tenths pounds is...well...it's not really a good idea to try to eat two and two-tenths pounds of ripe Mirabelles. At least you won't gain weight. The correct, in this case, response to "un kilo?" is not "oui!" its "Non! un demi-kilo s'il vous plait" (a half kilo) or deux deci-kilos (two tenths of a kilo).

The market was very early Sunday morning and the locks didn't open for business until 9:00 a.m., by which time we were back aboard and ready to move to Pont d'Ouche. The locks were closed from noon to 1:00 p.m., the lockkeepers lunch hour, and we tied to the bank below a closed lock for our lunch. At 1:00 the lock did not open and there was no sign of activity. Fifteen minutes later, there was still no sign of a lockkeeper, no activity of any sort. It was a warm, sunny and profoundly peaceful Sunday afternoon on the Burgundy canal. So I leaned on the air horn button. Still no activity, no lockkeeper appeared, the gates did not swing open, nothing happened. I walked up the tow path to the lock to see what the hold-up was and yelled "Bon Jour" as I approached the lockkeeper's house. The problem was a sun bathing lock-

---

50 Mirabelles are another French, or really European, goody that is basically unavailable in the United States. Mirabelles are grown in Oregon and a few other places, unfortunately they are converted into Brandy or Eaux-de-Vie and not marketed as fresh fruit. Bonne Maman® in France and Hero® in Switzerland make Mirabelle preserves that are excellent, but I have never found them in the United States either, although other flavors from both firms are available.

keeper. The young blond lockkeeper[51] was sun bathing on a large towel, sans bikini, both bits, and she had fallen asleep. To put it mildly, she did not appreciate being interrupted by a loud "Bon Jour", at least not from me. In military terms, I immediately executed a rapid strategic retreat. She returned to a bare semblance of decency and opened the lower lock gates. We moved *Nova Cura* into the lock and she got her revenge. Filling the lock she opened both upstream sluices all the way, immediately, giving us two minutes of wild, rough and dangerous water while the lock filled. I did not help her open the uphill gate and as Betty drove us out of the lock, she made a face and stuck out her tongue.

Gissey sur Ouche to Pont d'Ouche was thirteen kilometers and thirteen locks, and between our late start and that lunch time delay, it was a long day. At Pont d'Ouche there was a small hire-boat base, but *Nova Cura* was too long and heavy for their pontoons, and was not welcome, something we got used to at hire-boat bases. So we moored to the canal bank in front of two large hotel barges and went in search of a dinner ashore. The only restaurant in the tiny village turned out to be an Irish Pub. A real Irish Pub, run by a real Irishman: Irish pub food, Irish music, Guinness and Harp on tap and a dart board on the wall. The place was crowded with Brits off one or both of the hotel barges. Dinner was Sheppard's Pie, salad, and a pint of half & half. Although because of slow service caused by the hotel barge crowd, dinner grew to Sheppard's Pie, salad and two

---

51 On the old historic canals that carry little, if any, freight and are closed through the winter, such as the Canal du Nivernais south of Vermenton and the high part of Canal de Bourgogne, the lockkeepers were often seasonal hires—students, retirees, old barge captains, local farmers. Some were good, but many were not. On the larger rivers and the modernized canals with large locks that were still used commercially, and in any canal or river section that used traveling lockkeepers, the lockkeepers were VNF professionals and always very competent.

pints. Desert was a third pint. By the time we left, the Hotel Boat crowd was in fine form. All those good Brits were trying to sing along with the sound system; belting out Irish revolutionary classics with gusto, and a few actually knew the words. Off in one corner a group of people from the hire-boats, people of unknown national origin, were standing around with strange expressions. They had thought they were in Burgundy.

Easy, slow half days suited us. Monday we moved on to Vandenesse en Auxois, yet another of the attractive, old, small, gray, stone towns that seemed to be a specialty of this part of Burgundy. This one boasted a municipal halte nautique with electricity and water available for a nominal fee, the fee to be paid in town at the cafe/restaurant—which was closed on Mondays. Oh well. After a quick lunch on board, the bicycles went ashore and we rode to Chateauneuf. Coming up the canal in the morning the fairytale walls and towers of Chateauneuf, perched high atop a steep rocky hill had been visible for miles and hours. Originally built by the Lords of Chaudenay in several stages, between the end of the eleventh and the middle of the twelfth centuries, the chateau was given by Philippe the Good, Duke of Burgundy (and father of Charles the Bold) to his godson Philippe Pot in 1457. Philippe Pot, a Burgundian diplomat and military leader said to have been the greatest knight and warrior of his time, massively enlarged and strengthened the chateau and rebuilt the main buildings in the Gothic style. The compact little village of Chateauneuf lay just below the chateau and was separated from it by a draw bridge. Many of the buildings in the village dated to between the fourteenth and the seventeenth centuries and now housed a couple of auberges, a cafe, and a number of art galleries and gift shops. The village wall, really an outer defensive perimeter for the chateau, was largely intact. All true fairy tale castles are high up on steep rocky hills. Riding, and then pushing our bicycles up that hill was hard, hauling up the stone for those massive walls and towers must have been brutal. Feudal Lords who lived in iffy neighborhoods and built castles on steep rocky hills needed serfs...lots of serfs.

The eighth lock up the canal from Vandenesse en Auxois, the Escommes lock—a two and one half meter rise and our last up lock for this trip—was lock number one on the Saone/Rhone side of the Canal de Bourgogne. Escommes was on the dividing pond. It was Tuesday July 31, 2001, after eleven days of climbing up hill, covering eighty-two kilometers and transiting seventy-six locks, *Nova Cura* had reached the Yonne-Saone water shed. We were on the summit, at The Roof of the World. In the morning we would go through the Pouilly tunnel[52] to Pouilly en Auxois and, the following day, begin the long decent to the Yonne River.

---

52 The Pouilly tunnel, the final segment of the Burgundy canal to be constructed, was built between 1826(?) and 1832. It is a marvelous testament to the skill of the early nineteenth century French engineers. The tunnel, three and three-tenths kilometers long, was built from both ends toward the middle and when the ends met the two sections were only centimeters apart. The almost perfectly straight tunnel was cut through difficult fractured, faulted and, in places, water logged rock. Rock falls and cave-ins killed an unknown number of workers.

Going south on the Burgundy Canal
near Longcourt en Plaine

Nova Cura on the canal bank at Fleurey sur Ouche

Entering the Pouilly Tunnel - the "Roof of the World"

7. Down, Through History, to the Yonne

A multi-lingual sign beside the mooring basin in Escommes listed the tunnel transit requirements and said that a VNF representative would come by in the late afternoon to check *Nova Cura*. If everything was in order, he would give us permission to go through the tunnel and our transit time. The tunnel is narrow and traffic through the tunnel is one-way, the directions alternating, and carefully controlled by the VNF. I put the search light on its mount, plugged it in and tested it, and tested the horn. Betty took two of our shiny new life jackets out of their plastic wrappers and hung them prominently in the wheelhouse. In the evening, just as dinner was being served, the VNF agent arrived to inspect *Nova Cura*. He tested the search light and horn, glanced at our life jackets, measured the height of the wheelhouse, asked if it could be taken down, and after telling us not to get underway, not to leave the quay, until our assigned time, he handed me a small slip of paper—10:30 the next morning.

After breakfast on tunnel day, even though the VNF agent had not required it, we took down the wheelhouse for the first time—discovering in the process that there was a fair amount of rotten wood in some of the roof panels, and around several of the windows. Once the wheel house was down, there was little to do except sit and wait. Our instructions had been very clear. Do not leave; don't even undo the mooring lines, until 10:30. We thought that another barge or boat was making an early south-bound trip through from the other end. No other vessel appeared and at 10:30 Betty started our motor,

I undid the last two mooring lines, and we started through—vaguely worried that someone coming from the other end had started late, we would meet in the middle, they would be bigger than us, and we would be the ones who had to try to back out of the tunnel. The trip through was anti-climatic. The tunnel was lighted, almost perfectly straight, and from a hundred meters in, the little spot of daylight at the far end was clearly visible, like the bulls-eye on a target. At the north end, when we emerged from the narrow tunnel approaches and entered the wider basin of the Port de Pouilly en Auxois, our VNF agent from the evening before was waiting. He waved to us and then signaled to a hotel barge that they could now start through. The Port de Pouilly en Auxois was large, well equipped and charged a nominal daily use fee for water, electricity, trash service, and showers. The afternoon was spent putting the wheelhouse back up, going to the local Supermarche and exploring the old part of town adjacent to the canal. Putting the wheelhouse back together took longer and was more difficult than it should have been, because two pieces of deteriorating window frame kept falling off. Dinner in the evening was at the Hotel la Poste, and was surprisingly good.

Between Pouilly en Auxois and another Gissey (but this time without the "sur Ouche") there were twelve locks, seven of them in the first two kilometers and, for the first time, a traveling lockkeeper accompanied us, riding a motor bike along the canal path from lock to lock. *Nova Cura* was alone, the only barge or boat, but had the canal been busy, boats and barges would have been grouped into small convoys, each large enough to fill a lock. Grouping boats going through the canal helped conserve water, and lockkeepers. The traveling lockkeeper left us at Gissey and we continued north for another ten and a half kilometers to our last lock for the day, at Pont Royal. The ten and a half kilometers between Gissey and Pont Royal is the longest lock free stretch on the entire Burgundy canal. The large basin at Pont Royal, a former commercial port and lay-over spot for freight barges, was managed by Locaboat Plaisance, but at this hire-boat base there was no problem with space for *Nova Cura*, there must have been a hundred meters of empty stone quay. Following lunch at the Locaboat bases bar/restaurant, we pedaled back along the canal for three kilometers to St. Thibault and visited the elegant thirteenth century priory church built by Robert II, Duke of Burgundy, to house the remains of the towns (and churches) namesake saint. The town also had an interesting old Chateau that was open to the public, but rapidly changing, deteriorating, weather—thickening low dark gray rainy looking clouds, a rising wind and a dropping temperature—suggested that skipping the chateau in favor of a fast ride back to Pont Royal might be a good idea.

From St. Jean de Losne to Pont Royal, the weather had been good, consistently warm and sunny, and no rain. Burgundy did have a summer after all, sort of late and short, but maybe there was some hope for all those little wine grapes. Back in Pont Royal we found the reason for the rapid change in the weather. Pont Royal and the Canal de Bourgogne had been invaded. Eight rather unusual little houseboats had arrived, on trailers, towed from the U.K. The boats were "Beaver 23s" and they looked like small house trailers (caravans) mounted on flat bottomed aluminum rafts with a five or six horse power long handled outboard motor centered on the stern. The long handle on the outboard motor provided both engine control and steering. The owners, who were busy launching their floating caravans, drinking beer, fiddling with their motors, drinking beer, taking pictures of each other and drinking beer, were a friendly and happy bunch. If I could hold that much beer, I'd probably be friendly and happy too. The British Beaver Boaters told us that six more Beaver 23s had put in (launched) further north and would be arriving shortly; they were only a lock or two from Pont Royal. They were members of the "Wilderness Boat Owners Club." A club exclusively for Beaver 23 owners and aficionados; and the club was exploring the upper Burgundy canal on its annual extended cruise. I had a hard time equating traveling on the Burgundy canal with wilderness exploration; but both Betty and I were sure that the Wilderness Boat Owners Club had precipitated the abrupt return to unseasonably cool, cloudy and wet weather. They brought it with them, it was typical U.K. weather. The rain started as the reinforcements arrived, bringing more beer. In the morning as the British Beaver Boaters prepared for further wilderness exploration, the sky was slate gray, it was flat out cold and a stiff wind was blowing intermittent rain. Betty and I were wearing blue jeans, sweaters and sea going foul weather jackets. The BBBs were wearing light rain jackets and shorts—they were on vacation and it was mid-summer.

From Pont Royal to Venarey les Laumes, on the canal, is only twenty-two kilometers, but there are forty-one locks. For us it was twenty-two kilometers, forty-one locks and two and a half, cold, wet, windy days. We were accompanied the entire way by the same poor, soggy, suffering, traveling lockkeeper. On the second of those days, August fourth, engine on in the morning to engine off in the evening was nine and one half hours. Nine and one half hours during which the sun never appeared, the rain never stopped, the wind never quit, and the temperature never made it above fifty degrees Fahrenheit (it felt like October, maybe the end of October, possibly the end of November, on the Chesapeake Bay). Nine and one half hours to move just over five kilometers, transit nineteen locks and drop fifty meters in elevation. The whole day was spent waiting on locks, entering locks, tying up in locks, riding down in locks and leaving locks. Late morning on the third day, when we finally reached the pleasant and well equipped halte nautique at Venarey les Laumes (water, electricity, showers, etc., nominal fee), we gave that poor lockkeeper two bottles of good wine, then plugged in our power cable, turned on the cabin heater, popped the cork on the best bottle of wine in the wine locker, fixed a good lunch and spent the afternoon trying to warm up and studying our travel guides.

Things to see and do, electricity for the cabin heater, a laundromat with dryers that actually worked, and on Wednesday, a large early morning open air market kept us in Venarey les Laumes for four days. It was August, high summer and peak vacation season in France, but the weather never varied: low gray clouds, intermittent rain, a cold west wind and temperatures that seemed to never get much above fifty degrees Fahrenheit. Several other canal boaters—English, Dutch and American—that we met at the halte nautique told us this weather, at this time of year, was very unusual. At least the Americans and the Dutch thought it was unusual, the Brits thought it was summer, they were running around in shorts.

Despite the weather we toured. We took a taxi to the Chateau de Bussy-Rabutin, owned by Roger de Rabutin, Count of Bussy. Count Roger, during the early years of the reign of Louis XIV, could not resist the urge to write satirical verses, songs, and pamphlets about court life and his King. Some of his writings went a bit far in the Kings opinion[53] and Roger spent a lot of time at his chateau, exiled from court—much to

---

53 *Histoire Amoureuse des Gaules*, for which he spent over a year in the Bastille.

the benefit of modern tourists. The Count was an articulate, artistic, cultured and talented man and the Chateau's architecture, interior design, paintings and artwork, and the gardens and park around the chateau, are well worth visiting. Also worth visiting, for the food, is the Auberge Bussy-Rabutin, located just outside the Chateau's gates, our lunch was excellent.

The next two days were spent taking long, damp-to-water-logged, bicycle rides; first to Alise St. Reine and Mont Auxois and then to Flavigny sur Ozerain. At Alise St. Reine we visited the Musee Alecia and the fascinating (and ongoing) archeological dig at the Gallo-Roman oppidum (town) of Alecia, had a late, expensive and not very good lunch at Le Cheval Blanc (Red Book), and before returning to *Nova Cura*, stopped at the imposing statue of Vercingetorix. Mont Auxois and Alecia, on it's west end, are the site of the battle/siege of Alecia, the climactic battle of Julius Caesar's conquest of Gaul. In 52 B.C., somewhere near Alecia, a settlement and hill fort of the Mandubii Gauls, Caesar was attacked by an army of Gauls under Vercingetorix. The Gauls were defeated, fell back to Alecia, and Caesar laid siege to them there. Caesar's Legions build two rings of earthwork and timber fortifications completely around the settlement, the hill fort and most of the hill—one ring faced in, the other out. An army of Gauls gathered outside the fortifications and in the fall they launched a strong attack on the outer ring of the Roman fortifications. The attack was coordinated with an all out attempt at breaking through the inner ring by Vercingetorix. The Romans suffered heavy casualties; but the Gaul's assault failed. Vercingetorix was captured, or surrendered, and the besieged Gauls were slaughtered or enslaved. The battle of Alecia ended significant resistance to Rome and in the

following century a blended Gallo-Roman culture took root
in much of what is today France.

The gloomy, gray, cold, wet and windy day was perfect for
visiting the Alecia excavations and the statue of Vercingetorix.
Standing on the observation platform at the feet of that tower-
ing statue of the proud, doomed, Gaulish warrior—Caesar
kept him a prisoner for eight years and then had him stran-
gled—while looking out over the Laumes plain and the long
slope leading up to the site of the Mandubii Gauls settlement
and hill fort was unexpectedly moving. The place seemed
haunted by the whispering ghosts of armies that clashed and
died more than twenty centuries ago.[54]

Our last full day at Venarey les Laumes we went to the
weekly outdoor market, it was a good market and very crowded,
and then rode to Flavigny sur Ozerain, a longer and harder
than expected ride. Guide books tend to be written for people in cars and little matters like steep hills and narrow roads
with a lot of traffic and no shoulders, are rarely mentioned.
Flavigny sur Ozerain is another of those places with almost
too much history[55]. Today it is a charming old town with a
very medieval feel, almost intact walls and fortifications, a
year round population of approximately four hundred and
fifty people and, because of second homes owned primarily by
Parisians, a noticeably larger summer population. The town's
economic base is tourism: auberges, gites, small restaurants,
cafes and art galleries dot the narrow medieval streets. The
church of St. Genest and the ruins of the ancient abbey of
St. Peter and the abbey crypt are well worth visiting. The

---

54 The information on Vercingetorix and the battle of Alecia came from several
tourist brochures picked up at the Musee Alesia in Alise St. Reine.
55 The towns' site has been inhabited since prehistoric times. For the details see:
Flavigny sur Ozerain, A Medieval Town in Burgundy, by the Societe des Amis de
La Cite de Flavigny, translated by Kay Werner-Simonson, June 1988.

abbey house now houses the small shop that produces the—much too intensely flavored—Anis de Flavigny candies. There are good self guided walking tours of the ramparts and gates and of the filming locations for the movie *Chocolate*, for which many of the exterior scenes were filmed in the town.

On Thursday, August ninth, eight locks and thirteen kilometers, down the canal brought us to Montbard. This section of the canal follows the River Brenne and the countryside was very different from the area between Dijon, the "Roof of the World" and Venarey les Laumes. In many ways this area reminded me of southern Ohio. It had the same low rolling hills with a few rocky outcrops, corn and wheat fields, scattered woodlands, and farms that looked large and prosperous. In Montbard there were two halte nautiques. A smaller but still well equipped VNF/Municipal one that was free, and a large, almost luxurious, one that was owned and run by a hire-boat company. All of the barges were at the VNF/Municipal facility so we went there.

We had now been traveling the Burgundy canal for three weeks and the statistics were starting to come in; expenses—groceries, beer, wine, dockage, souvenirs, miscellaneous items, eating out approximately four times a week (average per meal cost FF 150.00, for two), and diesel fuel—were averaging approximately FF 2,000.00 per week ($280.00). Canal cruising, ignoring startup costs, was reasonable. In general *Nova Cura* was operating well, but our DAF Diesel had an oil leak that I could not locate, that was slowly getting worse. The engine was losing a third to a half liter of oil per day, the lost oil going into the bilge. I was afraid the leak might be in the oil pan gasket, which would be a big problem, as the engine was hard mounted—welded to its bed—and access to the oil pan was by touch only; reach down, feel for a nut, and hope you don't drop your wrench.

Montbard, a small industrial city with a population of seven to eight thousand people, known for high quality steel tube, pipe and pipe fittings, is the second largest town, after Dijon, on the Burgundy canal. While the older part of town, between the canal and the River Brenne, is still very attractive, the newer sections north and east of the river look post World War II industrial modern. The day after arriving in Montbard I tried to buy a newspaper, the local news stand was closed; the proprietor was taking a two week vacation. But I did discover that it was market day in Montbard and the market, befitting a large town, was excellent, we loaded up: fresh rabbit, good vegetables, fruit and several cheeses. After the market we explored Buffon in Montbard. Montbard was the birth place and home of Georges-Louis Leclerc de Buffon and he remains the town's chief tourist attraction. The older part of town blankets the north, east and south slopes of a hill crowned by the walls of the Chateau de Montbard, which dates to the ninth century. Buffon bought the chateau in 1735, demolished almost everything—supposedly most of the interior was already in ruins—except for the two principle towers and the curtain wall, which he had restored. He then turned the area enclosed by the curtain wall, and the slopes around the chateau, into the gardens that today are the lovely Parc de Buffon. Between the gardens and river, he built his personal residence, a mansion which, for a man of Buffon's time and status, is surprisingly modest, but it fits its site perfectly and does not overwhelm the town. In addition to the park we spent a lot of time visiting the Musee de Buffon and the Cabinet de travail de Buffon (Buffon's study), the room in which he wrote most of his *Historie naturelle*. During our visit the Cabinet's walls were thickly hung with superb colored engravings of birds from the *Historie naturelle*.

The next morning, our second in Montbard, it was fifty two degrees Fahrenheit in the cabin, with the electric heater going, and fog thick enough to mask the far side of the canal obscured everything. In late morning when the fog finally began to lift, we put the bikes ashore and rode six kilometers to the Abbaye de Fontenay. The Abbaye was founded by St. Bernard, Abbot of Clairvaux, in 1118. The Abbaye was large and prosperous until the religious wars of the sixteenth and seventeenth centuries when it began to decline. During the French Revolution the Abbaye, by that time largely a ruin, was sold by the church and became a paper mill. In 1906 it was bought and restored to the way it was believed to have looked in the late twelfth century. The Abbaye was lovely and very interesting; but it felt restored, a bit pristine and theme parkish. The Abbaye was also very crowded. Large tour groups were being shoved through too close together and the loud voices of the tour guides—English, French, German—mingled and merged. We enjoyed a good, and very inexpensive, lunch at a Salon de Thé (tea) that was associated with, but was not in the Abbaye, and then rode back to Montbard along a route that took us past the railroad station. Outside the station there was a small tabac with a large newspaper rack on which was the English edition of the International Herald Tribune.

Both of us were already questioning our Michelin Red Guide's restaurant ratings, our opinions frequently did not agree with the opinions of Michelin's reviewers, and our visit to the Abbaye de Fontenay caused us to start questioning, our Michelin Green Guide's ratings of tourist sites. The Green Guides use stars to rate general tourist attractions: one star means "interesting", two "worth a detour" and three "worth a journey". The Abbaye de Fontenay had three stars, while the much more interesting Chateauneuf and Flavigny sur Ozerain had only one and the whole complex at Alise St. Reine, which I found incredible, moving, and in a way, more spiritual than most religious sites, had no stars. We stopped paying attention to the Green Guide's stars, but kept using the guides; they were well written, fun to read and full of information.

The day we left Montbard for Ravieres, twelve locks and twenty kilometers, summer returned: a clear almost cloud free sky and warm weather. Our lunch stop was at Buffon, the site of Buffon's family estate, and the location of his iron works, but we did not visit the old forges even though our guide books and tourist literature said they were very interesting and water transportation, to supply raw materials to the forges and carry away the products, had been one of the principle reasons for building the Burgundy canal. From above Venarey les Laumes to past Montbard, the canal had followed the Brenne River, a tributary of the Armancon River. At kilometer mark ninety-seven, between St. Remy and Buffon, the Brenne joined the Armancon and from there to Migennes and the Yonne River, the canal closely followed the Armancon.

After lunch, just as we were leaving the quay, a large Crown Blue Line hire-boat operated by a crowd of young looking people, blasted past at what must have been full throttle; making a wake (the wave produced by a moving boat) that, had *Nova Cura* not been equipped with good fenders, would have slammed us into the stone quay hard enough to possibly do damage. Up to that point the day had been very pleasant, a warm, sunny, peaceful ride down the canal, but from Buffon to Ravieres, the crowd on that hire-boat confirmed, and re-confirmed, our belief that on the French canals anyone could rent a hire-boat: common sense, courtesy, a rudimentary knowledge of boats and boating, probably even a functioning brain, were optional. They constantly varied their speed and occasionally stopped to land or retrieve walkers or cyclists. If we passed them after one of their stops, they would blast past us again, a cute trick they performed several times. On one occasion they squirted past just as Betty was lining up to enter a lock, a very dangerous thing to do,[56] then they tied to the middle of the lock wall, leaving no space for us—if they had moved all the way to the front of the lock, there would have been plenty of room. The lockkeeper refused to cycle the lock until they moved forward, which they finally did, with ill grace. No one from that boat assisted with opening or closing the lock gates.

In Ravieres, I had hoped to visit the chateau of Field Marshal Louis-Nicolas d'Avoust (May 10, 1770 – June 1, 1823), Napoleon's "Iron Marshal" and one of the Emperor's greatest military commanders. But it was closed. However, Ravieres was an attractive small village with a number of interesting, and very old, houses and the remnants of its old city wall, most notably a well built, heavily fortified, and rather Germanic looking gate and gate tower. The town felt old, sad and in decline, as though it had once been a more important place with a much larger population. Tourism and the second home boom had not reached Ravieres. The hire-boat full of young people, unfortunately, had. They spent the night on the quay too close to us, drinking and partying loudly until the early hours of the morning, which left no doubt about their ethnic origin.

---

56 Betty had to throw the barge into hard astern to keep from hitting them. Eighteen plus meters and forty-five or so tons of sharp bowed iron barge hitting a cheaply built fiberglass hire-boat would not work out well for the hire-boat.

The next morning the Germans left early, and loudly. We had a short day planned, just five locks and nine kilometers, to Ancy le Franc, and upon arrival, were pleased to note that the Germans had not stopped there. Chateau Ancy le Franc was interesting but over hyped, it was not as nice, or as interesting, as Chateau Bussy-Rabutin, and not even close to Chateauneuf. What was interesting was a museum in the chateau's out-buildings. The museum, which was almost unmentioned in our guides, held a wonderful collection of old bicycles, motorcycles and cars. The cars were nice, but the bicycles and motorcycles, all fully restored and in working condition, were fascinating. The town of Ancy le Franc itself was very pleasant: attractive, clean, with a nice selection of shops, cafes and restaurants and with a good halte nautique.

Ancy le Franc to Tanlay, the next day, was a long, long day on the canal. The number of locks, nine, and the distance, twenty-one kilometers, would have been fine except the first four locks of the day were automated[57] and the automated systems on two of them were out of order. At each of the broken locks Betty had to put me ashore so I could walk up to the lock and use a signal button to summon a lockkeeper—press the button and a bell rings at another lock to alert the lockkeeper to the existence of a problem. The lockkeeper then had to finish whatever he was doing, drive to the lock we were at,

---

57 Approximately a quarter of the locks we transited during our seasons on the barge were automated, no lockkeeper. The automated locks used two, different, activation systems. Some, less common, used motion detectors mounted a hundred meters or so above and below the lock which sensed an approaching vessel and activated the lock. The more common system used an electrical relay activated by twisting a pole that hung down over the middle of a canal—it took a good, firm twist too. Once a vessel was in a lock and tied up, pushing a button on a junction box mounted near the center of the lock completed the cycle. The pole locks were more reliable although both systems seemed to malfunction regularly. The biggest source of problems was groups of three or more hire-boats traveling together.

over-ride the automated system, cycle the lock and then re-set the automated system. We were hours getting through those locks and, as a result did not arrive at the halte nautique in Tanlay until after 5:00 p.m.

Wednesday, August 15, 2001, the day after we reached Tanlay, was a French holiday and the locks were closed. It was also the first really hot day we had experienced in France, by early afternoon the temperature in *Nova Cura's* iron and steel walled cabin reached ninety-three degrees Fahrenheit. We spent most of the day visiting the Chateau de Tanlay which was genuinely impressive. Built in the mid sixteenth century[58] on, and partially incorporating, the remains of a medieval fortress, the chateau had been owned by just two families and had never been looted, burned or badly damaged. The original ceiling frescos were intact and the chateau was filled with three hundred plus years of superb, original, furniture, tapestries, rugs, art and artifacts. Rare in France, much of the interior of the chateau was climate controlled, to help preserve the contents. The air conditioning may have had something to do with why we spent most of the day there. Late in the evening the heat broke with a violent thunderstorm, hard rain and strong gusts of cool wind, the leading edge of a cold front that brought the return of unseasonably cool, damp and windy conditions.

Getting our usual late start we moved to Tonnerre, six locks and nine kilometers, a short three and a half hour trip enlivened by hard rain and very gusty winds that made

---

58 The Chateau de Tanlay was built by Francois de Coligny d'Andelot, one of the principal leaders of the Huguenots (French Protestants) and the circular room at the top of one of the retained, medieval, towers was a meeting place for Huguenot leaders during the French religious wars. The ceiling in the meeting room is painted and the painting makes an interesting political/religious statement. It depicts the principal Catholic and Protestant leaders, with the Catholic leaders generally shown less than fully dressed and often in suggestive poses.

going through the last lock and tying up in Tonnerre's spacious port de plaisance (free, with water and electricity) difficult. Tonnerre—French for "Thunder"—was the last town on the Burgundy canal that we really wanted to visit, and linger in for a of couple days. The town is located at a spot where the Armancon River could be forded and there has been a settlement, generally fortified at the site since at least pre-Roman Gaul. Because of a devastating fire in 1640 and the frequent wars that have ravaged the Armancon valley, particularly the Franco-Prussian War and World War I, little is left, above ground and visible, of ancient Tonnerre. The street pattern hints at an old inner wall and a much larger and more recent ring of fortifications. There are still a number of lovely old houses (I think most have been rebuilt more than once) and the hospital, built between 1293 and 1295 by Margaret of Burgundy (and fully restored), is magnificent. Tonnerre is also a wine town, the center of the Tonnerrois AC (Appelation Controlee), and both excellent white Bourgogne Aligote and a light, clean and very good red Burgundy are produced[59].

Approaching Tonnerre *Nova Cura* developed a noticeable vibration, which I attributed to aquatic weeds fouling

---

59 Tonnerre has an additional, rather odd, claim to fame; Charles-Genevieve-Lou-ise-Auguste-Andree-Timothee Eon de Beaumont, Le Chevalier d' Eon, known as the "Lady-Knight of Eon", was born here in 1728. He had a strange and complicated career: he was a competent and respected military man, a successful diplomat and a very successful diplomatic spy. In his diplomatic spy role he frequently dressed, lived and traveled as an upper class, often noble, women. He was physically slim, almost delicate, reputedly very attractive, and he apparently made an elegant "lady". In the early years of the French Revolution he fled to London where he continued his peculiar life style, possibly spying on France for the British and for the exiled French Royalists. During the Chevalier's lifetime there was considerable speculation about whether "he" might not, in fact, be a "she." He died in London in 1810, still an exile, an autopsy performed soon after death was definitive, he was indeed a he. There is a small, but good, museum devoted to the Chevalier in Tonnerre—a tourist is a tourist...an attraction is business.

our propeller—something that had already happened once. In Tonnerre I checked the propeller and it was clean. A quick check in the engine room showed the problem. The head of one of the shaft coupling bolts, the four bolts that secured the connection between our gearbox and our propeller shaft, had sheared off and a second bolt was visibly lose. The shaft coupling was still in place and two of the four bolts were tight but it was no longer perfectly aligned. There was a narrow, almost a hairline, gap on the side secured by the broken, and lose, bolts. I tightened the lose bolt and then tried to remove the remains of the old bolt so that I could put a temporary replacement in, but that large old bolt would not budge. There was already an engine oil leak, which I had not been able to find, and we had planned to go to Chantier Fluvial de Migennes, the barge/boatyard owned and managed by Jo Parfitt, the New Zealander who had surveyed *Nova Cura* to have that problem taken care of. Now there were two problems that needed a boatyards attention.

The next morning, the morning of what turned out to be our one full day in Tonnerre, breakfast was rudely interrupted by a loud Poooh, like the sound of escaping air, followed by the sound of running water, and then the water pressure pump came on. Noises like that coming from the engine room on a boat…well, they never mean anything good…your fairy god mother has not just waved her magic wand over you…the Easter Bunny has not brought you a large basket of chocolate eggs. I turned off the water pressure pump and climbed down into the engine room. Our, possibly very old, hot water heater was no longer sitting flat, the way all good hot water heaters should, its bottom was now convex, not concave. It also had a six or seven centimeter split along the braised seam at the base of the tank (the sudden appearance of which probably caused that loud Poooh). Twelve gallons or so, fifty liters, of fresh water had gushed out onto the engine room floor and run down into the bilge (that sound of running water), adding to the mess of leaked engine oil and canal water already down there. Stuff happens on boats, bigger and better stuff happens on big old iron barges. Now there were three problems that needed attention.

I turned off the valve between our water pressure pump and the hot water side of the water system, thankful that I had put one in. The water system was now cold water only. While I was doing that, Betty called Jo Parfitt, told him about our assorted problems and that we would be there sooner, rather than later. Jo said to arrive on Tuesday, the twenty-first of August, and he would have a spot ready for us. Betty then called our mail service in the United States and arranged for our mail to be sent to Chantier Fluvial de Migennes[60]. The boatyard is on the Yonne River, just outside the entrance to the Burgundy canal and just past canal kilometer mark zero. We were just upstream from kilometer marker forty four and today was August seventeenth...five days....forty-four kilometers, OK, relax, the barge isn't sinking, the engine runs: put the bicycles ashore, go see a bit of Tonnerre, tour the old hospital, have a good lunch, try a little Tonnerrois Aligote. The trek to the boatyard could begin on Saturday.

Tonnerre to Flogny la Chapelle was four locks and thirteen kilometers. Lunch was at an attractive small canal side Auberge in Dannemoine. Back at *Nova Cura* following lunch, we watched a totally incompetent hire-boat operator try to get his boat off the bank and headed up the canal. After he had slammed into the bank for the third time, Betty could stand

---

60 Chantier Fluvial de Migennes, Route de Charmoy, Gare d'Eau, 89400 Migennes, France, phone and fax : 33 (0)3 86 92 93 13, and e-mail fluvialmig@aol.com

no more. She jumped onto the hire-boat, gave the poor man at the wheel a quick fifteen minute lesson in boat driving, brought the boat back to the canal side and jumped off. As we headed down the canal he was successfully following a more or less straight line up the canal. After tying up for the evening we took a bicycle ride around Flogny la Chapelle and found nothing much, it seemed to be a poor and rather shabby little town with a large proportion of Arabs and Africans in the population. It had been another hot day and just after sunset the heat broke with another of those violent evening thunderstorm.

Flogny la Chapelle to St. Florentin was seven locks and twelve kilometers, and on the way we passed through the deepest lock on the Burgundy canal. Lock number one hundred and six, at Germigny, dropped us five and two tenths meters. The lockkeepers were a happy Moroccan couple who had a neat, well maintained lock house, beautiful flower gardens, at least six little kids and were peddling good Tonnerrois wine on the side. In stark contrast to Flogny la Chapelle, St. Florentin was a lovely village with a compact medieval center, a few remaining bits and pieces of a defensive wall, and a beautiful sixteenth century church. The church crowned a small but steep hill on the edge of the oldest part of town, and had wonderful, apparently original, stained glass windows and, unlike many of the older churches, was clearly still being used for its intended purpose. A sign by the church informed us that the site had originally been a Roman (and later a Gallo-Roman) fort. The village also had a lot of very old half-timber houses, many of which had second and third levels that projected progressively further out over the street. All the small shops that help define a classic French village were there along with several restaurants that looked as though they might be pretty good. On the canal, just outside the village, there was a large and fully equipped port de plaisance operated by the Rive de France hire-boat company. I wanted to know more about St. Florentin but, except for our chart kit, which was not a great font of historic knowledge, none of our guide books even mentioned the town. If there was a tourist office, it was well hidden, and the only signs or historical markers were the ones near the church, and a lone sign on the road by the port de plaisance that stated, without elaboration or explanation, that St. Florentin had been designated an historic village.

St. Florentin to Brienon sur Armancon was four locks and ten kilometers, and, on arrival, another big and well equipped port de plaisance. The town's compact shape and medieval street pattern, and the remnants of a town wall, indicated a long history. Unlike St. Florentin, in Brienon sur Armancon there was a large and easily located tourist office. A lady in the tourist office who spoke good English told us that the town had suffered major fires in both the seventeenth and eighteenth centuries and had then been badly damaged during both the Franco-Prussian War and World War I, so little is left from its past. She directed us to a remaining part of the old town wall which had some fifteenth century graffiti carved into it and to an interesting eighteenth century washhouse.

Tuesday, August 21, 2001; Brienon sur Armancon to Migennes, the Yonne River and Chantier Fluvial de Migennes, was four locks and nine kilometers, and the end of our trek to the boatyard. We had completed our trip through the Burgundy Canal and our transit of the "Roof of the World".[61]

---

61 If we had missed the opportunity to do the Burgundy canal, we would probably not have been able to do it. 2002 was a relatively dry year and the canal was not open all the way through and it was not again open for its entire length during the rest of the time that Betty owned *Nova Cura*.

As promised there was a space for us, second barge out in the middle of the quay. After a lunch in town, we went to the Boatyard office, where a DHL box containing a full month of our mail was waiting, and talked to Jo Parfitt about the work that needed to be done. In addition to the three must-dos on our work list, there were a number of want-to-dos, three of which were big jobs. Jo did not think they would be able to get to the big want-to-dos. But, the three repairs that had brought us to the boatyard and the smaller want-to-dos were possible. Work was to begin in the morning.

8. Barge Work, and Home in a Changed World

Bright and early in the morning the boatyard carpenter was knocking on the roof, ready to get going. *Nova Cura's* forward cabin had two narrow single berths arranged in an L. One of the berths was too short, and the other was too high off the floor. When our friends Mac and Nancy visited Betty and I slept there and thought it was rather uncomfortable; but, when the weather turned really cold the forward cabin—close to the bathroom, the cabin heater and the early morning coffee—was warmer and more comfortable than the aft cabin. High on our list of want-to-do's was removing those single berths and building in an adult-sized double. The carpenter did an excellent job and two days later there was a well built double berth in the forward cabin, and the two new, single mattresses that we had purchased in Dijon more or less fit. From that day on the forward cabin was our cabin. Guests could sleep back aft unless it was really hot—the aft cabin had better air flow and was cooler than the forward cabin.

While the carpenter was working on the forward cabin, Jo Parfitt, with some marginal assistance from me, removed our large water heater and carried it into the shop to see if it could be repaired. He then located, and fixed, our oil leak. I had looked for the leak numerous times, but always with the engine off. Jo started the engine, let it come up to full temperature and, with the transmission out of gear, advanced the throttle to seven hundred rpm (normal cruising rpm), and found the leak immediately. Oil was dribbling out low on the block where an oil pipe attached. A pipe fitting on the end of the oil pipe was connected to the block by a threaded pipe nipple. Jo thought either the fitting on the oil pipe was loose or the pipe nipple was loose, or cracked. Trying the most probable first, he put a wrench on the fitting and gently tested to see if it was tight. It came right off the block. Jo removed the oil pipe and instead of part of a broken metal pipe nipple, he found a piece of PVC pipe; a piece of plastic. The metal pipe nipple threaded into the engine block had broken off almost flush with the surface of the block and someone had "repaired" it by jamming a piece of PVC pipe into the remains of the old pipe nipple and using a reducing coupling to connect the oil pipe to the piece of PVC.

Maybe it was a quick-and-dirty repair, a temporary fix intended to last a day or two, long enough to try to get to a place where parts could be obtained and a proper repair made. If so, the problem was never fixed. The oil line involved was a return line and the oil was not under much pressure, but when the engine was at full temperature (hot), oil leaked. Extracting the remains of the broken pipe nipple from the engine, threading in a new one, putting a properly sized coupling on the oil pipe and re-attaching everything, was a matter of minutes. I thought back to May seventeenth and the first time we had boarded *Nova Cura* after purchase, and that murky pool of oil and water in the bilge. To this day I believe that someone at H_2O knew exactly where that oil came from and I have a hard time understanding how the "mechanic" who did our engine survey failed to find that little jewel. When the big oil leak problem had been solved, Jo told me how to remove the oil filter attachment from where it was, low on the engine, and where to remount it on the forward engine room bulkhead; a location that would make changing the engine oil much easier and neater. He also told me where, in town, to buy the remote oil filter mounting kit I would need and, as he was leaving, where to dispose of the oily mess in the bilge.

The old water heater was well past resuscitation. The same "antique" model water heater was still available[62] and a drop in replacement being the line of least resistance, one was ordered. The source of the problem had been the pressure relief valve at the top of the hot water heater, it failed. Hot water and steam, which should have vented to the bilge through the relief valve and a hose whenever the pressure became too high, could not vent. The water heater was basically a copper, or mostly copper, cylinder, with a concave bottom and a convex top. Copper is a relatively weak metal, when the relief valve failed and the internal pressure became too high, the water heater expanded...sort of. The concave bottom became convex and then a weak spot in the braised seam around the bottom of the tank let go. The estimated time for delivery of the new hot water heater was eight to ten days. *Nova Cura* was going to be in the boatyard for at least another week, without hot water, and our Jekyll and Hyde weather which had been warm and humid, even hot, since Tanlay, was threatening to revert to its cold, gray, rainy alter ego.

While we waited for the new hot water heater, Jo removed and replaced our broken shaft coupling bolt. I finished moving the engine oil filter, and Betty and I continued the seemingly endless projects of cleaning the bilge and removing rust from the steel top of the main cabin. Replacing the broken

---

62 An interesting difference between Europe and the United States was, and is, that everything is not perfectly up to date in the old country. People care for and maintain boats, engines, cars, etc. long after they would have been discarded in favor of the latest and greatest in the US. We could buy a new "antique" hot water heater, essentially unchanged from the 1930s. Our DAF diesel was long out of production, but new parts made by an aftermarket firm were readily available.

shaft coupling bolt turned out to be a major job. Jo removed the remains of the old bolt with a humongous wrench. When the bolt was out, he found that it had unusually deep threads and the thread was not Metric, SAE, Wentworth or any other thread he was aware of. Further, the holes in both halves of the shaft coupling were threaded. To drill out the holes would require removing both halves of the coupling from the boat, about which Jo said "don't even think about it". Instead he machined a new bolt from a piece of large diameter steel rod and made two nuts for it. He preferred using two nuts to welding a head onto the new bolt. The heat of welding might distort the threads. The new bolt fit perfectly and was still in place when *Nova Cura* was sold.

Betty and I fought the war of the rusty deckhouse roof from purchase (almost) to sale, and I suspect that the people who bought *Nova Cura* are still fighting, and losing, that war. The main cabin roof was made of thin sheet steel strips, approximately eighty centimeters wide, which were supported by long pieces of angle iron bent to the contour of the roof. The sheet steel strips and roof supports ran from side to side across the full width of the cabin: the strips were welded to the side walls of the deck house, edge welded to each other and spot welded to the roof supports, but, the sheet steel was too thin, the welding had been badly done and the roof strips were slightly buckled and in a few places, noticeably uneven. To make the roof look smooth and perfect, whoever built it slathered it with a thick layer of something that resembled automotive body putty, and then sanded it and painted it. Over the years the thin and buckled steel strips moved, flexing when people walked on them, expanding in hot weather, shrinking in cold, and the body putty and paint cracked. Water seeped in and the steel rusted...rusted badly. Working off and on over our first season on the barge, we ground large parts of the roof down to bare steel, primed it and painted it—no new body putty or filler. But every year the paint would crack, or get scrapped and scratched, water would find a way in, thin runnels of pale orange rust formed...and the never ending war went on. Anyone who buys and restores old boats or barges gets used to rolling large rocks up hills. Brings to mind the wooden deck on a boat we once owned...and the seven hundred and eighty or so counter sunk and plugged screws that almost held it place...and the dozen tubes of caulk that almost sealed the seams...and a large, stringy blob of black deck goo that ended up in my hair?

Between working on the barge and waiting for parts to come in, what was supposed to have been a short stop in the boatyard swelled to fifteen days. Our return flight from Paris to Philadelphia was October third and it was already September fifth. When we left St. Jean de Losne our plan had been a round-trip, a loop cruise, north through the Burgundy canal to Migennes and the Yonne River and then back via either the Canal du Nivernais to the Canal Latéral a la Loire, the Canal du Centre and the Saone River or via the Yonne River and the Canal du Loing, Canal de Briare, to the Latéral a la Loire, etc. Given our newly acquired experience on the Burgundy canal, both return routes were clearly overly ambitious. So... enjoy Migennes, explore part of the Yonne River, and lay up *Nova Cura* for the winter at Chantier Fluvial de Migennes. *Nova Cura* could be lifted out of the water for winter storage, and Jo thought that the three big jobs on our wish list could be done over the winter, while the barge was on land, and we would be good to go when we came back in early May 2002. Also, leaving the barge in Migennes for the winter would be convenient, both leaving and returning: Migennes was right on the main line between Paris, Dijon and the Mediterranean, a train to the Gare de Lyon in Paris, or directly to Roissy-Charles de Gaulle airport, was no problem, the boatyard was only a few minutes' walk from the train station, everything we would need in the spring was a short walk or bike ride from the boatyard, and there was a good small hotel between the train station and the boatyard—if a place to spend a night or two turned out to be necessary.

The general area of Migennes, the confluence of the Armancon River with the Yonne River, has been inhabited for thousands of years, and the site of the modern town has probably had a settlement of some sort since deep into pre-history. An important trade route that followed the Seine, Yonne, Armancon and Brenne River valleys and was continuously in use from prehistoric times through the medieval period passes close to Migennes. Today's roads and rail lines between Paris and the Mediterranean via Dijon and the Rhone Valley, to some extent, follow this ancient trade route. Unfortunately many of the Armancon Valley towns suffered grievously during the Franco-Prussian War, World War I and World War II. Migennes, a major rail center with a large rail marshalling yard and important inter-city connections, suffered more than most. In World War II the allied air forces, in order to deny the retreating Germans use of the rail facilities, devastated the town in multiple massive air raids. Not much of Migennes that pre-dates World War II is still above ground. What is left and what has been found in various archeological excavations and during construction digs indicates a very long and probably fascinating history: there is a very old church, built on the remains of one or more earlier structures, there are Gallo-Roman mosaics, buried streets and foundations, traces of defensive walls and fortifications, and a lot of artifacts.

Modern Migennes, although not quaint, cute or touristy, is a great place for cruising boaters. The town has everything that anyone on a boat could possibly need, the rail and road connections are excellent, and there is a lot to see and do within a reasonable bicycle ride, or a short train ride. As a result, the large port de plaisance in Migennes (the old commercial port), managed by Crown Blue Lines—which maintains a full service hire-boat base and a maintenance facility here—is popular with transient boats and barges and is used as a hotel barge passenger pick-up and drop-off point. There is also still some freight barge traffic to and from Migennes. Although most of the freight barges that call load or discharge either across the canal from the port de plaisance, or further up the canal near Bas d'Esnon, in the late summer and early fall barges still occasionally load grain, brought in by truck, on the quay in the port de plaisance. We made frequent use of a French big box chain store called "Mr. Bricolage"[63], a massive hardware/home improvement store that made me think of a Home Depot with a large Best Buy added in. We also parted company with a lot of euros at Le Cellier, a very good wine shop off the Avenue du Port, near the ATAC Supermarche. In addition to an unusually good selection of bottled wine and beer, Le Cellier had what amounted to a wine filling station. Behind a counter at one end of the store there were six gas pump type hoses that dispensed bulk wine. Bring in your wine jug or barrel, stick the hose in and pay by the liter. If you didn't have a bulk wine container, and felt the need for one, they had a good selection in a full range of sizes, styles and types.

At the end of August the weather turned cold and rainy, and our new water heater had not arrived; when the cabin

---

63 www.mr-bricolage.fr Bricoler: odd jobs, fix up. Bricolage: do-it-yourself.

temperature dropped into the low fifties in the morning having no hot water became a quality of life issue. Finally, on Monday, September third, a miserable cold, windy and rainy day, the thing arrived, at the end of the day of course, and the next morning I installed and tested it, working along to the merry sound of hard rain on the roof. Wednesday morning, cold gray and hazy but not actually raining, we topped off our water tanks, paid our boatyard bill, confirmed our return date with Jo Parfitt and left; moving down the Yonne River to the Locaboat base in Joigny, where our hire-boat trip on the Canal du Nivernais the previous fall had ended. Because of *Nova Cura's* size they did not really want us there; but they allowed us to stay one night—to enjoy an excellent "we're out of the boatyard" dinner.

Leaving Joigny headed down stream, the fist lock of the day, at the village of St. Aubin sur Yonne with its twelfth century chateau overlooking the river, was a lock with sloping side walls. The Yonne River's sloped wall locks are large locks originally constructed in the 1840s as part of a major project to improve navigation on the river. The engineers who built them thought that vertical lock walls in large locks constructed in soft, unconsolidated sediment in a river subject to spring floods would not be strong enough. Therefore the walls of the lock chambers were built of large granite blocks laid on a forty-five degree slope. In the years since they were originally built, many of these locks have been rebuilt with one or both of the lock chamber walls vertical. But nine of the original locks remain in use on the Yonne River, all in the section between Montereau faut Yonne, at the confluence of the Yonne and the Seine, and St. Aubin sur Yonne. The sloping side walls make these locks difficult, even dangerous because a barge crew cannot simply put a line around a bollard on the lock wall and rise or fall along the wall with the change in water level; lines must be taken to both sides of the lock so that the barge stays safely in the middle of the lock. Most of these locks have had small floating docks added at the downstream end for small boats to tie to. We took to using the floating docks even though they had clear, generally multilingual, signs on them saying that they were for pleasure boats less then fifteen meters long (the size of the largest "sans permis" hire-boats).

Eighteen cold, gray, misty, damp kilometers and three locks, two of them with sloping sides, down the Yonne from Joigny brought us to the Quai de Bretoche below the walls of Villeneuve sur Yonne. As we were docking a small Dutch Barge, about *Nova Cura's* size and flying an American flag, was getting underway. The name on the stern was *Liberté*, and we had seen it in the Port de plaisance in Migennes. There was power and water on the quay, locked; but the key was available for a small fee, payable in the tourist office, during normal business hours. I walked up, paid our fee and got the key—to be returned immediately—so that we could plug in and warm up.

Nova Cura was tied up a hundred meters downstream from the Pont de l'Yonne and just past the Auberge La Lucarne Aux Chouettes...our primary reason for stopping. Our cruising guide claimed, and Jo Parfitt affirmed, that the Auberge la Lucarne Aux Chouettes, the "Owls' Nest"—a Red Book rated (two couverts) auberge owned and managed by the Paris born American actress and dancer Leslie Caron—was a wonderful place to have lunch or dinner or to enjoy a night ashore, with excellent food, service and ambiance.[64] While I was hiking to the tourist office for the key to the electric box, Betty walked

---

64 www.lesliecaron-auberge.com, phone 03 86 87 18 26

over to the auberge and made dinner reservations. It was Friday and even though Betty made our reservations early in the afternoon, they were for the nights last seating; the auberge's restaurant was booked almost to capacity. Dinner was everything expected, and more. The restaurant was built into three seventeenth century river bank warehouses: white stucco or bare stone walls, gray stone floors warn smooth by centuries of use, and massive old roof beams. Our dinner was the equal of any we ate in France, the service was impeccable, the wine exquisite, and from our table we had a beautiful view out over the lighted quay and the dark river.

The day after our excellent dinner was yet another dreary, cold, gray and rainy fall day, and we opted to stay in Villeneuve sur Yonne and, in the intervals between rain showers, explore the town. Villeneuve le Roi (the original name) was founded in 1163 by King Louis VII as a moated and walled strong point on his border with the County of Champagne, at that time, not under the control of the King of France. The city's military importance declined when independent Champagne was incorporated into France in 1314; but resumed during the religious wars of the sixteenth century. In 1594 after a siege, the city was captured, looted and burned. During the French Revolution the Royal Chateau was largely torn down and the city's name was changed to "sur Yonne" from "sur Roi". Today most of the original wall, two of the gates and the impressive gate tower of the old Royal Chateau remain. The former defensive moat, outside the medieval wall, has been converted to a ribbon of park that runs almost completely around the old town. The park has a very nice pedestrian and bicycle path running its full length. Inside the ring of the park and the old walls, the town still has a medieval feel and is a delightful place for walking, looking or just sitting in a cafe enjoying a good glass of wine.

Sunday another seventeen kilometers, and four sloping sided locks downstream brought us to the ancient and historic cathedral city of Sens. The first three locks were no problem, the small boat float was available. In lock number four, unfortunately, a pair of hire-boats beat us to the small boat dock and we ended up floating down as the water level dropped, without a line to shore. The lockkeeper let the water out of the lock very slowly so there was little current and Betty, using the engine and rudder, did a good job of keeping *Nova Cura* safely in the middle. I like to think we would have let the hire-boats have the small boat dock, but... In Sens *Liberté* was docked on the Quai Dr. Albert Schweitzer, along with a large hotel barge, a yacht and several hire-boats, and the people aboard directed us to a spot directly astern of them and helped with our lines. When *Nova Cura* was secure, we finally met, and introduced ourselves to, Stu and Judy Miller, from Fort Lauderdale, Florida, the owners of *Liberté*. Like us, their alternate, non-barge, home was a sailboat. In the afternoon an exploratory walk around the area near the river turned up a clean modern laundromat, a news stand (with the Herald Tribune), a barber shop—which I needed rather badly—a large boulangerie, several patisseries, a number of other food shops of various types, and several cafes and restaurants.

Monday, after a stop at the tourist office for a thick handful of brochures, guides and booklets, Betty and Bill did Sens. Sens (Roman Agedincum Senones) was the capital and principal oppidum of the Senones, one of the largest and most powerful of the Celtic tribes of Gaul[65] and archeological

---

65 Julius Caesar's conquest of Gaul was the concluding chapter in a long history of conflict between Rome and the Gauls (or Celts). Approximately four hundred BC part of the Senones, crossed the Alps into northern Italy, drove out or assimilated the Umbrians and settled on the Adriatic coast between modern Ravenna and Ancona. Their capital is believed to have been where modern Senigallia now stands. In

discoveries in and around the city indicate that the area was inhabited long before the Senones moved in. The Senones oppidum became a Roman fortress and administrative center, a Gallo-Roman city, and a center for early Christianity. The first and longest stop in our day of touring was the cathedral and the adjoining museums, which were housed in the cathedral treasury, the Bishops palace and the library and archives. Although the cathedral was established in 972, the existing Gothic cathedral, the oldest Gothic cathedral in France, was built primarily between 1130 and 1170, on the site of (and the remains of) at least one earlier church. The museums were wonderful. The treasury had a magnificent collection of religious artifacts and historical religious objects including the robe of St. Thomas à Becket, while the rest of the museum housed art and artifacts from the history of Sens and the area: stone age tools, the remains of a Neolithic house and tombs, Bronze and Iron Age weapons, tools and ornaments, Gallo-Roman stone work, medieval weapons and armor, etc. Included in our museum tour was a visit to an ongoing archeological dig in the courtyard of the Bishops palace. In a large roofed, dug out area, sides and roof supported by steel beams and massive wooden timbers, were the remains of a fourth century bath, a bit of a stone paved street or court and some other foundations. A sign told us that a test well (?) had indicated the presence of even older, possibly pre-Roman structures under the bath—layers and centuries of history vividly on display. The old part of Sens retains much of the Roman city's street plan, there are still a few parts of the Gallo-Roman and medieval city walls, and there were whole blocks, streets, of

---

391 BC they invaded Etruria and in 390 they captured and looted Rome. After a century of intermittent conflict the Romans finally defeated them and, in a series of campaigns between 290 and 280 BC, drove them east into Macedonia.

thirteenth to sixteenth and seventeenth century buildings, several of which were open for tours. The Grande Rue, a narrow cobblestone paved pedestrian shopping street running up the river bluff from the Yonne River bridge to the cathedral, was lined with restored fifteenth and sixteenth century half-timber houses.

Late in the afternoon, when we returned to *Nova Cura*, a large Locaboat hire-boat was tied up astern of us and a group of people were sitting on the boat or standing nearby on the quay enjoying some evening refreshments and talking—in American English. They turned out to be three couples from the Washington, D.C. area, two of whom owned sailboats which they kept at our home base, Herrington Harbour North. Herrington Harbour is a large marina and we didn't know either of them. After a few minutes talking with the new arrivals, I went, with Stu from *Liberte*, he and Judy had a car (an old Citroen 2cv), to two large brocantes (second hand stores) that he knew about. He thought that I might find a coal or wood fired stove or, even better, a small gas space heater, but there was nothing worth buying, nothing usable or restorable. The weather had not improved, it was cold and getting colder, and the only heat on *Nova Cura* was our small electric heater and the two burner gas cook top. Our cruising guide was positive that there was electricity available on the quay in Sens, but neither Stu nor I could find it, and Betty and I wanted some form of usable, bigger and better, non-electric cabin heater. That night dinner was beef stew, because it would have to simmer on the stove for a long time—cabin heat—and I ran the big DAF diesel, in neutral, for an hour to make hot water for showers.

Tuesday, September eleventh, the morning was spent walking around Sens and doing a little shopping. I bought two long-sleeved, warm, shirts. Lunch was at a Japanese restaurant, the Miyabi, on the square in front of the cathedral. The food was excellent and today it would probably be called French-Japanese Fusion Cuisine, or something else equally trendy. After lunch we walked across the Yonne River Bridge to a large wine shop, "le Marche des Vins", that Judy and Stu had told us about, and spent a pleasant half hour picking out some bottles of wine. When we returned to *Nova Cura*, the three American couples from the hire-boat were standing on the quay beside the hotel barge talking excitedly to the captain. They waved us over and said that something terrible had happened in New York. The World Trade Center had exploded and was on fire. The barge captain said a passenger jet coming in for a landing had hit one of the buildings. Over the next hour, as more information reached us, the situation clarified and we learned that two hi-jacked airliners had been deliberately flown into the World Trade Center towers, a third had been flown into the Pentagon, the Defense Department Headquarters in Washington, D.C. and a fourth had crashed in Ohio or Pennsylvania, somewhere out in the country. One of the men from the hire-boat remembered that a cafe-bar on the Grande Rue had a television, and we all trooped up there. On the cafe-bars television video clips of the two planes hitting the Trade Center, and of the plane crashing into the Pentagon, of the towers burning and falling, of people jumping and of others running, played over and over behind a calm French reporter as he read one bulletin after another. There were tears on his cheeks. Except for the television there was not a sound in that bar. After twenty minutes or so the bar tender switched to CNN Europe, an English language station, and we learned as much as was known at that point. The whole group stayed, silently watching and listening, until well into the evening, the bar tender switching back and fourth...English to French...French to English. When Betty and I left and I went to pay for our wine, the bar tender refused payment.

In the morning, after a quick trip to the boulangerie and the news stand for the Herald Tribune, we left for Villeneuve sur Yonne. Almost the entire edition of the Herald Tribune, all of the news content, was devoted to the attacks on the World Trade Center and the Pentagon. The news was grim and disturbing.

Other than the news, the only thing of interest in the paper was the weather forecast, particularly the analysis and the week ahead. The weather had been bad—cold, gray, overcast, intermittent mist and rain, wind, colder cold—since the beginning of September and the forecast indicated that it was unlikely to magically improve over night. There was a very large embedded upper level low, the paper called it a "macro meteorological feature", squatting like a great gray toad over western Europe from the U.K. to Poland, the Pyrenees to the Baltic, and it was not going anywhere fast. It would be at least the weekend, possibly a full week, before the low hopped off somewhere or dissipated. We knew where the electrical outlets on the quay in Villeneuve sur Yonne were, and how to get the key. Once the shore power was plugged in and the heater turned on, I went to the presse for an afternoon paper, or updated information of some sort, but found nothing new.

The next day the rain fell in rivers, sheets and waterfalls. Except for a short trip for a paper, bread and something for dinner, neither of us left the barge. The Herald Tribune was again devoted to the events of 9/11, and this issue contained information on the large number hijackers, now called suicide bombers and terrorists, and about a man named Osama bin

Laden, the leader of an organization called Al Qaida. Al Qaida and its leader brought to mind the Assassins, the perverted medieval Nizari sect of the Ismaili Shias, and Rashid ad-Din Sinan, the Old Man of the Mountain.

I spent the afternoon reading, sitting in the wheelhouse where, between paragraphs, I watched the rain and the river. In early afternoon two hotel barges passed, one headed up stream, the other down, and late in the afternoon a third tied up in front of us. The passengers, each clutching a large umbrella, marched ashore to see the village. They were paying a hefty fee for six days on a floating hotel; the weather was a secondary concern. *Nova Cura* was not expected back at the boatyard until September twenty-eighth, so we opted to spend the next day, Friday, in Villeneuve, there was electricity for the cabin heater and hot water, a nearby presse and boulangerie and the next morning, the weekly market.

By the time we had had breakfast, read the paper and gone to the market, the morning's misty rain had stopped and a few small windows of blue pierced the clouds. Taking advantage of the opportunity to stretch our legs and get a little exercise, we set out to walk the bicycle and pedestrian path that followed the old moat. A third of the way around, a group of young, late teens or possibly early twenties, Middle Eastern or North African looking men were sitting on, and standing around, a pair of benches on the side of the path. Betty and I were talking to each other in our somewhat southern and distinctly American English and as we passed the group a large, muscular guy stood up and walked directly into me, hitting me in the chest with his shoulder hard enough to almost knock me down. It was a very intentional act, followed by a lot of laughter and a number of loud comments, in what sounded like Arabic, many of which included "Osama". There were a lot of

people of Middle Eastern and North African origin in
Villeneuve sur Yonne, also in Sens and Migennes. Prior to
Tuesday 9/11, and now this, I had not paid much attention to
them. Now I started watching them. There had been articles
in the Herald Tribune, the London Times and U.S.A. Today
about the celebrations that followed 9/11 in parts of the Is-
lamic world and among some Muslims in Europe. Many, probably most, of the Middle Eastern and North African people that
we saw in the towns and cities along the Yonne and the canals
were a visibly poor socio-economic underclass, immigrants,
legal and illegal, looking for work and a better life. But many
were unassimilated, and a minority flaunted the trappings of
their culture and religion, perhaps not wishing to assimilate. I
started to think that France had, or was going to have, a problem. The next morning we started back up the Yonne. We had
decided to return to Migennes and were considering changing, moving up, our return to the United States.

Leaving the lock at Laroche St. Cydroine, the last lock
before the entrance to the Burgundy canal and Migennes, we
executed an abrupt change of plan and went to the small halte
plaisance in Laroche St. Cydroine, a new concrete dock with
water and electricity (both free). When we passed Joigny on
the way up the river, five Penichettes were leaving the Locaboat base, and they all followed us up the river and then
crowded into the St. Cydroine lock behind us. It was late
afternoon and they were going to have to spend the night
at Laroche St. Cydroine or in Migennes, it was too late for
them to go any further. In a lock, the first boat in is the first
boat out, and Betty blasted out of that lock and straight to
the dock, no messing around. Within seconds I had two lines
ashore and less than a minute after Betty brought us alongside
the dock, our power cord was plugged into the one and only

electrical outlet on the dock. The hire-boats followed us. The dock was not large and *Nova Cura* took almost half of it. After an amazing amount of flailing around, two of the penichettes managed to get alongside the dock and tied up, and two more rafted to them. The fifth, and largest, milled around in the river, the crew looking forlorn, until I directed them to come alongside us. There were eighteen or twenty people on the hire-boats, all Dutch, all from the same town, all employed by the same firm, and almost all spoke English. They were on the first day of a one-week, one-way, hire-boat cruise up the Canal du Nivernais, the trip leader and organizer was aboard the large Penichette rafted to us. We met a lot of Dutch on the canals and they almost all spoke English. They were also friendly, courteous and they generally handled their vessels, small sailboat or large barge, competently and skillfully. Hire-boats, well you make allowances for them.

The next day it rained all day...again. The herd of penichettes managed to get off the dock and headed up river toward Auxerre, the four little ones chugging along in line behind the big one. We spent almost the entire day aboard *Nova Cura*, leaving only to walk up to "Aux Rives de l'Yonne", a small hotel in Laroche St. Cydroine, for lunch. The hire-boat crowd had eaten dinner there the night before and they recommended it.

Monday the weather improved, there were breaks in the rain, and we pedaled into Migennes for a newspaper and a few groceries. In the early afternoon *Liberte* came up the river, slowed as they passed us, and shouted that they were going to the port de plaisance in Migennes. That seemed like a good idea, so we followed them through the lock and tied up between *Liberte* and an English sailboat named *Gloriana*. Although we talked about cruising up to Auxerre for a couple of days, we stayed on the quay in the port de plaisance until the twenty-eighth when, as originally planned, we moved *Nova Cura* around the corner to the boatyard and took the train to Paris.

Our eleven day stay on the quay in Migennes turned out to be very pleasant in spite of the weather, the embedded upper level low finally dissipated and a high built in bringing a northeast wind, bright sun, crisp, clean air and night time temperatures that dropped to forty degrees. There was a nice community of cruisers on the quay. Twice groups of us went to a Chinese place, the Auberge du Peking, for dinner. The English couple aboard *Gloriana* were interesting, they were en route south for the winter and were experienced sailors who had made the trip from England to the Mediterranean several times; once the long, rough way around, out in the ocean. When the weather dried out, Betty and I took day trips by train to Auxerre and Joigny and by bicycle to Cheny, where we visited the tenth century chateau (rebuilt in the sixteenth century).

I found an old, but restorable, iron coal/wood stove in a brocante; too late to be useful as a cabin heater this season but restoring it was fun. I scraped down the inside, replaced some of the fire bricks, sanded and wire brushed the outside, put high temperature epoxy on a couple of places where rust had pitted the surface, and then painted it with a dull black high temperature paint. There was no chimney so it was a pretty useless stove, but it looked great, particularly with a small potted plant on it.

Several groups of gypsies had come to Migennes for seasonal work in the vendange (the harvest of the wine grapes) and one group, a half dozen caravans, camped in an unpaved parking area that bordered a part of the quay adjacent to the port de plaisance. They ignored the boaters, and were, in turn, ignored. There were a lot of ducks in the canal, mostly Mallards and odd looking crosses between Mallards and domestic ducks: fat, well fed, semi-tame ducks. A number of the town's older residents had a close relationship with those ducks. Every afternoon, bags of day old bread or what looked like dry dog food in hand, several of them would come down to the canal to feed—and sometimes talk to—the ducks, and the ducks would gather...good things were about to be served. Every time someone on a boat or barge appeared on deck, or walked down the quay, a few ducks would paddle over and sit there, quacking softly and looking hopeful. If you made the mistake of feeding the few...the multitude quickly arrived. In the late afternoon or early evening, after the elderly residents of Migennes had left, a young woman would emerge from one of the gypsy caravans, go down to the canal side, and toss bits of bread to the ducks. Three or four days after she started her duck feeding routine, I was sitting in the wheelhouse having a glass of wine before dinner when she came down to the canal, bread in hand, accompanied by an older man. She started tossing bits of bread and when the ducks had gathered close to shore, her companion's arm swung, a cast net flew and the ducks, mostly, scattered. What looked like three or four, wrapped in the net and complaining loudly, disappeared with the master of the cast net into an area between several of the caravans, an area well shielded from view. The loud quacking ended quickly. In a way the ducks were partially right, in this case a young woman on the canal bank tossing bread did mean good things were about to be served. Ducks clearly have small minds and short memories, the next evening the young woman was back at the canal side, tossing bread, and the ducks gathered.

On the twenty-fifth *Gloriana* and another, recently arrived, English sailboat left for the Mediterranean. On the twenty-sixth *Liberte* departed for their ordained appointment at the boatyard and Betty and I rode over to the boatyard to find out where to park when our time came. After lunch on the twenty-eighth we left the port de plaisance and moved to Chantier Fluvial de Migennes, parked *Nova Cura* in the designated spot, and spent the rest of the day changing the oil, doing laundry, cleaning, packing and preparing for our return to the United States. Saturday we completed our preparations for departure and had a very enjoyable lunch with some sailing acquaintances from the U.S. who were in Migennes for the start of a two week Crown Blue Line hire-boat trip. After lunch, we left the keys to *Nova Cura* at the boatyard office and caught the 4:00 p.m. TGV to the Gare de Lyon, and Paris.

Arriving in Paris, we took a taxi to the Hotel Joanne d'Arc[66] in the Marais and then enjoyed a long, pleasant evening walk past the Pl. de la Bastille and the Port de l'Arsenal to the Village of St. Paul where we had a lovely dinner, sans reservations, at the Bistro Vins des Pyrenees.[67] We had three days to enjoy Paris before our return flight and we did. We explored the Marais and the Village of St. Paul, walked to Sacre Coeur, the Louvre and the Trocadero and rode the Batobus down the Seine and, then back up. Betty had a map that gave the address, phone number and a brief description of what were claimed to be the one hundred best bistros in Paris and we ate every lunch and dinner in a different one. All the ones we tried were good and one, Baracane[68], was

---

66 Hotel Joanne d'Arc le Marais, 3 rue de Jarante, 75004 Paris, phone: 33 (0) 1 48 87 62 11

67 25 rue Beautreillis, 75004 Paris, phone: 33 (0) 1 42 72 64 94

68 Baracane, Bistro de l'Oulette, 38 rue de Tournelles 75004 Paris, phone: 33 (01) 42 71 43 33, www.1-oulette.com

suburb. Unusual in our experience, the weather stayed good the whole time we were in Paris—sunny, crisp, clean, dry, and cool but not too cold—and none of the unions were on strike.

When we checked into the Joanne d'Arc the desk clerk had told us that because of new security measures at the airport we should be there several hours before our departure time. She recommended at least three. On the morning of October third we took the train to the airport immediately after breakfast, and got there a full four hours before our scheduled departure. We needed the time. In the end we had, maybe, fifteen minutes to spare. Heavily armed soldiers and police officers were everywhere. The check-in lines snaked out the doors and filled the normally busy road in front of the terminal. Every piece of checked luggage and every carry on item was searched twice.

9. Agitez la Brique - Trois

The flight from Paris to Philadelphia was smooth, not overly crowded and it arrived on time. In Philadelphia airport security was much tighter than it had been, tighter than either of us had previously seen. Soldiers in combat fatigues and carrying automatic weapons were stationed in the international arrival area. Although by the time they reached the arrival terminal anyone bent on hi-jacking or blowing up an airliner, unless they had left a bomb on the plane, was a failed terrorist. The immigration agent went through our passports page by page, with frequent glances at us. Betty and I both had a lot of entry and exit stamps in our passports: European trips, numerous trips to The Bahamas, and dozens of assorted Caribbean island in and outs from spending a couple years in the islands aboard *S/V Walkabout*. Customs carefully searched everything, even though we had nothing to declare and we were getting off a plane, not boarding one. A few of the Customs Agents were wearing side arms. Things had very definitely changed.

My sister picked us up at the airport and, after a night visiting with her, we took the train to Maryland where friends met us and drove us to down to Herrington Harbour North. Even though *Walkabout* was dusty, dirty and splattered with sea gull crud after her long summer on the hard, it felt good to be back aboard—familiar, comfortable and safe. A week of living aboard on the hard cleaning and taking care of the annual maintenance chores and we were back in the water, headed south.

That winter was a mild one on the U.S. East Coast and in The Bahamas. We moved slowly, enjoying the trip, and did not reach Norfolk, Virginia, at the bottom of the Chesapeake Bay, until October twenty-fourth. In Norfolk boats traveling the Atlantic Intracoastal Waterway have to motor directly past, and close to, the U.S. Navy's sprawling naval base: past the carrier piers, the cruiser/destroyer docks, the submarines, the supply ships, tankers, and all the support facilities. Motoring past the base just six weeks after 9/11 was a surreal experience. Security was tight, vessels of all types, from small speed boats to mega yachts and container ships, had to travel slowly in a narrow traffic corridor under the watchful eyes, and machine guns, of the men aboard half a dozen fast patrol boats. Thanksgiving was spent in the old colonial city of New Bern, North Carolina, Christmas at Vero Beach, Florida, where the afternoon temperature reached seventy-five degrees, and the next day we were running our diesel cabin heater, and on January 18, 2002 we left Miami for The Bahamas. In The Bahamas I had the best year fishing that I have ever had; the dinner menu aboard our boat featured a lot of good, really fresh, fish. I also managed to fall off the boat, breaking three ribs in the process. By early May we were back at Harrington Harbour North laying up *S/V Walkabout* for the summer— again ready for a season of slow comfortable canal cruising, chateaus, ancient churches, good food and good wine aboard *Nova Cura*.

The day before our departure for France, I walked into Clipper Bay Yachts, the yacht brokerage in the marina, and listed *S/V Walkabout* for sale. I wasn't at all sure that I really wanted to sell the sailboat, but we had decided to shake up our lives a little more—agitate those bricks. Besides, if anyone actually made an offer on the boat I could always turn it down.

Pre 9/11 flying to France and staying for five months was not a problem, buy a ticket on-line or over the airport counter, hop on the plane and buzz off to Paris—"welcome to France, we hope you enjoy yourself." Post 9/11 things were different, particularly internationally. As ordinary tourists with no formal visa, buying tickets for an international round-trip with departure and return dates more than ninety days apart was barred by the new security rules. Rules like that are begging to be bent and a ticket broker sold us what was, basically, two sets of one-way tickets; although they were priced like round-trip tickets. Our flight from Philadelphia to Paris's Roissy-Charles de Gaulle airport landed at 9:30 a.m., May twenty-first, on time. French immigration stamped our passports—the arrival date clearly shown—and "welcome to France, we hope you enjoy yourself." There were some expensive marine electrical bits and pieces for the barge in our luggage, but customs whisked us right through without comment. By 2:00 p.m. we were checked into the Hotel de Terminus in Migennes, and enjoying the first lunch of our 2002 canal season.

We were also getting used to the euro and it was having an odd effect on our thinking. During our first year on the canals, France had been transitioning from the franc to the euro. Prices were given in both, but the franc always came first and the franc-to-dollar ratio ran approximately 7:1. The transition period was over. France was on the euro, and when we arrived the euro-to-dollar ratio was around 1.15:1(85 euro cents = $1.00). Spending francs at 7:1 had a small element of play money to it. The mental translation between dollars and francs was not intuitive and instant, and often we were not really conscious of how much money we were actually spending. In 2002, the euro, mentally, was a dollar. Prices had not changed but things seemed more expensive and we were very much aware of how much real money we were spending.

After lunch we walked over to Chantier Fluvial de Migennes, *Nova Cura* was just inside the gate: dirty, a tarp covering the wheelhouse, grass and weeds standing tall around the keel, prop and rudder. There was no sign that any of the jobs we had thought would be done over the winter had been done. At the office, Jo seemed surprised to see us, even though Betty had sent several e-mails with our projected arrival date and had received at least one in return. I took a ladder from one of the boatyard sheds and we climbed aboard, aside from being dusty and dirty, everything was just as we had left it— nothing had been touched, nothing done. Déjà vu all over again! Weren't we in this neighborhood just a year ago? The hotel room might be necessary.

The previous fall when we left the barge for the winter we had talked with Jo about three big jobs that we wanted done: removing decades of old tar from the hull, rebuilding and extending the deck house and modifying the access to the aft cabin. We had also discussed two smaller, desirable but not critical, jobs: rebuilding, leveling and strengthening the double berth in the aft cabin and restoring the wooden trim around the interiors of the cabin windows. We had gone off to the United States under the happy delusion that everything would be taken care of while we were gone. At the very least the one job, removing decades of accumulated tar from the hull, that had to be done with the barge out of the water, and was the reason the barge had been stored on land for the winter, would be done.

The hulls of old iron barges were generally painted with tar. Boiling roofing tar was brushed on below, and often above the load line. Over time repeated applications resulted in a thick, gummy, layer of tar that was unattractive and, on hot days, would literally melt, sag in ripples and waves, and creep down the sides of the barge. When the tar build-up reached the creepy-crawly stage a barge would be dry docked, the accumulated layers of tar would be chipped, scrapped and sand blasted off, and the layering could begin again. Removal was generally done in cold weather when the tar was stiff and mechanical grinders and chippers could be used to remove it. *Nova Cura* had years and years, probably several decades or more, of accumulated tar on her hull and the time to clean it up and start over was well past due. There were ripples on her sags.

Nova Cura's wheelhouse had been designed and built to be disassembled when it was necessary to get under very low bridges. From having taken the wheelhouse down to go through the Pouilly Tunnel, we knew that there was rotten wood in several areas; parts' falling off is a pretty good clue. We also knew, because both Jo Parfitt, and Philippe Gerard at H_2O, had told us about it, that current French and European Union regulations mandated shatter-proof safety glass in the wheelhouse windows. Ours was old, thin and easily broken, window glass. We wanted the wheelhouse structurally stabilized, rebuilt where necessary, and fitted with approved shatter-proof safety glass.

The aft cabin had been the original crew's area in *Nova Cura's* previous life. The forward end of the aft cabin was

composed of the aft engine room bulkhead and the aft wall of
the wheelhouse. Access to the aft cabin was from the wheelhouse through a narrow old style scuttle[69] and down a steep
wooden ladder. That scuttle was one of the things both of us
had disliked about *Nova Cura* from the very beginning. It was
too narrow and too low. Access to the aft cabin was difficult
for tall, or unusually wide, people. If the wheelhouse was
to be worked on anyway, why not extend it aft, over the aft
deck house as far as the aft edge of that awkward scuttle? The
scuttle could be cut off and replaced by a simple hatch. The
forward seventy centimeters, two and a half feet or so, of the
aft deck house's roof would then be inside and across the back
of the wheelhouse, and could be used as a bench, a place where
guests or whichever of us was not on the wheel, could sit comfortably out of the weather.

Our first morning back in France, breakfast, bread and coffee, at the hotel was eleven Euros. After breakfast we walked over
to the boatyard, said good morning at the office, climbed aboard
Nova Cura, connected our hose, broke out our cleaning supplies
and went to work. Just before we broke for lunch, I plugged in
our electrical system and turned on the battery charger and refrigerator. On the way back from lunch we stopped at the ATAC
Supermarche and bought as much food, wine and beer (life is not
food alone) as we could carry. We might be sleeping in the hotel
for a while but our breakfasts, and most of our lunches and din-
ners would be aboard *Nova Cura*. In the afternoon we continued
cleaning and I flushed and filled the water tanks and made sure
that all of the onboard systems, except for the toilet, were up

---

69 Scuttle (nautical usage); a small protected opening or hatchway in the deck of,
or in the roof of a deck house on a ship, that is large enough for a person to enter
and/or exit a lower deck, a cabin or a deckhouse.

and running. Then we cooked and enjoyed a nice dinner before pedaling back to the hotel for the night.

In the morning, back at the boatyard, with our breakfast, the newspaper, and more groceries in hand, Jo and a yard worker were looking at the tar on *Nova Cura*. Tar removal was about to begin. Before he left Jo showed us some faded white chalk marks on the bottom that he had made during his original survey. Those chalk marks were interesting, one of the jobs Betty had paid H_2O to do while the barge was in the dry dock was to power wash the bottom and apply a fresh coat of tar. When Jo left, the yard guy donned his cover-all and respirator/face mask, started an air compressor, and began the long, noisy job of removing all that ancient tar. Removing the old tar, applying two coats of new tar and welding up an old exhaust pipe outlet hole in the hull took until Thursday, During tar removal, when the compressed air chipper was in use and the noise was absolutely intolerable, we took long bike rides to Joigny or out into the countryside around Migennes. In the middle of tar removal, work began on the wheelhouse. Some of the roof panels, both the sliding doors and the rear wall were removed and taken into the carpenter's shop. The missing parts temporarily replaced by wooden slats and a tarp.

Betty renewed the insurance on *Nova Cura* (again using H_2O's address), and sent the application for our annual waterway use permit to the VNF. The European Union had been adjusting and standardizing residency requirements, and 9/11 seemed to have accelerated the process. For a non-citizen to register and operate a pleasure vessel in a member country, you now had to be able to prove that you had a residency permit, in France a "permis de séjour", which we did not have, or you had to have paid taxes for at least three years in the country in which the vessel was registered, and we were about three years short on that one. When Betty sent in the usage renewal, she included copies of the previous year's papers, which carried the former owners address in England. Much to our relief, the 2002 usage tag was returned promptly. But, we were going to be cruising around France on an old barge with very improper papers and, for the last month of the 2002 cruising season, we would be doing it on expired tourist visas. If we were stopped at a check lock, or caused a major accident, and our papers were examined...

When the compressed air chipper was not in use, Betty and I ground, sanded and painted the roofs of both deck houses...again...and cleaned the bilge...again. Leaked engine oil and water from the burst hot water heater had flowed forward from the engine room and the residue needed to be cleaned up. *Nova Cura* had three iron bulkheads, one between the forward cabin and the forepeak and one at each end of the engine room. None were water tight. There was a drain hole approximately five centimeters in diameter at the lowest spot in all three and, the bulkhead at the aft end of the engine room also had three large cut-outs: one for the propeller shaft, and two for the steering chains. VNF regulations stipulated that private barges over fifteen meters in length registered in France must have at least two bulkheads that were water tight from the keel to the deck, and each of the three resulting hull sections had to have its own, large, automatic bilge pump. So we cleaned the bilge under the main cabin and in the engine room and I sealed the drain in that bulkhead by driving a lead plug into it[70]. The

---

70 The drain was too low and too hard to reach to weld a patch over it, so...a two kilo hammer and a lead plug did the job. The drain was the only hole in the bulkhead, several bundles of electrical wire, both DC and AC, as well as the fresh water hoses to and from the water heater were already routed over the bulkhead, through the wheelhouse.

only bilge pump we had was a large, new, automatic one in the main cabin under the kitchen (galley) that had been installed by H_2O, so I installed a second one in the engine room and the boatyard put in a through-hull fitting for the outlet hose. We now had one water tight bulkhead and two big bilge pumps. Betty's long term goal was to register her barge in France; but to do so it had to comply with the VNF's requirements. *Nova Cura* was now two thirds of the way to satisfying the VNF on bulkheads and bilge pumps.

Friday, May thirty-first, ten days after our arrival in Migennes, with a smooth, clean, hull, a coat of new tar, and ten new magnesium anti-galvanic corrosion anodes, *Nova Cura* was picked up by a very large crane, carried to the quay and set in the river. Watching that crane trundle forty five or so tons of iron barge through a crowded boatyard was interesting. We walked over to the Hotel de Terminus, retrieved the few items still there, checked out, and were once again live aboards. Our costs went down and our quality of life went up.

On any given day a half dozen, plus or minus, of the boats or barges nestled into the three or four deep raft of assorted vessels moored along the boatyard quay, had people living aboard, all working hard, trying to get their cruising season underway. Every day or so somebody left, headed down river to Sens or Paris or up river to Auxerre; each departure was accompanied by waves and shouted good wishes from those of us still working. Each departure seemed to be followed by an arrival, every day or so someone would arrive by train or car to commission a boat that had been laid up for the winter, or a boat would cruise in to do a little work or have something repaired, before continuing on to somewhere. Probably somewhere interesting that we had not been to, but wanted to visit, if we could ever get out of the boatyard. Two days

Trundling through the boatyard

after *Nova Cura* was launched, Stu and Judy Miller of *Liberté* arrived. It was nice to see them and compare notes on our winters and our plans for the summer. That same day a sailboat from England motored in and rafted to us. The couple aboard were moving their boat south to the Mediterranean; he worked for the Foreign Office and had been assigned to one of the British Consulates in Spain, but the trip was taking too long, and they had decided to have the boat trucked from Migennes. They lay alongside *Nova Cura* for a week, waiting for their truck to arrive.

Since our arrival the weather had been nearly perfect, warm sunny days, comfortable nights and no rain, a definite improvement over the preceding year. But during our first week in the water that changed. Low thick gray clouds moved in, the temperature dropped and the rain came. Interior work, modifying the access to the aft cabin, rebuilding the marine toilet (an annual chore on all boats), and interior painting could continue, but half our wheelhouse was still in the carpenter's shop, and two days without rain were needed to fit the wheelhouse sides and roof and install the hardware that held it all together. Then, a deadline, four friends from Herrington Harbour were arriving in Paris on Saturday, June eighth, and expected to meet us, and *Nova Cura*, in Auxerre the following Thursday. The end of the week the rain broke, the tarps and temporary wood frame came off, the last of the welding and metal work on the modified aft cabin access was done and, except for the doors, the newly extended wheelhouse went up.

We spent the weekend sanding, priming and painting the steel sections inside the wheelhouse and applying a first coat of a wood stain/sealer to all the woodwork. The steel inside the wheelhouse was white, and Betty had decided to paint it an antique dusty burgundy. She found some paint that looked like it might be about the right color and while she was rolling and brushing the paint on, while it was wet, it looked like just what she wanted. But, as it dried it...well...there was a change. The final dry paint was a more than vaguely risqué cherry pink, possibly appropriate for the boudoirs of a certain type of business establishment often found in sea ports. It was not exactly what Betty had in mind. The man on the sailboat rafted to us thought it was some sort of primer. But it was there, and there it stayed. Three months later it didn't look too bad...it had mellowed, or ripened or something, or maybe we just didn't notice it anymore. The last two working days before ready or not this barge is off to Auxerre, the carpenter did a temporary installation of the wheelhouse doors, made a few adjustments to the wheelhouse side panels, not the final ones, and installed the new wooden aft cabin hatch and doors. I tested the engine and changed the oil, and Betty arranged for a local seamstress to make cushions for the new seating area in the expanded wheelhouse.

Wednesday morning, after talking with Jo about the work that still needed to be completed, we left for Auxerre—twenty-two kilometers and nine locks up the Yonne. Lunch was cheese and slices of a baguette eaten at the wheel while we held our position in front of a lock for forty-five minutes, because we had forgotten that the locks closed for an hour at midday. Betty had not forgotten how to drive the barge and the deck hand didn't flub the line handling. The trip up-river was completed without any unfortunate incidents—anyone watching probably thought we actually knew what we were doing. In Auxerre we tied up in the large and well equipped port de plaisance just upstream from the foot bridge over the Yonne, a spot from which there was travel poster view of the Cathedral of St. Etienne and the heart of the ancient city.

Within minutes of docking in Auxerre, while I was still tidying up our lines, a large hire-boat came alongside and honked at us. At first I thought it was someone who wanted us to move or who wanted to raft to us, but, to our surprise, it was Bob and Julie Norman and another couple we had met, more friends from Herrington Harbour; they were on a one-way hire-boat trip down the Canal du Nivernais from Chitry les Mines to Migennes. They tied to us briefly and we talked about their trip and Nova Cura. We had shown them photos of Nova Cura while we were at HHN getting ready to come to France and knew they were planning a hire-boat cruise, but the meeting in Auxerre was a surprise to all of us. They had come down the canal from Accolay and, when they reached Auxerre, there we were. They had dinner plans but said they would come to *Nova Cura* for lunch the next day.

Our guests rolled in just past noon. Mike and Brenda would be staying on the barge with us while Harlan and Linda stayed at a Gite, a centuries old fortified farmhouse, several miles south of Auxerre. Half an hour later Bob and Julie's hire-boat pulled alongside and rafted to *Nova Cura*, and for the next several hours ten people, all boaters who knew each other from a marina on the Chesapeake Bay had a fine time— sipping wine, talking, opening more wine, eating lunch, and drinking just a bit more wine—on a barge in the middle of France. When the hire-boat finally cast off and headed down the Yonne, the rest of us took a long walk through Auxerre, and ended the day with a leisurely and excellent five course dinner at La Salamandre[71], the perfect finish to a great day.

---

71 Still in the Red Book; La Salamandre, 84 rue de Paris. Phone: 03 86 52 87 87. E-mail: la-salamandre@wanadoo.fr

The following morning, with some of us feeling less than perfectly fit, we crowed into Harlan and Linda's rental car and spent the day touring and wine tasting. The day began with a visit to Vezelay and a guided tour of the Basilica of St. Madeleine. From the spirituality and high culture of Vezelay, we descended to the possibly less spiritual, but equally cultural, wine caves and tasting rooms of Chablis for a little tasting and buying. After Chablis, with everyone fully restored and feeling much better, we moved on to St. Bris for a bit more wine tasting and a tour of a medieval wine cave before returning to Auxerre and an alfresco cabin top dinner aboard *Nova Cura*—a dinner heavy on the cultural products of Chablis and St. Bris.

Saturday Harlan and Linda drove off to Provence and Mike, Brenda, Betty and I spent the day walking Auxerre. The day began with a predawn thunderstorm but by the time we were all upright and ready to march the sky had cleared and the sun was out. While we walked most of the older parts of Auxerre, half the day was spent at the Cathedral, the ancient Abbey, the museum and the associated archeological excavation. Auxerre, originally a Gaulish village, became the large and important fortified Roman city of Autessiodurum, a strong point on the military highway between Lyon and Boulogne. The Roman city morphed into a walled Gallo-Roman city that became one of the early Christian centers in Gaul. The principle religious structures in Auxerre are the Gothic Cathedral of St. Etienne, built on the site of an earlier Romanesque Cathedral, and the sixth century Abbey of St. Germain, built by Queen Clotilda (wife of Clovis) over the tomb of St. Germain (died 448). The Cathedral was interesting and it's Romanesque crypt, with the famous fresco of Christ riding a white horse, flanked by armed angels, was impressive (and full of tourists); but the Abbey of

St. Germain, the museum of St. Germain and the on-going archeological excavation were fascinating.

The four-euro fee to tour the Abbey of St. Germain, the museum and the archeological dig was one of the most worthwhile admission fees I have ever paid. St. Germain, Bishop of Auxerre, died in Ravenna, Italy, on July 31, 448, and his body was returned to Auxerre and buried in the Oratory of St. Maurice, which St. Germain had constructed. Between 493 and 545 Clotilda had the Oratory replaced by a Basilica which became the foundation for the present Abbey-Church. Between 841 and 849, the crypt below the church, with the tombs of St. Germain[72] and others was given its present form by Charles the Bald. The frescos painted on the walls in the crypt are original to that time and may be the oldest in France.[73] The museum, built into the abbot's residence, the fourteenth-century cellars, the monks' dormitory and part of the convent, houses a large and well-displayed collection of historic and pre-historic artifacts from Auxerre and the surrounding area as well as a number of well-executed displays recreating life in Roman/Gallo-Roman Autessiodurum. Under the main church and the courtyard of the Abbey, a major archeological excavation was in progress and a tour of the site was included in our four-euro admittance fee. The tour was self-guided, no babbling tour-guides, and children were not allowed. The

---

72 St. Germain is no longer actually in his tomb and presumably the others aren't either. The remains, relics, of St. Germain were preserved and revered at the church until 1567 when, during the religious wars, the French Huguenots captured Auxerre and desecrated the shrine, tossing whatever was left of Germain out into the street. A legend in Auxerre claims that after the desecration of the tomb, Germain's relics were retrieved and interred in the Abbey of St. Marion; but the Catholic Church has not recognized the remains in St. Marion.
73 The information about St. Germain and the history of the Abbey-Church came from *The Catholic Encyclopedia* and from tourist brochures picked up in the museum.

archeologists had uncovered a whole series of previously un-suspected Gallo-Roman, Carolingian and Merovingian tombs, along with the foundations of some probable Gallo-Roman religious structures. At one point in the tour we walked over a steel grate laid across a dimly lit five or six meter deep pit—remember we were deep under a medieval Abbey-Church. In a side wall of the pit there were three or four stone sarcophagi, one above the other, and far down in the deepest corner part of a stone arch that may have been the top of a door, or window had been exposed, hinting that still more lay below. Auxerre was full of tourists that warm summer Saturday, but there were few down in the dig. The few who were there stopped on that steel grate and stood, silent and thoughtful, gazing down on eons of man's faith, almost seeing the very face of time.

Mike and Brenda needed to return to Paris on Monday. To go to Paris by train from Auxerre, you go first to Migennes; so the Auxerre to Migennes leg of their return to Paris was by barge. Sunday was gloriously sunny and the hottest day we had experienced yet in France. The locks opened for business at 9:00 a.m. and we were on the river and ready, along with what seemed like every hire-boat in Auxerre. Despite the hire-boats we made every lock, and even with an extended lunch stop in Gurgy, reached the Port de plaisance in Migennes in time for Mike and Brenda to get their train tickets to Paris and do a quick load of laundry before dinner. In the morn-ing, another very hot day, our guests left on the TGV, and we returned to the boatyard to finish the wheelhouse and the interior carpentry, and have the 12 volt alternator looked at—it had decided to alternate inadequately.

Ever the optimist, I thought we'd be in the boatyard for two or three days while things were wrapped up. *Trox* inter-vened. *Trox* was a large Dutch barge, in beautiful, absolutely immaculate, condition that, according to the boatyard rumor mill belonged to the director of City Bank's European operations or, maybe, to his wife. In any case, the owners would take *Trox* on a three or four week cruise each season, apparently with, according to the rumor mill again, a hired crew. The rest of the year *Trox* stayed at and was worked on, extensively worked on, by Chantier Fluvial de Migennes. The year before the owners had had the interior floors done in Dutch tile. The tile was not what they wanted after all, so, this year the tile was coming out and hardwood was going in. We were a couple of small jobs, a day's work. *Trox* was a career, and the career was being prepared for its annual cruise.

The time spent waiting wasn't entirely wasted. Although the International Herald Tribune, and sometimes the London papers, were generally available I often felt cut off and unable to keep track of the rapidly changing post 9/11 world. In Migennes and in Auxerre, I tried to buy a small, portable, shortwave radio receiver—one with a band splitter, that could pick up the BBC, the Voice of America and the United States Armed Forces Network—but was unable to find a satisfactory one. During the wait for *Trox*, the information deficit problem was solved. Satellite television came to *Nova Cura*.

Stu and Judy had satellite T.V. aboard *Liberté*, as did several of the other boats and barges in the boatyard. Our first morning back in the boatyard, I hitched a ride to Mr. Brico with Stu; it was much too hot to ride the bike up there. While at Mr. Brico, I noticed that they had a sale on televisions and satellite dishes. I wanted to buy one of each for *Nova Cura*, but because of the residency requirement and the television tax, I couldn't. It was against French law for me to buy a television and for the store to sell me one. Satellite dish? Eh...no problem, how many? But no television. By law, a legal street address was required to buy a television <u>and</u> to pay the television tax, and the purchaser had to provide legal proof of residency. The television tax applied to both you and your address. The tax was a one-time thing per address. You had to pay the tax when you bought the first television for any residence you rented or owned. Once you had a tax receipt in your name for a specific address, you could buy as many televisions as you wanted—for that address. If you moved, or bought a vacation home, well... I don't remember what the amount of the tax was; but it was above trivial, I would still have paid it, but as a foreigner, with no "permis de séjour" and no legal street address, it was a crime for me to pay it. Stu said I needed a friend with a tax receipt who could provide a little assistance. When he bought their system he had a little assistance. I needed a little assistance.

That afternoon, back at the boatyard I was talking with an Englishman off a long narrow boat that had a satellite dish on its cabin top, about how nice a satellite television system would be. No problem said he, I have a receipt for an address in France, and we'll just go buy one—voilà...a little assistance. Stu drove us to Mr. Brico. I picked out the television I wanted and, while the assistance paid for it, I bought a satellite dish, some coaxial cable and a few other things. When we were clear of the store and on our way back to the boatyard, I reimbursed my benefactor. As soon as we reached the boatyard, the plunder was carried aboard *Nova Cura* and, with help from Stu and my new English acquaintance, I set up the dish, ran a temporary cable through the forward hatch and connected it to the television, switched the set on, and as we slowly turned the dish until it pointed in the right direction CNN Europe—English Language edition—came into focus. The tube stayed on until nearly midnight.

The next day I bolted the satellite dish to the front of the deckhouse and ran a permanent cable from the dish to where the television would sit in the main cabin (add television shelf to the carpenters work list). The mount for the rather large dish had a swivel hinge so that it could be laid flat on the deck and out of the way when the barge was underway. Once the dish was properly set up and the cable run, I spent the rest of the day playing with our new toy. The dish would bring in the signals from seven satellites, a total of one hundred seventy-three channels.[74] About half of the channels were "free to air" and would come in clearly. The rest were scrambled and to receive them we would have to subscribe to a satellite service and get a decoder box. The service would need our address, and our tax number, and...well, maybe we'll just be happy with free...free is good.

Among the eighty-five or so free-to-air channels were the European versions of CNN, CNBC and NBC, one of the BBC channels and several other English-language stations. There were numerous European channels, whatever your language of choice: French, German, Dutch, Norwegian, Russian, Polish,

---

74 The dish was a passive receiver and not tracking or motorized. To tune in a particular satellite, the dish had to be very slowly turned by hand until it pointed at the desired satellite. We would open the roof top hatch and I would slowly turn the dish while Betty watched the screen and hollered (loud enough for me to hear through the hatch) "left, "left", "right", "no left a bit" until the desired signal came in. The satellites were all geostationary and in an equatorial orbit. As an aid in tuning, the dish manufacturer had provided a reference sheet with the degrees east or west of the prime meridian and the altitude (angular distance above the horizon) of each satellite when viewed from various places in western Europe. A list of the channels beamed from each satellite was also provided. With a bit of practice the system worked very well but a good compass was a necessity. A lot of barges and canal boats used the same system and several times we found ourselves moored to a canal bank or tied to a quay next to another barge with both of us adjusting our dishes to a bellowed chorus of "left", "left", "á la droite", "back a bit", "non, Non! á la DROITE!"...

Spanish, Italian, etc. We got a handful of channels that were new, and sometimes a bit weird: several Turkish channels, T.V. Algeria, T.V. Dubai, T.V. Libya, etc. Among the odder channels were two that broadcast, without sound, the views from panning video cameras: one showed alpine ski resorts from the French Alps to Austria—need to know what was happening at Courchevel?— and the other showed the central squares and the area in front of the main train stations in many of Europe's larger cities. We could see the weather on CNN, always useful—more rain was on the way and a major anti-cyclonic storm was hitting northern New Zealand. CNBC told us, in case we had failed to notice the dollar-to-euro exchange rate, that our mutual funds and the dollar were dropping like rocks. The French and German stations had really great ads—some of which would have driven the family purity crowd in the U.S., and all the other self-appointed custodians of all things prim, prissy and proper, absolutely berserk. There was something for everyone and for all occasions; but whether or not the T.V. improved our quality of life or not was a question open to debate. Several days later I was looking at the sales receipt for the television and the address written on it, an address in St. Jean de Losne, looked familiar—it was H_2O's address.

In the fullness of time work on *Trox* was completed and, a week after our return from Auxerre, our turn arrived. The carpenter and mechanic, possibly making up for previous neglect, showed up at 7:00 a.m. Three days later all the carpentry work was finished, the alternator was alternating, the seamstress had delivered the new cushions for the wheelhouse bench, and Betty's barge was good to go. Friday, after settling our appalling bill, we left Chantier Fluvial de Migennes to the usual waves and shouts and headed down the Yonne, bound for the valley of the Loire and more fine wines.

The original wheelhouse, note the scuttle

The new better, bigger, improved wheelhouse

The new aft cabin access hatch and wheelhouse seat

Brenda, Mike and Betty getting ready for dinner

10. On to the Loire

Over the winter and spring the VNF had tinkered with the lock operating schedules. The historic canals such as the Burgundy canal and the Nivernais canal which were already seasonal and were overwhelmingly used by pleasure, particularly hire, boats were unchanged. The principle commercial rivers and canals were also unchanged. But a few sections of river and canal that had large locks and no longer carried significant amounts of commercial traffic now operated on a restricted schedule, and the Yonne River, between Joigny and its confluence with the Seine, was in this group. On the Yonne, during the pleasure boating season the locks now opened once an hour, between 8:00 a.m. and 7:00 p.m., Monday through Friday. On Saturdays there were only six openings and on Sundays the locks were closed. Our first day on the river, adjusting to the new lock schedule, the five locks and twenty- two kilometers between Migennes and Villeneuve sur Yonne took eight hours, two of which were spent sitting in front of one lock—first the lockkeeper enjoyed his lunch, then when he decided to open, we were in the middle of enjoying ours. Late in the afternoon we tied up astern of *Liberté*, and Stu, rather gloomily, informed us that the water faucets and power outlets on the quay were locked. The tourist office lady who was custodian of the key, apparently the one and only key, was on vacation. Oh well, our water tanks were full, the alternator was doing its thing, our batteries were fully charged, and we were right next to a great restaurant. Betty walked over to the Auberge La Lucarne aux Chouettes and made reservations.

Later that evening, while sitting in the restaurant en-joying a pre-dinner aperitif and the beautiful view over the Yonne, a hotel barge pulled up directly in front of the restau-rant. As soon as the hotel barge was secure, a crew member came in to the auberge. He spoke to the lady at the reception counter, and she handed him a key. He went out and removed the padlocks from one of the water faucets and from the box with the electrical outlets, and then returned the key. After dinner, as we were leaving, I asked the same lady about the key to the water and power. She looked surprised and asked if we were on a peniche? Pointing to *Nova Cura*, I said yes, one of the little ones. Ah...no problem! She opened a drawer in the counter and handed me a key attached to a small square of wood with "2" painted on it. We removed the lock from faucet number two and I returned the key. The electrical out-lets were all in one, already unlocked, box. The previous fall, when the key had been in the custody of the lady in the tour-ist office, there had been a nominal fee for power and water. When I returned the key to the lady in the restaurant, I asked about paying the fee. With an airy wave of her hand, she said that we had dined in the restaurant... Never underestimate the power of a good restaurant in France. As I was returning to *Nova Cura*, the passengers from the hotel barge, dressed for dinner, filed down the passerrelle and into La Lucarne aux Chouettes.

On Sunday, a fine sunny and warm day, the locks were closed so we could not move down to Sens. In the afternoon there was a rather comical little sailing regatta on the river next to us. A dozen or so small sailing dinghies of mixed size, design and vintage, competed on a short race course laid out across the river, so that the dinghies were broadside to the current. There was very little wind and as the sailors crossed the river the current did what it does and slid them down stream and off the course. They ended up "sailing" a triangular route, mostly off the race course. First across and down the river, then back to our side but still further down the river and, finally, back up the river attached to one end of a rope, the other end of which was attached to a power boat. Nothing goes up stream as well as a good, reliable, motor. I am not sure what this was doing to improve their sailing skills; but everyone was having a great time.

Sunday night *Nova Cura* had visitors, uninvited and definitely unwelcome. It was a warm night and Betty and I were sleeping in the aft cabin. The two opening ports, wide open. In the very early morning hours, well before dawn, the sound of someone stepping aboard woke me. I sat up to the sound of soft, careful footsteps on the side deck, and then a muscular, dark skinned hand and arm came in through one of the ports and started groping around on the shelf below. I should have grabbed that arm and twisted it hard. Instead I jumped up, ran up to the wheelhouse, threw the door open and yelled. A Frenchman of African origin looked at me said something, probably obscene, leaped off the barge and took off down the quay; followed by at least two companions. Stu and Judy, docked just ahead of us had a Citroen 2cv and an antique Czech built motorbike. Both were parked on the quay, chained and locked. Or rather both had been parked on the quay. In the morning the 2cv was there, but it was alone. The motor bike had been stolen.

Once again a little tired of Villeneuve sur Yonne we left for Sens in time to make the 9:00 a.m. opening of the first downstream lock. Stu and Judy stayed to report the theft to the local police. Late in the afternoon *Liberté* arrived in Sens, and Stu told us that they had gone to the Police Station, filed a theft report and given the police a photo of the motor bike and a copy of their bill of sale. The police were most sympathetic, but indicated that there was very little chance that Stu and Judy would ever see that motor bike again. The police were right. I wished that I had grabbed that groping arm and twisted it three hundred and sixty degrees; but I kept that thought to myself. It wouldn't have helped and, besides, I'm the sort of person who just doesn't actually do that type of thing; but my inner Walter Mitty is alive and doing well.

During our visit to Sens in September 2001, we had been unable to find the electrical and water connections that our cruising guide said were there. This year, while securing our dock lines, I almost tripped over an electrical connection and in the lovely flower bed that edged the paved part of the quay there were multiple water faucets. In Sens dock-side water faucets are like flowers, they live in mulch, bloom in the summer, and disappear as soon as the weather turns cold and rainy. I have no idea where electrical outlets in metal boxes set into concrete pylons go when the weather turns cold. Sens was as delightful as it had been the previous fall although it was difficult not to think about 9/11 and everything that had happened since.

Two American college girls doing a summer in Europe, Betty's brother's niece and a friend of hers, were to join us in Sens and spend a few days traveling with us before moving on to Spain. The girls were to arrive in Sens by train from Paris late on the afternoon of Wednesday, July third. Early that afternoon, the *Ancloute*, a large hotel barge arrived, tied up and unloaded their passengers, and the passenger's luggage, into a pair of tour buses. This was unusual as most hotel barge trips were weekend to weekend. Being nosey and thinking that maybe the hotel barge had a mechanical problem or some other equally interesting problem; I walked down to see what was going on. The Captain and Chef were on the Quay. When the last passenger was safely seated and the busses had left, the Captain told me that the passengers were being transferred to a barge on the Canal lateral a la Loire; because the Yonne River section of the Lockkeepers Union was walking out—going on strike—the locks would not open on Thursday. Duh... strike? The lockkeepers are walking out? Great! We have two guests coming who think they are going to be spending several days traveling down the Yonne to Moret sur Loing and the Canal du Loing with us. Well...this is France...strikes are a way of life, and most are one day affairs. We'll adjust and leave on Friday, there was a lot for the girls to see and do in Sens. When our guests arrived, we welcomed them with a bottle of fine Burgundy, took them to dinner at a nice bistro and explained the lockkeeper problem.

Unfortunately, the strike was not a one day affair[75] and our guests did not get to cruise the Yonne aboard *Nova Cura*. Thursday was the Fourth of July, and the girls took the bicycles and went for a ride around Sens and visited the Cathedral and the museum. While they were gone, Betty and I went to the butcher shop and bought a fine, large, fresh Belgian hare and then to the wine shop for a couple of bottles of good champagne. In the

---

75 The lockkeepers felt that they had a real grievance and it took their union and the VNF a full week to sort things out, come to an agreement and get the locks back into operation. Remember the changes in the Yonne River Locks operating schedule? We were told that when the VNF put the locks on a restricted schedule they also cut the number of full time professional lockkeepers. At that time, there was a thirty five hour work week in France and 8:00 a.m. to 7:00 p.m., Monday through Friday, plus a chunk of Saturday, equals a bit more than thirty five hours. When the union and the VNF finally compromised and the keepers returned to work, the locks operated on an even more restricted schedule; although the hours of operation still equaled more than thirty five hours a week.

evening I fixed Lapin a la Dijonnaise for dinner and we celebrated the Fourth with a champagne toast. During dinner one
of the girls said that she had never had chicken in mustard sauce
before and that it was very good. When I told her it was Belgian
hare, rabbit, both girls paused, looked at their plates, looked at
me, and resumed eating. I don't think either of them had ever
had rabbit; but they both claimed it was good. I suspect that in
the fall when they were back at school and regaling their friends
with tales from their summer in Europe, one of the stories was...
The Rabbit. After dinner we were all sitting on the deckhouse
roof enjoying a final glass of champagne when a brief fireworks
display lit up the river. The fireworks were for an event at a river
front pavilion upstream from where we were docked, a party of
some sort, maybe a birthday or a wedding. The fireworks may
not have been in honor of the Fourth of July, or us, but they
were a fitting end to the day.

Friday, the day after the Fourth, when it was clear that
the strike was not over and wouldn't be over the next day
either, our guests decided that, as nice as Sens was, they would
move on. Some people they knew were at Ibiza in the Balearic
Islands, and a warm, sunny beach on a Mediterranean island,
with people their age, sounded better than a tin boat on a
river in central France.

There were seven vessels "locked in" on that quay: *Nova
Cura*, *Liberté*, the hotel barge *Ancloute*, a cargo peniche on its
way to Migennes to load, and three yachts. There was nothing we could do except wait and enjoy Sens. Each morning
the prisoners of the Yonne would gather on the quay, mugs of
coffee in hand, look at the morning papers, trade rumors and
speculate about how long the strike would last. Each evening
the routine was repeated, with a glass of wine or a cold beer
playing the role of the mug of coffee. Early in the morning on

Saturday, strike day number three, the Dutch owner of one of the yachts, a television and documentary film producer who spoke excellent French and English, called the VNF to discuss the situation. At the end of the call, he thought the VNF had agreed to make some sort of exception and let the prisoners of the Yonne, at least the private vessels, move down river to the Seine, starting at 9:00 a.m. In a mad scramble everyone, except for the hotel barge and the cargo barge, got under way and paraded down to the first lock. Wrong! The VNF may have agreed but someone forgot to clear the idea with the Union. In response to a chorus of honking horns, the lockkeeper came out, looked at all of us, made a classic French gesture, and said something along the general lines of "kiss off." The parade returned to the quay. Then, one of the men off the cargo barge told us that the lockkeepers union was affiliated with the PCF, the French Communist Party, and that Communist unions never permitted irregularities—like letting five captive pleasure boats escape a just and honorable strike. Our morning and evening social gatherings continued.

On Tuesday, July ninth, strike day seven, the front page of "LE SENONAIS Libéré, Le Journal de l'Yonne," the local daily, devoted its entire front page to a few headlines and a large, color, photo of the quay and our row of barges and boats. The headline, in big bold letters set right on the photo, read "Sens: escale forcée pour les Plaisanciers!" roughly a forced layover in Sens for some pleasure boaters. The large front page photo of the quay had the hotel barge *Ancloute*, the largest and most impressive vessel, front and center. Their guests had been speedily transferred to another hotel barge and the crew, except for a lone boat keeper, was gone. That afternoon a woman from the tourist office came down to the quay and told us that the strike was over, and that the next morning the locks would resume operation. Half an hour later the keeper of the first downstream lock drove onto the quay and told us the same thing—the strike was over. He would test the lock early in the morning and the first official opening of the lock would be 9:00 a.m. Then he wished us bon voyage and accepted a glass of wine, several glasses of wine, one from each of us. Once again we were all friends and colleagues on the river. That night the prisoners of the Yonne held a final social event, a celebratory dinner on the quay.

Prisoners of the Lock

The next morning the cargo barge headed upstream, *Liberté* and the three yachts headed down stream, *Nova Cura* and the *Ancloute* went nowhere. On Monday I had taken a pair of shoes in for repair and they would not be ready until late Wednesday afternoon at the earliest and possibly not until Friday. We consoled ourselves with an excellent dinner at the restaurant Le Clos des Jacobins,[76] two couverts, in the Red Book. Late Wednesday I checked on my shoes and they were not ready but the proprietor said I could pick them up when the shop opened the next morning. Thursday morning, while Betty took in our electric line and filled both water tanks, I ran to the shoe shop. The shoes were ready and we were off the quay in time for the 9:00 a.m. lock opening. The lock was a little slow to open and loitering in front of the lock gate, *Nova Cura's* stern got too close to shore. The propeller hit a large block of submerged granite that had fallen from the locks approach works.[77] Once in the lock Betty pulled the rpm back to idle and tested the gearbox, shifting several times from forward to neutral to reverse and back again. Everything seemed to be in order. Leaving the lock Betty accelerated slowly to cruising rpm with no apparent problems, so we kept going. Eleven hours, nine locks and fifty-five kilometers later we tied up to the hotel barge dock at Moret sur Loing, despite a large sign that said a hotel barge would be arriving in the morning.

---

76 Le Clos des Jacobins, 49 Grand Rue, Sens. Phone: 03 86 65 31 08. www.restaurantlesjacobins.com. The restaurant's name comes from the Jacobins, a loosely organized group of politically active writers and intellectuals who wrote about, supported and popularized revolutionary thoughts and ideals during the French Revolution. During the revolution, local Jacobins may, or may not, have met in an old building, parts of which are incorporated into the restaurant.

77 A locks approach works are the bulkheads, aids to navigation, docks, wing dams, etc. on each end of a lock. On a small canal they generally don't amount to much but on a large river lock they can be quit extensive.

Friday, well ahead of any possible arriving hotel barge, we moved from their dock to the pleasure boat dock, a large new and well built floating aluminum dock, where *Liberté* was already tied up. Late Thursday, coming down the river, Betty had commented that she thought there was a slight vibration in the engine or steering that had not been there before. This morning the engine started, and ran in neutral while warming up fine, but in gear there was a noticeable, although small, vibration. I checked the gearbox oil level, and it was dry—no measurable oil, nothing, not a drop, on the dipstick. I added a quart of thirty weight engine oil which brought the fluid level back up to the full mark. The oil level had been all the way up when we left Migennes and there was no sign of where the leak was. There was no oil on the sides or bottom of the gearbox, but there was oil in what had been a clean bilge. With oil in the gearbox we started the engine and, at low rpm, put it in gear and there was no vibration—not in forward, not in reverse. *Nova Cura* had a long propeller shaft which was partially supported by a large carrier bearing mounted approximately a meter aft of the gearbox. The carrier bearing was strongly bolted to a heavy steel mounting bed that was, in turn, welded to the steel engine stringers. While looking for our gear oil leak, I noticed that the carrier bearing was visibly no longer flat on its steel mounting bed. One corner was up high enough for a seven millimeter feeler gage to slide in under it. When our propeller hit, the shock had been strong enough to move the carrier bearing. It was possible that we had bent the propeller shaft and/or damaged the propeller. I crawled all the way aft to the stern gland, to where the propeller shaft passed through the hull, there was no visible damage and there was no water leaking in.

The Bastille Day weekend was starting and I was sure that I would have to wait until Monday, possibly Tuesday, to talk to anyone about this problem. Never the less I called Chantier Fluvial de Migennes intending to leave a message for Jo Parfitt, but he answered the phone. I explained what had happened and what I had found. He asked a few questions and then said that he had a friend, a mechanic at Chantier Naval, a large commercial boatyard located where the Loing met the Seine (we had seen it on our way in) and he would see if his friend had time to look at our gearbox and propeller shaft. I then called H_2O; they had installed our gearbox and replaced the carrier bearing, and discussed our problem with Philippe Gerard. Philippe asked a number of questions, said that he needed to check a few things, and asked me to call him back on Monday or Tuesday morning and he said not to move the barge until I had talked to him. With that we decided to enjoy the Bastille Day weekend.

Moret sur Loing and the area immediately around it became part of the Kingdom of France in the eleventh century. Throughout the medieval period the town was a heavily fortified military strong point on the warring frontiers between the Kingdom of France and the Duchies of Burgundy and Champagne. The Loing river bridge, the massive fortified "Porte de Bourgogne" (gate), the central keep from the old chateau, the remnants of the defensive walls and towers and parts of the Benedictine monastery date to that period. Following the Hundred Years War and the incorporation of Burgundy into France Moret sur Loing's military significance ended and, although Henry IV kept his mistress here (and made her the Countess de Moret) and Louis XIV used the chateau's central keep as a state prison, the town became a peaceful retreat from Paris. In the nineteenth century the town's attractive location near the Loing's confluence with the Seine and its proximity to Paris and Fontainebleau made the town an early tourist center and a favorite of the Impressionist painters. Alfred Sisley lived in the town from

1889-1899 and his house is now a museum. Today the town lives on tourism and is a destination for day-trip bus tours from Paris. Despite the swarming horde of tourists we liked Moret sur Loing. In the late afternoon or early evening, after the tour buses had departed, or early in the morning before they arrived, a walk up Rue Grande from the Loing bridge, through the Burgundy Gate past the Hotel de Ville to the tourist office and the ramparts was delightful—particularly with a stop for a café au lait in the morning, or an aperitif in the evening.

Saturday afternoon, surprisingly, an Englishman (I think) named John Faulkner knocked on the wheelhouse, introduced himself and said that Jo Parfitt had asked him to look at our gearbox and prop shaft. He looked at the carrier bearing and used several clean, dry paper towels to feel all around and under the gearbox; they stayed clean and dry. Then he started the engine, let it idle for several minutes and tried shifting into forward and reverse at low rpm. Next he used a brass rod with the ear piece from a trumpet welded to one end as a sounding rod to listen to the gearbox while I moved the shift lever from neutral to forward, to neutral, to reverse and back. With the engine warm and in forward, he again felt around with a clean, dry paper towel. This time he found a small amount of oil. I shut the engine off and he told us that he thought the shock of our propeller hitting the granite had damaged the carrier bearing and had damaged the rear oil seal on the gearbox. With the engine running and in gear, shaft turning, there was a slow oil leak where the drive shaft exited the gearbox—at the rear oil seal. He also thought that we had probably damaged the propeller, that one of the blades was bent or dented, and it was possible that the propeller shaft was bent and the stern gland damaged. He had heard nothing unusual in the gearbox, and he thought that the vibration we were feeling was most likely caused by a combination of damage to the propeller and no gearbox oil. To repair the damage, the barge would have to be dry docked. Then he really surprised us, he suggested that we just continue on to St. Jean de Losne, if we traveled slowly and paid close attention to the gearbox oil level, we would probably make it without doing any additional significant damage. With that, he gave us his business card and phone number, said that if he could help in any way to give him a call, wished us good luck and left. That night there were Bastille Day fireworks over the Loing.

Monday morning, as soon as I thought Philippe might be in the office at H_2O, I called. He was there. He listened to what John Faulkner had said, told me that he was acquainted with John Faulkner, and said that he had talked to both Westinghouse, the manufacturer of our marine gear, and to the mechanics at CBV in St. Jean de Losne. Both Westinghouse and CBV felt that if there were no unusual noises in the gearbox, the oil leak was slow and we were able to shift smoothly and easily into both forward and reverse, damage to the gearbox was probably limited to the rear oil seal. I told him that we were thinking about continuing in the direction of St. Jean de Losne. He said that, in our position, he would do the same thing and to call or send an e-mail every few days and let him know where we were and how things were going. If the situation really deteriorated, he knew of (and knew people at) several boatyards along our route where repairs could be made. Betty and I looked at each other; walked back to *Nova Cura* started the engine and prepared to cast off. I was wondering if I would recognize an "unusual" noise if I heard one. Both of us hoped that we reached St. Jean de Losne. If we stopped en route for repairs, wherever we stopped was probably where this canal season would end.

Leaving Moret sur Loing, we entered the short Canal du Loing. Forty-seven kilometers long, with only nineteen locks and an elevation change of just thirty five meters, the pretty and placid little Canal du Loing climbs from Moret sur Loing to the small town of Buges, where the Canal de Briare, the Canal du Loing and the now closed Canal d'Orléans meet. Originally built by the Duc d'Orléans between 1719 and 1724 as a link between the Loire River—via either the Canal de Briare or the Canal d'Orléans—and the Seine River, the canal was upgraded to the Freycinet standard in the late nineteenth century. It is still an important link between the Loire and the Seine, and in regular use by cargo péniches carrying grain and other bulk cargos, hotel barges and large numbers of pleasure boats.

Our destination for the night was the ancient town of Nemours. The weather was clear and warm, we had a short day planned and it would have been a pleasant day on the water. Would have been if there had been no "sans permis" hire-boats also on the canal. At the second lock of the day, an automated lock, a heavily loaded grain barge was very slow leaving the lock and the automated system timed out, which tripped the emergency breaker. As the grain barge cleared the lock a trio of hire-boats zipped around us and crowded in. They tied to the lock wall and sat, waiting for the lock to cycle, waiting for something to happen. When nothing happened, a couple people from the hire-boats started running up and down the side of the lock trying to figure out what to do. Betty finally put *Nova Cura's* bow on the canal bank; I stepped ashore, walked up to the lock and pressed the large red button next to a sign that read "reset lock" in multiple languages. We stopped for lunch early, tied to the bank and enjoyed a long lunch, trying to put some space between the hire-boats and us. I complain a lot about the hire-boats, and some of them

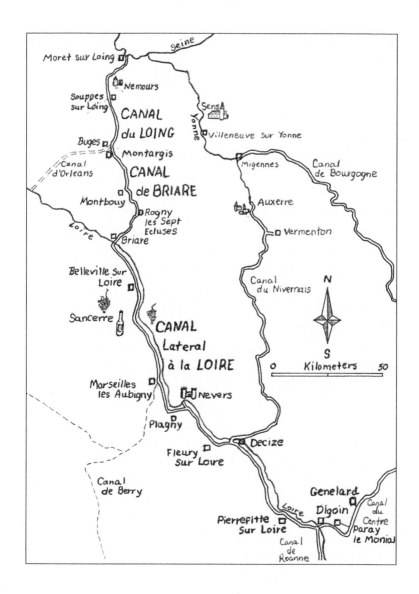

Map 4. The Loire Valley Canals

were a real pain. But it's the hire-boats and the hire-boat companies that pay most of the canal usage fees, the people who
rent the boats spend a lot of money in the canal side towns
which means jobs, and the hire-boat companies themselves,
provide a lot of jobs.

Our guide books said that Nemours had a chateau and
church, both twelfth century, and a good historical museum—
all three worth a stop. Our cruising guide had generally been
very accurate with regard to the location, quality and facilities
available at the various marine stopping places. In Nemours,
the guide showed a halte nautique with power, water and
trash facilities located right downtown, near the chateau and
church. The location was correct, and from the dock there was
a view of the chateau. The chateau, church and museum may
indeed have been well worth a visit, but we never found out.
We never got off *Nova Cura*. We were afraid to leave the barge
unattended. The halte was a deteriorating dock adjacent to
a squalid, trash-strewn park occupied by a group of ragged,
dirty, mostly drunken, men. On the dock the water taps were
gone, the naked rusty pipes capped off. The electrical power
box gapped open, devoid of receptacles and wiring. At the
land end of the dock's ramp, a single trash bin sat, overflowing
and surrounded by a mound of filth. We should have moved
on, but it was late afternoon, the locks would be closing soon,
and our cruising guide showed no good stopping spot for
three or four more locks. So, we stayed. I double-looped our
dock lines on the bollards—they could be cut; but double
looped, twisted over, under tension and with both ends of each
line on the barge, they could not be removed.

Neither of us slept much that night. The sounds of
drunken men and breaking glass made sure of that. Shortly
after dawn we left, even though that entailed loitering in the

canal until the locks opened. There was a little loose rubbish on our deck and puddles, stains and the smell of urine clearly showed that during the night a couple of the parks habitués had relieved themselves on *Nova Cura* from the dock. While we waited on the locks, I used buckets of water, soap, bleach and a brush and tried to scrub away Nemours.

Above the first lock of the day we were back in rural France, cruising slowly up a calm, well maintained canal bordered by poplar trees. On one side of the canal a paved tow path was in use by early morning walkers and bicycle riders. It was the classic image of a French canal and we could have tied to the canal bank and been very comfortable. Just past the third lock of the morning, in the little village of Bagneux sur Loing, we passed an obviously new concrete quay with large bollards painted a bright, cheerful, yellow. The quay was bordered by a small grassy area with a couple of picnic tables and a trash bin, and it looked very inviting. We both commented that we should have spent the night there. Just one lock, four kilometers, further and well before lunch we stopped at a halte nautique outside the post card village of Souppes sur Loing. The halte was new, large and had water, electricity, picnic tables and, unusual in France, a barbeque grill. Neither the attractive quay at Bagneux sur Loing nor the excellent new halte nautique at Souppes sur Loing were mentioned in our cruising guide. Taking advantage of the water, we gave the barge a proper bath, trying mightily to erase the final traces of Nemours. But, one of the fine gentlemen from the park had relieved himself on the wheelhouse door and that stain would not wash off. In the end the door had to be sanded and refinished. Once *Nova Cura* was clean we pedaled into town, ate lunch at the local bar-restaurant and looked around town: a small tabac with the English edition of the International

Herald Tribune, a nice boulangerie, an épicerie, several other shops and an exhibit (not really a museum) about the hemp-growing industry. Before the development of modern synthetic fiber, hemp for rope was extensively grown in the area and the hemp fiber was processed in Souppes sur Loing.

From Souppes sur Loing we moved up to Cepoy, where we met an American couple aboard a twenty four-meter converted Luxemotor who gave us some very unwelcome news. According to a VNF notice they had read in Briare, the Canal du Centre, one of the links on our path to St. Jean de Losne, was to close for the season in mid-August because of low water; although heavy rains in the interim could affect the closure date. It was Wednesday, July seventeenth. If the Canal du Centre closed on August fifteenth we had less than a month to reach Chalon sur Saone and the Saone River. We were going to have to act like a hire-boat, pick up our speed and skip some of the interesting places. Despite our perceived need to move a little faster, leaving Cepoy we left late and then travelled all of six kilometers, to the port de plaisance in the city of Montargis. Going through the second lock of the day, at Buges, we entered the lock from the Canal du Loing and exited the lock into the Canal de Briare. Just above the transition lock (above because we were climbing) we passed the entrance to the Canal d'Orleans.

The Canal de Briare, linking the Loire River at Briare to the city of Montargis, was begun in 1604, during the reign of King Henry IV. Work was stopped in 1610 when the King was assassinated, resumed approximately ten years later, and the first barge from Briare and the Loire River reached Montargis in 1642. The Canal d'Orleans, linking the Loire River at Combleux to the Loing River at Buges and canalizing the Loing between Buges and Montargis was opened to barge traffic in 1693. Montargis, or Buges, remained the head of navigation until the Canal du Loing between Buges and the Seine was opened to barge traffic in 1724. Today, after several modifications, the Canal de Briare is fifty-seven kilometers long and has thirty-five locks. Locks one to twelve climb from Briare and the Loire to the Loire/Seine watershed and the dividing pond. Locks thirty-five (the Briare-Loing transition lock) to thirteen climb from Buges to the dividing pond. The Canal d'Orleans was taken out of service in 1954, but most of it has been preserved and there is a long range plan to restore at least part of it for use by hotel barges and pleasure boats. The canals former tow path, for the full length of the canal, is in use as a bicycle and hiking route.

Montargis, is a clean little city crisscrossed by numerous small canals and rivers. The Canal de Briare runs right through the city, hemmed in by red brick walls and the facades of three and four-story homes that open onto the old tow paths, here on both sides of the canal. The canal forms two sides of the oldest part of Montargis and makes a blind ninety-degree turn at the corner. Coming from the north, there is a green and red traffic light to control barge traffic approaching the right angle turn because a barge driver can not see around the turn and the first of two closely-spaced locks is immediately past the turn. Approaching the right angle turn we had a red light and stopped well back. A large hotel barge came out of the lock and around the turn and needed the full width of the canal to make the turn. The in-town locks are an attraction, popular with locals and tourists. Both ends of both locks were crowded with gawkers and there was a Gelato (Italian ice cream) cart at the second lock. It was not the place to miss a throw with a mooring line. The locks are manual, with full time lockkeepers and helping the lockkeepers with the heavy work of pushing the long levers that opened and closed the lock gates was part of the fun—at least on warm, sunny, summer days. Past the second lock and on the edge of the oldest part of Montargis, there is a nice fully-equipped port de plaisance and we were docked in time to enjoy lunch at an outdoor cafe on the central square and visits to the Musee du Gatinais, the local historical museum, and the Musee des Tanneurs, an interesting museum devoted to leather tanning, an important local industry until the middle of the twentieth century.

Seventeen kilometers, and six locks—four in a closely spaced automated chain that took less than thirty minutes— south of Montargis, we stopped for the night in Montbouy, where there was something new, to us, on the quay, coin operated electrical power outlets, a half-euro coin in the slot bought two hours of power. We stopped because a tourist brochure picked-up in the Montargis tourist office mentioned, without detail or explanation, that when the Canal de Briare was being modernized and the locks up-graded, the engineers working on the canal discovered a previously unknown Ro-man or Gallo-Roman amphitheater, and a large area of associ-ated ruins between the towns of Montbouy and les Lorrains. We rode out to the amphitheater, paid the two-euro entry fee and spent an hour and a half walking the ruins. The site was only partially excavated and several exploratory trenches, roofed and protected by fencing, showed where archeologi-cal work was in progress, although nothing was currently happening. An explanatory sign showed a map of the hypo-thetical layout of the Gallo-Roman city with known build-ings and sites marked and with modern roads and the canal superimposed. The Canal de Briare cut through the site a safe distance from the amphitheater itself. A second sign told us that modern researchers believed that when the canal was originally built some of the old stone had been used for canal construction, and that some had also probably been used in building a nearby chateau. The amphitheater was protected by a fence and there was an attendant and a small fee to explore the ruins, but foundations and scattered stone, covered with brush and brambles, broke the surface in a number of places, generally unprotected.

Returning from the ruins, we left the bikes on the barge and walked through the part of the village near the canal: one small shop, a café/bar (closed), several dozen tightly-clustered courtyard farm houses, some built on older foundations, and a large old, distinctive and attractive church. A sign in front of the church identified it as the "Eglise Notre-Dame de Montbouy, a Historic Architectural Monument of France, built between the thirteenth and sixteenth centuries." The church seemed much larger than would have been remotely necessary for a small village, the doors were very tall for their width, portions of the rear wall and of one side wall were of noticeably different, older looking, stone work, and what looked like traces of old foundations around the church hinted at outbuildings. The church was locked so we could not go inside and look around.

Except for the historical marker in front of the church, there were no informational markers or signs in the village, and none of our guide books mentioned Montbouy or its church. But none of them, not even the green guide, mentioned the Gallo-Roman amphitheater and related ruins either, although they were marked on our canal chart. France has so many artifacts, churches, chateaus, fortresses, etc. that no single guide can hope to cover them all. For the price of the guide book, you get the authors opinion of what is, or should be, important, interesting and popular.

Getting into the comfortable half day on the water cruising mode that we had enjoyed on the Canal de Bourgogne, we moved seventeen kilometers and eight locks further up the canal to Rogny les Sept Ecluses (Rogny of the Seven Locks) and moored to the canal bank behind several other barges and a couple of large hire-boats—the small halte de plaisance was for little boats. During the day we passed the town of Chatillon-Coligny, one of several towns that the canal rumor mill said was the home of the one and only marine sewage pump-out facility on the in-land waterways of France. It may have been there, but if it was, it was well hidden. The village of Rogny les Sept Ecluses takes its name from a ladder (one lock emptying directly into the next) of seven locks that were part of the original Canal de Briare. The preserved remains of the seven step ladder are a tourist draw and just outside of the town—they were in our green guide. We spent the night because Betty wanted to have dinner at L'Auberge des 7 Ecluses, which was prominently mentioned in <u>Watersteps Round Europe</u>, by Bill and Laurel Cooper;[78] her current inspirational book. Dinner in the Auberge was worth every minute of the overnight stay. In the morning a fast operating chain of six automated locks took us up almost twenty-five meters—from Rogny les Sept Ecluses and the valley of the Loing—to the summit pond in less than a kilometer and a half. Across the summit pond to the Loire/Seine watershed, and then down through twelve locks, and *Nova Cura* was in Briare, and beside the Loire River.

---

78 <u>Watersteps Round Europe</u> (ISBN 1-57409-016-X), by Bill and Laurel Cooper, published by: Sheridan House, 1996. <u>Watersteps Through France</u> (ISBN 0-7136-4391-9), by Bill and Laurel Cooper, first published by: Metheun, London, 1991.

11. Through the Wine County

Briare (Roman Brivodorum) was a minor Loire River port and a center of mosaic and enamel work until the construction of the French canal system made it a major center for barge traffic between the Rhone/Saone, the Loire and the Seine. The old in-town commercial port, connected to the Loire by several locks, declined in importance when the Canal lateral a la Loire was extended across the Loire on the Briare Aqueduct in 1896 and freight traffic on the Loire essentially ceased. A new, larger commercial port was constructed outside the town where the Canal lateral a la Loire joined the Canal de Briare. The commercial port still handles some freight barges but, as in St. Jean de Losne and many other in-land ports, the focus today is on pleasure boats, including hotel barges and a large number of hire-boats. The old in-town commercial port and the short section of Canal leading to it were redeveloped for pleasure boat use in 1989, and the old port is now a large, attractive, well equipped port de plaisance surrounded by ca-fes, restaurants and shops. Everything a transient boater needs is within a short walk or easy bike ride and, again like St. Jean de Losne, Briare is a popular wintering-over place for full-time canal cruisers.

At lock number six during the decent to Briare, we caught up with an, English built eighteen meter long barge that had been designed to look like an old Dutch barge, named *Bengta*—owned by George and Maggie Pringle, the Scots couple who had been our fellow students during barge driving school. They too were enroute to St. Jean de Losne. In the port de plaisance, the Briare harbormaster directed us to a spot alongside another barge that would be leaving in the morning. He also showed us a letter from the VNF that said the status of the Canal du Centre with regard to closure remained uncertain, but that closing the canal would be a last resort, and before the canal was closed for the season, the frequency of lock openings would be reduced to conserve water. To be safe, the harbormaster thought we should plan on reaching Chalon sur Saone and the Saone River by mid-August. It was Sunday, July twenty-first and Chalon sur Saone was three hundred and three kilometers and ninety-nine locks down the road.

Our stay in Briare passed too quickly. A morning in the Maison des deux Marines (The House of the two Waters), a small but good museum devoted to commerce on the Loire and the Canal de Briare. An afternoon in the much larger Musee de la Mosaique et des Emaux (Museum of Mosaic and Enamel Work), an impressive museum that explained and illustrated the local mosaic and enamel industries, including the making of enamel buttons. An afternoon and evening was spent aboard *Bengta*, visiting with George and Maggie. George was a retired Marine Engineer and the engine room on *Bengta* looked like an engineer's engine room, spotless and perfectly laid-out. An afternoon showing George and Maggie *Nova Cura*, during which George looked at our gearbox/drive train problem and agreed that, if we were careful and kept an eye on the gearbox oil level, we should make St. Jean de Losne with no additional problems. I sent an e-mail to Philippe at H_2O, telling him that we had reached Briare, to our surprise he sent a mechanic (from H_2O?) to look at our gearbox. The mechanic also thought that we should keep going, carefully. The next morning, July twenty-fifth, with two more favorable opinions on the gearbox providing moral support, we bought two hundred liters of diesel, crossed the Loire on the aqueduct and started down the Canal lateral a la Loire.

Before the construction of the Canal lateral a la Loire, barges carrying freight between Briare and the head of the Canal du Centre at Digoin used the Loire—a river subject to both drought and floods. Attempts to control the Loire using wing dams, dredging, channel stabilization, and other conventional measures were unsatisfactory and in 1822 construction of a canal paralleling the Loire between Digoin and Briare was authorized. Briare is on the right-bank of the Loire and the original plan was a right-bank canal; but because of terrain, urban areas and roads, the canal was constructed on the Loire's left-bank. Right Bank-Left Bank? A rivers right and left banks are relative to its downstream direction. Stand on the bank, or on a bridge, facing downstream, that is facing in the direction in which the current is flowing, the left bank is to your left and the right is? Yes! It's on your right!

Canal construction began in 1827 and by 1838 the canal was operational to Chatillon sur Loire, on the left-bank six kilometers upstream from Briare, where a lock gave access to the Loire. Until 1896, when the Briare Aqueduct carrying the Canal lateral a la Loire across the Loire was completed, barges entered the Loire through the lock at Chatillon sur Loire, crossed to a lock on the right-bank at les Combles and entered a short section of right-bank canal that took them into the old port in Briare. Today, after several modifications, the Canal Lateral a la Loire, between Briare and its junction with the Canal du Centre at Digoin, is one hundred and ninety-five kilometers long and has thirty-eight well spaced locks. When traveling from Briare to Digoin all of the locks are upstream, ascending, locks.

In the United States if you cruise the Atlantic and Gulf coasts from northern Maine to south Texas, every marina, boatyard or municipal dock has the same, standard, electrical outlets and water taps. If you crisscross the country in a mobile home, every camp ground and RV park has the same, standard, electrical outlets and water taps. But in France...in France local individuality rules. In the late afternoon of our first day on the Canal Lateral a la Loire we tied up at Belleville sur Loire. The long canal side quay was crowded with boats and barges, many racing to beat the possible closure of the Canal du Centre. Electricity and water were available on the dock and Le Bistro de l'Ecluse was right next door. When I tried to plug in *Nova Cura's* power cord, there was a small problem—the plug did not match the outlet. Our plug was clearly not going into that outlet. I needed an adaptor. OK, we'd been through this routine before, several times. Down in *Nova Cura's* engine room there was a box with four electrical adaptors, and several water tap adaptors. Down to the engine room for the box of adaptors, nothing matched. We needed another adaptor and it was too late in the day to try to buy one. A man from the hire-boat tied up just ahead of us, a plugged-in hire-boat, pointed me to a small sign at the far end of the dock, which informed me in six languages, that power adaptors were available for rent at Le Bistro de l'Ecluse—for two and one-half euros per night. We walked up to the bistro, enjoyed a fine dinner and, even though plugging in was not really necessary, rented an adaptor. In the morning, after breakfast, I pedaled to the local hardware store and, for only sixteen euros; they made an adaptor for me, our fifth. It was never needed...never used—in France, individuality rules.

Between Bellville sur Loire and Sancerre, we stopped for an hour and a half just above the lock at les Houards. The lockkeeper had a side gig selling wine and the old stone lockkeepers' house had been turned into a tasting and display room, crowded with stacks of artfully arranged wooden wine cases. Across the lock a local farmer had set up a cheese shop where boaters could taste and, maybe buy, some of his goat cheese. Betty and I sampled, and bought, at both shops. Several bottles of the wine turned out to be old and vinegary, corked. The lockkeeper either didn't know his wines, or (more likely) he was buying up out-of-date wine, cheaply, and selling it to passing boaters, knowing there was little chance he would see them again. The cheese was a different story, the Crottins de Chavignol (literally translated: goat droppings) were excellent, smooth and almost creamy, not chalky and dry like many crottins.

The village of Menetreol sous Sancerre, kilometer marker one hundred and fifty-seven on the Canal Lateral a la Loire, has the nearest halte nautique to Sancerre. As at Belleville sur Loire, the dock at Menetreol was crowded with boats and barges trying to get to somewhere past the Canal du Centre before the possible mid-August closure. Several boaters already on the dock moved two small barges, one forward and the other back, to make a space large enough for us, and then helped slide us in. It was a close fit.

Aboard Betty's Barge, a day at Menetreol, to visit Sancerre and buy some of the fine wine that carries the villages' name was a requirement of life. Sancerre sits high atop an unfortunately steep hill, a very healthy bike ride—for the last kilometer, push—from Menetreol. It was a hot day and when, gasping and sweating, we finally reached the village, we parked and locked our bikes beside the tourist office and collected a handful of tourist brochures about Sancerre, the village, and Sancerre, the wine. Most of the towns in France seem to be old, and Sancerre was not an exception. During the Gallo-Roman period a temple dedicated to Julius Caesar stood on the hill and the name may be derived from "Sacrum Caesaris (sacred to Caesar)." The village is very pretty, with narrow, twisting, cobblestoned streets, numerous fourteenth to seventeenth century houses and buildings, and with just enough of the old chateau and defensive walls left to give it a pleasant atmosphere. During the religious wars Sancerre was a Huguenot (Protestant) center and it took a brutal eight month siege (1572-73) by the Catholic forces to return the city to the King. Then in 1640, because of continued religious unrest, the King had most of the chateau and the defensive walls torn down to prevent their use as a center of armed resistance.

We walked the entire heart of the village, climbed to the top of the Tour de Fief, the only remaining piece of the Count of Sancerre's chateau and then had lunch at La Pomme d'Or, a Red Book one couvert restaurant on the Place de la Marie. The Pomme d'Or had a wide variety of Loire Valley wines, including many from Sancerre, available by the glass and we tried several. After our wine...or lunch...whichever...we went in search of wine vendors and, if possible, wine tastings; without luck. The tasting rooms that were open were selling souvenirs (how about a nice cork screw that says "Sancerre"?) but they were not tasting and they had little wine to sell. A man at one of the tasting rooms tried to explain the lack of wine for sale, but his French was way too fast and heavily accented for me. Basically, it was either too late, or too early, in the year, or maybe both. However, at one of the stops on our fruitless search, I discovered that Sancerre also produces pretty good beer—the Brasserie Sancerroise, 258 Route d'Amigny, 18330 Sancerre, brews up some fine suds. A visit to the brewery by bicycle didn't seem like a good idea, the brewery was at the bottom of the wrong side of that hill, but, after sampling, I bought a six pack each of "Biere Blond" and "Biere Ambree."

Sans wine, we rode back to *Nova Cura* and I quickly became devoutly glad that I was not trying to ride down that hill with my beer, and a case of wine, strapped to the bike's luggage rack.

A half hour or so before sunset Betty and I were on the dock talking to the French owner of the small barge astern of us, a Luxemotor a meter or so longer than *Nova Cura*. He had helped us tie up when we arrived, was Parisian, and did something in television. He spoke excellent English, knew more about American politics than I did, kept his barge at the Port de l'Arsenal in Paris, and was one of the few actual French barge owners that we met. There were a lot of French boaters on the canals, but most were aboard sailboats, power yachts or hire-boats—almost never barges. During our conversation, to get him off Washington politics and the policies of the current administration, which seemed to get him rather worked up, I told him about our visit to Sancerre and about our disappointment at being unable to buy any good wine. He looked at me, looked at his watch, and said to meet him on the dock in twenty minutes.

Twenty minutes later he was on the dock with a two-wheeled cart. I took a minute to grab our wheeled, folding, airport luggage carrier, and then followed him into the rapidly darkening night. Off the dock, past a bistro, down a street, through an alley, up another street, down two more alleys— I was lost—to a house on a narrow dark street. My guide knocked softly on the door. The door opened a crack. A brief, quietly spoken, conversation in rapid French. A man emerged, led us a hundred meters further down the street, into an alley to a door in a large shadowy building. He unlocked and opened the door and when the three of us were inside, and the door closed, he switched on the lights. I took a quick look around and realized that the building was a complete winery, one whole side wall stacked almost to the high ceiling with racks of bottled wine. My guide whispered that the wine was Sancerre and it would be fifty-six euros, cash only, for a full case of twelve bottles. He bought two cases, I bought one, and neither of us received a receipt. The unknown vintner, or worker, retrieved three unmarked cardboard wine cartons from the rear of the building and filled each with twelve bottles, which I noticed had no labels. When the cases were secured to our carriers, the vintner (I had decided without any real evidence that he was the owner) turned out the lights, opened the door and we filed out. The vintner left and, without a word my guide took off at a rapid pace in a different direction, with me close behind. I had no idea where I was and I was afraid that if I lost sight of him it would be past sunrise before I again saw *Nova Cura* and Betty. I was also worried about being stopped by the gendarmes while running around in the dark with a case of label-less wine: wine for which I had no receipt, did not know who the seller was, and had no idea where the winery I had purchased it at was.

Safely back aboard *Nova Cura*, even though the wine was at room temperature and it was hours past dinner, Betty pulled the cork on a bottle. Out of the bottle and visible, the cork had Sancerre and some other stuff stamped on it. It was far and away the best Sancerre I have ever tasted. I am sure that in a good wine cave in France, and only a good one would have had that wine; it would have been very expensive. In the United States, if it was available at all, it would have been far above our budget—and I only bought one case...

Leaving Menetreol, we finally put in close to a full day, Menetreol sous Sancerre to Marseilles les Aubigny, thirty-two kilometers and nine locks. Marseilles les Aubigny used to be an important barge center. The town is where the Canal de Berry, now closed, met the Canal lateral a la Loire. The Canal de Berry, built between 1809 and 1839, linked the lateral a la Loire (and the Loire River) at Marseilles les Aubigny, via St. Amand and the Cher River to the lower Loire River at Savonnieres and Tours, by-passing much of the flood and shoal plagued Loire. A secondary branch of the Canal de Berry extended south from St. Amand to the iron mines and forges around Montlucon. Because of limited water supplies for the gravity fed canal, the Canal de Berry was initially built on the model of the English narrow canals and narrow two meter wide barges called "Berrichons" were used. Commercial traffic peaked in the late nineteenth century when hundreds of Berrichons plied the canal. The water supply problems could not be solved, the canal was never up-graded to the Freycinet standard, traffic declined to nothing during the first half of the twentieth century and the canal was closed for good in 1955—which ended the town's economic importance. There was a halte nautique in town, but the only section suitable for a barge was forty or so meters of new concrete quay which was occupied by a hotel barge that appeared to have no one on board. The rest of the halte was a dozen or so short, spindly little pontoons, suitable for skiffs and jet skies, which were set perpendicular to the canal side. Past the halte nautique there was a long stretch of old commercial dock with good, large bollards but no facilities, we docked there as did several hire-boats and another barge. Walking around town later we found very little: a boat/barge yard that did have a dry dock, a restaurant/bar, a small boulangerie (closed) and a couple of shops that looked permanently closed.

In the morning our remaining bread was moldy and the milk had an unfortunate smell. I walked to the boulangerie for a baguette...closed. I returned to the barge and we both walked to the little restaurant/bar, hoping for a coffee, or two and a croissant...also closed. Nothing in town was open. We had been stopping in towns every night and had fallen into the habit of buying just what was needed, day to day, and that habit had just bitten us. Sans breakfast we headed on up the canal to a very early lunch stop at le Guétin, where both a cafe and a small epicerie were open. Well fed and with a large bag of groceries from the epicerie, another nine kilometers brought us to Plagny, where a shady spot beneath some poplar trees near a bar/tabac looked like a comfortable, and maybe cool, place to tie up—the day had become very hot and humid, the air thick and still. Throughout the late afternoon and into the evening there was distant thunder and lightning, but there was no rain on the plain in Plagny. In the morning the bar/tabac was open and we went there for breakfast. A fair number of rural French, men and women, seemed to consider a glass of red wine and a couple of cigarettes at the local bar to be, if not breakfast, at least an essential part of the start of the working day. That morning in Plagny, the cigarettes and wine crowd was out in force. We enjoyed our café au lait and croissant out on the terrace, where there was a nice view of the canal and breathable air.

Day after day the march to the Saone continued. To Fleury sur Loire—the whole way in heavy thunderstorms—where we saw the remains of a Roman villa and road, and an intriguing twelfth century church that may have had earlier elements. To Decize, dating back to pre-Roman Gaul and mentioned by Julius Caesar, with its almost intact wall and lovely medieval center, where we could have happily spent several days. To Vanneaux where, in late afternoon, a hotel barge coming in to the quay passed much to close, missing us by less than a meter. To Beaulon, in steady rain, a cute town with all the usual shops and a lovely chateau that was in excellent condition but was not open for visits. To Pierrefitte sur Loire, where we were the only boat on the quay (everyone else knew better than to stop) and ate dinner at the Hotel du Port: the food was uneatable, the wine awful, the place dirty and swarming with flies. When I paid our bill the hefty woman at the cash register had a large fly crawling up her bloated, sweating face. She stood there and let it crawl. It was disgusting and I could not keep from staring at it. Betty and I were both getting tired and a little irritable.

Five and a half warm, rainy hours, twenty-six kilometers and six locks past Pierrefitte sur Loire, we reached Paray le Monial, passing through Digoin, crossing the Loire on an aqueduct, and transitioning from the Canal lateral a la Loire to the Canal du Centre en-route. In Paray le Monial, a sign on a bulletin board on the long clean quay told us that our dockage was free, courtesy of the VNF. A copy of the letter from the VNF that we had been shown in Briare, the letter saying that the Canal du Centre might close in mid-August, was also posted on the bulletin board. The town had a nice looking port de plaisance, but it was managed by a hire-boat company which operated a base there, and a prominent sign told the world that no boats, or barges, over fifteen meters in length were permitted. It was Sunday, August fourth, and Canal du Centre kilometer marker one hundred and two was on the quay. Assuming that the canal did close on the fifteenth, there were eleven days left to cover the remaining one hundred and two kilometers and fifty-seven locks. In the afternoon the sky cleared, the sun came out and our attitude began to improve. Ahead lay the wine country: the Cote de Beaune, the Cote de Chalonnaise, Santenay, Chagny and Chalon sur Saone.

In the afternoon we walked around Paray le Monial and visited the Romanesque basilica of the Sacred Heart, built between 1090 and 1109 by St. Hugues, Abbot of Cluny, and the Musée de la Faience. The town is yet another of the very old pre-Roman, Roman and Gallo-Roman sites that dot France. In a purely secular sense the town has no real importance; but it is a major Catholic religious center and a pilgrimage destination visited by tens of thousands of pilgrims each year. In 973 Count Lambert of Chalon and Mayeul de Cluny, Abbot of Cluny, dedicated an already old, possibly pre-Christian, temple to the Mother of God and established a Benedictine priory, and the monks of Cluny controlled the town until the French Revolution. The primary pilgrimage site is the Chapel of the Visitation where (now saint) Margaret Mary Alacoque believed she saw the sacred heart. In 1896, during the dedication of Notre Dame de Romay, Pope Leo XIII pronounced Paray-le-Monial "Cœlo gratissimum oppidum" (a town very dear to heaven).[79] During our visit the pilgrims were out in force. One group, mostly elderly and all dressed in black, were creeping slowly forward, down on their knees on the cobblestones, eyes closed, faces to heaven, rosary in hand. Two priests, one swinging a censer, the other a broom, lead the group. I think they were Spanish, not French.

The Canal du Centre, a visually attractive canal that follows the contours of the land and has no significant straight sections, was built between 1784 and 1792 by Emiland Gauthey, Chief Engineer of Burgundy, to link the Saone River at Chalon sur Saone to the Loire River at Digoin. The development of the coal mines at Montceau les Mines and the opening of the Canal lateral a la Loire in 1838 made the Canal du Centre economically important and it carried a lot

---

79 excerpted from the on-line Catholic Encyclopedia.

of cargo, mostly coal, until after World War II, when the coal mines began to decline in importance. The last mine closed in 2000, and today the canal primarily carries pleasure boats and barges, hire-boats, and some hotel barges; few freight barges are to be seen. As the canal's economic importance declined the money spent to maintain it also declined, and parts of the canal on the Loire side of the Loire/Saone watershed are now in poor repair with collapsing banks and shoals developing in the bends.

On the Loire side of the watershed the Centre is a mix of manual and automated locks organized into chains, or groups. Each chain is controlled by a traveling lockkeeper and without prior arrangements you cannot stop in the middle of a chain. Our first full day on the Centre our traveling lockkeeper showed up at 9:00 a.m. and pushed us up the canal twenty-one kilometers, through seven manual locks, to Génelard. Because the locks were all manual and our lockkeeper did not want me getting off *Nova Cura* to help with the locks, the trip took longer than it should have. In Génelard before he left us, our lockkeeper asked if we wanted to spend a full day in the town. Told no, he said be ready to leave at 9:00.

During the night rain arrived and by sunrise steady hard rain was falling, despite which we were ready to go at the appointed time; but, our lockkeeper wasn't. Shortly after 10:00 a.m., in a more moderate rain, a different lockkeeper showed up to shepherd us to Montceau les Mines, eighteen kilometers, seven locks and two drawbridges up the canal. The first day on the Centre we had traveled alone, but this day we were grouped with another barge about our size and a small sailboat. Some of the days locks were automated and this lockkeeper had a different philosophy regarding help opening and closing the gates of the manual locks, so we moved right along, and were tied to one of the pontoons in the port de plaisance at Montceau les Mines by mid afternoon—ten euros per night for dockage, water (needed) and electrical power. The late afternoon was spent walking around the down town area, buying a newspaper, an inner tube for Betty's bicycle and a few other things, and Montceau les Mines looked like it would have been a good place to lay over for a day. In and around the town there was a lot to see and do, some nice shops and a number of good restaurants, one of which "Le France," had a star in the Red Book. Unfortunately we had told the lockkeeper that we'd be ready to move at the usual time the next morning. Equally unfortunate, as dinner in a good restaurant would have been nice, Tuesday was apparently the night that all the restaurants closed. Every single restaurant in the central part of town was closed. A nice patisserie however was open, so dinner on the barge included a large and tasty desert.

Centre day three, Montceau les Mines to Montchanin, was practically a repeat of day two: rain, lockkeeper late, travel with the same boats, move twelve kilometers and nine locks up the canal and arrive in mid-afternoon. But, at Montchanin, dockage was free. Our spot on the quay was near Canal du Centre kilometer mark fifty-two and Montchanin was on the dividing pond, on the crest between the watersheds of the Loire River and the Saone River. We were more than halfway to the Saone and for the rest of the way to the river would be locking down—easier days had come again. Unlike the Loire side, on the Saone side all of the locks accept for the massive and very deep lock that connected the canal to the river, were automated. Although the locks were organized into chains, each of which had its own traveling lockkeeper, we could move at our own pace and stop where we wished. The lock-

keepers just patrolled their chain and took care of any problems that arose.

Along the canals most of the locks have both a number
and a name. A lock's number is its sequential position on the
canal and the name is generally related to some local feature
near the lock: a village, a chateau or a mill, even a bridge.
At each lock there is a sign, often a carved stone in the lock
house wall, giving the lock's name and number, its elevation
above sea level and the distance in each direction to the next
lock. There is also, generally, a sheltered bulletin board with:
VNF notices, tourist information, local restaurant menus and
sometimes an area map. Lock number one on the Saone side of
the dividing pond was named "Méditerranée" and a large sign
proclaimed that this lock was the gateway to the Mediterranean and told us how many kilometers it was to the Saone,
the Rhone and the Mediterranean in one direction and to Paris
and the English Channel in the other.

Scattered around the French canals are VNF control locks,
at which a couple of VNF agents, and sometimes other officials, check each barge or boat (except hire-boats) for required
equipment and look at the vessels papers and the identifica-
tion papers of the people on board. Most control locks are the
first lock inside France after a canal crosses the border or are
at major canal intersections. Exceptions exist, and "Méditerranée" was a VNF control lock.

This was going to be interesting. Act happy and confident. We had entered France on May twenty-first, our
ninety-day tourist visas were good for thirteen more days,
our annual canal usage permit was for the full season, *Nova
Cura* was fully insured, and Betty had her bill of sale (proof
of ownership); but, the usage permit had the former owners
address in the U.K. on it, the insurance papers had H_2O's

address in St. Jean de Losne on them, and Betty's bill of
sale had our mailing address in Florida on it. Finally our
licenses or permits to operate a vessel of *Nova Cura's* size on
the inland waters of France were, well...a bit incomplete.
We both held valid permits for category C vessels, private
pleasure vessels up to fifteen meters in length. Both of us
had been to barge driving school and taken the test to operate a category PP vessel, a private, pleasure vessel (barge)
between fifteen and twenty-four meters in length; but we
did not actually have the final category PP certificate, just
the notice that we had passed the test.

In the lock, trapped, I handed everything requested to
one of the inspectors. He shuffled through them, looked at
Nova Cura, shuffled the papers again, looked hard at us and
went into the lock house. He was visible through the window,
phone in left hand, right hand clutching our papers, right
arm flailing the air. A barge waiting to enter the lock honked
its horn. That phone call took forever. Finally he emerged,
handed me our papers without comment, and waved his arm
by way of saying that we could go. The lock was automated
but because it was a check lock there was a lockkeeper present.
I removed our stern line as Betty started the motor and
shifted into forward. The lockkeeper pushed his button, the
sluices opened, the water level dropped, the downstream gates
opened, Betty went briefly to neutral while I slipped our bow
line and then drove us out of the lock. When going through
a lock, operators of smaller barges often used only one heavy,
strong line running from the barges big forward bits aft to a
bollard on the lock wall. With the engine in slow ahead and
the rudder over, the barge would hold tight to the lock wall,
going up or down. The inspector stood and watched the whole
procedure. As we were leaving he pointed to two tires we

were using as fenders and shook his finger "Non!"[80] I was sure that in some VNF office we were now on the list of irregular, possibly undesirable people of questionable legality, character and, possibly, morals.

Freed from the control lock, we continued down the canal to St. Leger sur Dheune, nineteen kilometers and nineteen locks from Montchanin—even locking down, nineteen locks is a lot of locks. Several people had told us that St. Leger was a nice place to stop with an excellent port de plaisance. The port was modern, clean, with full facilities, even a laundromat, and had a competent, multi-lingual harbormaster who also ran the town's tourist information office. The village was a compact and very attractive classic rural French canal side village: boulangerie, patisserie, a small market, a bar/tabac, a cute cafe by the port and a couple of restaurants. It looked like it belonged in a painting and it was exactly the type of place both of us had fantasized about when we first started thinking, and day dreaming, about cruising the canals of France. Dinner that night was at the Hotel/Restaurant L'Amiral and after dinner we walked through the quiet little town just enjoying it.

In the early morning, before Betty was up, I walked into town for an International Herald Tribune, a cafe au lait and a loaf of bread. At the boulangerie, it was clear that we were back in Burgundy. In St. Jean de Losne, in Dijon, all along the Burgundy canal, in Migennes, in Auxerre and down the Yonne

---

80 Tires do not float unless there is an air bubble trapped in them and if they are ripped off or otherwise lost in a lock they can jam the lock gates and/or sluices. Because they don't float, the use of tires as fenders is illegal in France. But the prohibition is widely ignored and on barges, whether cargo, hotel or private, it seemed to be universally ignored. When Betty bought *Nova Cura*, there was one tire on board and we were given a second. We never heard of the prohibition on the use of tires actually being enforced, but if a VNF Agent chose to enforce the law, he could, and several lockkeepers made pointed comments about our tires.

as far as Sens, when I asked for a loaf of country bread or rustic bread (pain campagne, pain campagnarde), what I got was a small or smallish, round loaf of crusty, delicious, light brown bread. You would think that throughout France a pain campagne would be a pain campagne. But noooo...forget it. From Moret sur Loing to Montchanin, when I asked for country bread I was either handed a large boule (ball) of puffy, soft, characterless, white bread or I got a blank "what does this ignorant foreigner want" look. To get anything with texture and taste I had to ask for dark bread (pain bisse) or whole wheat/grain bread (pain complet) and even that didn't always work. In one village when I asked for a pain complet, I was handed a loaf of some sort of dense east European almost black, possibly pumpernickel stuff. It was so solid and of such course texture that a goat would have had a problem eating it. No doubt about it, it was complete. When I walked into the boulangerie in St. Leger sur Dheune, I stopped, looked around, and spotted a half dozen small, round, brownish, crusty loaves on one of the shelves. I asked for a pain campagne and one of those little loaves came down off that shelf. It was wonderful.

The harbormaster at St. Leger sur Dheune thought the VNF might still close the canal on the fifteenth, or modify the operating schedule even though there had been a lot of rain in the area. So, Saturday, August tenth, with an eye on the calendar, we moved down to the wine village of Santenay—a short easy trip, just four easy locks and seven kilometers. Once moored to the canal bank outside Santenay, the bicycles were put ashore and we rode down the tow path, over a bridge and up a quiet country lane into town. I wanted to visit the chateau of Philippe the Bold and see his famous dungeons, reputed to have been the state of the art back in his day. But the chateau is a privately owned wine estate, it was Saturday, and they were not doing dungeon tours. They may not have been doing dungeon tours, but they were selling wine and the tasting room was open. We pedaled off to lunch at Le Terroir,[81] a two couverts Red Book restaurant that should have been a one star place, with a half-dozen of Premier Cru Santenay in the saddle bags. Visits to two more wine houses and their tasting rooms filled the early afternoon—what else are you going to do in a Cote de Beaune wine village? After the second of the afternoons tasting rooms, our bikes loaded down with eighteen bottles of wine, sloshing, gurgling and enveloped in a cloud of wine fumes we wobbled unsteadily back to *Nova Cura* and a long nap.

Our guides told us that Chagny—another wine town just four kilometers and no locks down the canal from where we were moored—held a large, open air market every Sunday, and had a good selection of restaurants and a number of wine houses. Like Santenay, Chagny is in the border zone between the Cote de Beaune and the Cote de Chalonnaise. Unlike Santenay, in addition to its fine wines Chagny is a gastronomic destination famous for its restaurants. By the time our market purchases were stowed in the refrigerator and cabinets, it was mid-day and time to pull out the Michelin Red Guide. Our search for the perfect restaurant for lunch did not include Chagny's most famous restaurant, the three-star Lameloise (Chef Jacques Lameloise). We were looking at the other end of the scale and selected the two couverts Le Grenier a Sel, built into a sixteenth century wine cellar, where we enjoyed a really excellent lunch. After lunch we went in search of wine tasting rooms that might be open on a Sunday. Not a problem. It was August, peak vacation season in France. I think every wine

---

81 Still in the Red Book. Le Terroir, pl. du Jet d'Eau, Santenay, phone: 03 80-20-63-47, www.restaurantleterroir.com

house and tasting room in town was open, and crowded. This time we mostly looked, tasting little and buying only a few bottles.

In the morning we started early, intending to go through to the Saone River and Chalon sur Saone. There were a lot of boats on the canal, some of the automated locks were malfunctioning and painfully slow, and it took us nine hours to negotiate the twelve kilometers and eleven locks to Condemene, where the day ended, still, still several kilometers and one lock short of the river. After dinner that night, while perusing our guides, maps and other assorted literature, we discovered that the quay at Condemene was a reasonable bike ride from Place St. Vincent, the cathedral and the center of Chalon sur Saone, and there was a bike path for part of the way. Tuesday, leaving the barge where it was for a day, we rode into the city. After a stop at the tourist office for a map and a hand full of brochures, we left the bikes in a nearby bicycle parking lot and walked to the Ile St. Laurent for a look at the port de plaisance—and decided that *Nova Cura* was better off where she was. From the port we walked down Rue Strasbourg where, in two short blocks, there were five Red Book rated restaurants, enjoyed lunch in a sidewalk cafe on the Place St. Vincent, in front of the cathedral and surrounded by centuries old half-timber houses, toured the cathedral, and spent too much time in the Museum of Photography.[82] I wanted to visit the Musee Denon (the municipal museum of art and history) which was supposed to have a superb collection of Neolithic, Celtic, Roman and Gallo-Roman artifacts, but time ran out. On the ride back to Condemene we stopped at a magnificent patis-

---

82 Musée Nicéphore-Niepce. A large well laid out museum of photography named for Joseph Nicéphore Niepce, the father of photography, who was born in Chalon sur Saone.

serie/boulangerie (meter after meter of glass-fronted display counters held a seemingly endless array of delights), and at the best and largest fromagerie (cheese shop) either of us had ever seen. Chalon sur Saone was definitely worth a return visit.

Early on Wednesday, August fourteenth, one day ahead of the VNF's deadline, we left Condemene, moved down the Canal du Centre through an unattractive industrial zone where several self-propelled Rhone River barges looking as big as ocean going ships were tied to the quays, transited lock thirty-four B (no name), a huge eleven meter deep lock that had floating bollards set into grooves in the lock wall and reminded me of the locks on the St. Lawrence Seaway, and entered the Saone River. St. Jean de Losne was seventy kilometers, and only two locks, up-stream.

12. St. Jean de Losne & a winter of Discontent

Chalon sur Saone to St. Jean de Losne was two days of river travel in delightful late summer weather. The Saone is a big river that still carries freight and the channel is broad, deep and well marked. Our charts were full of warnings about this and that: "passage très délicat. (be very careful in this section)," "bien respecter le balisage. (pay attention to the buoys)," "ne jamais accoster en rive gauche (never land on, or moor to, the left bank)." Despite which, the going was easy, the river running surprisingly clean and clear, the banks an attractive mix of woods, fields and villages. At the confluence of the Doubs River and the Saone, we past the river town of Verdun sur le Doubs—where the Romans built a river port in the first century A.D., and there has been a town ever since. The town looked attractive and interesting; but it was still early, too early to stop for the night. Below the lock at Ecuelles, *Bengta* was waiting for the gates to open; they had spent the night at Verdun sur Doubs. We followed them into the lock and on to Seurre. Both of us tied to the town's main quay, along the river, for the night—both barges too big for the small, enclosed port de plaisance. George told us that they passed *Nova Cura* the day that we were in Chalon sur Saone.

The morning's wake-up call came just after 6:00 a.m., when the wake from a fast moving, heavily loaded freight barge leaving the lock just above town set *Nova Cura* to rocking and bouncing. That barge either spent the night in the lock or arranged a special opening. Because of the early departure, we were tied to the Quay National, in St. Jean de Losne in time to enjoy lunch at L'Amiral, and the proprietor welcomed us back. After lunch I walked over to the presse for a paper. The Herald Tribune was sold out, but I was recognized and welcomed back.

Friday we talked to Philippe and Catherine at H_2O about the repairs *Nova Cura* might need and scheduling the dry dock and an insurance survey. Philippe told us that he had reserved a week on the marine railway at CBV beginning Monday, September ninth, but there was a possibility that it would be a week earlier. The insurance survey would be done as soon as the barge was out of the water. He would keep us informed. Catherine told us that we would need a B&B or a gite for the week that the barge was out of the water. Unfortunately the great B&B in Losne that we had enjoyed so much the previous year, our "maison bourgeoise", was not available; but the gite in St. Usage was. Catherine called the gite and made us a tentative reservation. After the meeting, we moved *Nova Cura* to D pontoon at H_2O. It looked like the rest of this cruising season would be spent in St. Jean de Losne. This year, unlike Migennes the previous fall, sitting and enjoying life in a nice town was fine. Neither of us felt compelled to charge up and down the Saone. In the evening George and Maggie came over and we went to dinner at L'Amiral. They told us that they had decided to leave *Bengta* at Bourgogne Marine in St. Symphorien sur Saone, and go home to Scotland for the winter rather than follow their original plan and cruise down the Rhone to the Canal du Midi and winter over there.

The second half of August passed slowly: Betty lightly sanded and re-coated the wheel house. I cleaned out the forepeak, ground down some rusted spots, greased the inside of the bottom and painted the shelves and the floorboards, and both of us did a little work on the main deck house roof—no excessive exertion. On days when it wasn't raining, we took long mid-day bicycle rides to many of the little farming towns in the area, lunching in the local bar/restaurant or cafe. One cloudy, rainy day when a long bike ride had zero appeal, we paid our first visit to the Cafe de la Marine.

Having never been to the Cafe de la Marine, we didn't quit understand the program. The cafe, on the west side of the lock between the Saone River and the canal basin, off the road to the train station, was an old barge man's auberge, that was open only at lunch during the work week, and the clientele was mostly workers from the boatyards and H_2O. When we walked in there were two large tables full of men and several smaller tables near the windows; the woman behind the bar waved us to a small table and came over with two wine glasses. Betty asked for a menu, the lady looked a little surprised and pointed to a blackboard by the door which clearly said that the plat was "Bœuf Bourguignon," period. Um, OK, Beef Bourguignon it would be.

> Cafe lady, setting the wine glasses down: "Voulez-vous du vin?" (Do you want wine?)
> Betty: "Do you have an Aligote?"
> Cafe lady, to the restaurant at large: "La dame pense que nous avons une tres bon Aligoté". (The lady thinks we have a fine Aligote.)
> Cafe lady to Betty: "Voulez-vous du vin?"
> Betty: "Oui."
> Cafe lady to both of us: "Vous voulez manger ou quoi?" (Do you want to eat, or what?)
> Both of us: "Oui."

Without another word, she went behind the bar, took an empty wine bottle from a row on the bar, filled it from a barrel on the back-bar counter, plopped the filled bottle and a basket of baguette sections on our table, and disappeared into the kitchen. The wine was a nice, smooth red. Ten minutes later we were served the best Beef Bourguignon that I have ever eaten—the lady might have been a bit brusque, but she could cook. The main course was accompanied by a salad and, later, a cheese plate and coffee, good coffee. And the price? Sixteen euros was more than enough. The Cafe de la Marine served one menu, three courses plus wine and coffee, at lunch on work days only. The menu was posted both outside and inside the front door; if you wanted what was being served you just walked in and sat down. The wine was always whatever red was in that barrel on the back-bar counter.

There was a large international boating community in St. Jean de Losne: English, Dutch, German, Canadian, Australian, American, and others. The marinas, the canal basin and the Saone River quays were crowded with transient yachts making their way from the U.K. and northern Europe south to the Mediterranean and boats and barges coming in to winter over. We had a lot of boats and barges to look at, and people to socialize with. Everyone on D pontoon seemed to speak English. If it wasn't actually raining in the evening, a social event that ran the length of the pontoon was not unusual.

On Monday, September second, Labor Day in the U.S., our possible early haul-out did not materialize. *Nova Cura* would go on the marine railway on the ninth, as scheduled. The daily routine of life in the marina continued, but the weather was beginning to change, becoming just enough cooler, wetter and windier to notice. The electric cabin heater was out and occasionally in the mornings and evenings, turned on. Our

218

long bike rides became less frequent and outdoor boat work fell off. Fall was coming to Burgundy. Large North Atlantic low pressure systems were sweeping into the Bay of Biscay and moving across France with increasing frequency, each system bringing low gray clouds and rain. Sunny days were rare, the leaves were starting to fall and an end of the season melancholy began settling over the boating community. The Mediterranean bound transients were moving on. George and Maggie left for Scotland. An American couple we knew who lived on an old trawler in H_2O's marina, put their boat on the market, sold it in less than a week, and left for Florida. I noticed that in the morning the presse had fewer copies of the foreign language papers—they were all still there, just fewer copies, the market was declining.

Then, at the very end of the week, late Friday afternoon, Philippe came by *Nova Cura* and said he was sorry but CBV had called and told him a VNF tug boat had broken down, and the VNF wanted it fixed—immediately. On the rivers and canals La Navigation comes first. Our haul-out would now be on Monday the sixteenth. Another week on D pontoon. Betty went to the office and asked Catherine to call the gite and see if we could move our reservation back a week. It would not be a problem; the tourist season was ending too. The week passed slowly, a little boat work, a lot of reading and a few lunches out. Betty had developed an ear infection, had been to see a doctor, and did not feel like doing much. When I was working inside the forepeak I had gotten a splinter in my left eye (which I don't see well with anyway), and I needed to go to see a specialist at the hospital in Dijon.

Haul out day, Monday the sixteenth, was cold, windy and wet, the morning was spent getting ready for the haul out and our move to the gite. After lunch, because of the windy conditions Jean-Paul, H_2Os harbormaster, helped move *Nova Cura* to CBV. The barge was to be hauled on a side-haul marine railway and an obstruction in the river made approaching the railway slightly tricky. The barge had to end up parallel to the river bank, between the bank and the obstruction. With Jean-Paul at the wheel we approached CBV from downstream, close to shore. Just below CBV he made a jog to port (to the left, toward shore), then a small turn to starboard (right), which put us parallel to shore and positioned over the end of the marine railway. As we came into position, we had to get two of our long, heavy dock lines ashore and it was a long throw. I made the first, our bow line, but flubbed the second (I should have used a heaving line). As I retrieved the aft line and set up for a second throw, the wind and current began to swing *Nova Cura's* stern away from shore. I made what was probably the longest and best throw of my life and it worked, but only because a diver from CBV was standing knee deep in the river. He was in the water to make sure that we were properly positioned over the marine railway cradle. When both lines were ashore and under control, the railway cradle slide into the water and down to a position partially under *Nova Cura*. There were two steel up-rights on the landward side of the cradle and men onshore used our dock lines to pull the barge in until the port side was against the up-rights. The diver checked our position, put several braces into place, and we moved smoothly to shore and up, out of the water. With *Nova Cura* high and dry the source of our problems was easy to see, there was a large dent in one of the propeller blades. It was late afternoon, nothing more would happen that day, Betty signed some papers in the office at CBV, and they gave us a key to the lock on the pedestrian gate in their security fence. With that, we walked back to H_2O, retrieved our bicycles and took a few things to the gite.

In the morning we arrived at CBV a few minutes past 8:00 a.m., and were late. Charles Gerard and a representative from AXA, Betty's insurance company, had been and gone. The wheelhouse door key had not been left with CBV, or H$_2$O and the doors were locked, so they had gone to take care of something else. They returned at 10:00 a.m. and, with two men from CBV, spent the rest of the morning going over *Nova Cura* and discussing the damage. At the conclusion of the inspection, the insurance company representative shook hands all around, and left. Charles then gave us the verdict. There was considerable damage, but it was not as bad as had been feared, the insurance company would pay for almost every-thing, and we would probably be back in the water Friday afternoon. Between Tuesday and Friday, CBV would: remove and repair the propeller, remove the propeller shaft and check it on a lath, replace the damaged carrier bearing, machine and true the contact faces of both halves of the shaft coupling, replace the gearbox oil seals, and remove the stern gland and check it and the hull plate around it for damage. While all that was going on, a crew from H$_2$O would power wash the bottom and, on the starboard side aft where the hull had scraped something and was showing some rust, they would grind out the rust and red lead (prime) the rusted areas. They would then apply a fresh coat of tar to the entire bottom. It was going to be a busy four days in the boatyard.

During the survey, the insurance company representa-tive noted that *Nova Cura* did not have an external (outside of the engine room) emergency diesel fuel cut-off that could be reached from the steering wheel, or a security chain between the rudder and the hull. Both items were required if the barge was to be registered in France and both, were things that he (and therefore the insurance company) felt were necessary.

Welding the rudder and hull fittings for a security chain would have to be done while the barge was out of the water, so we added that item to the work list—paid for by us. The external fuel cut-off could be done in the spring; delayed until the next year's budget. During the survey one of the mechanics from CBV noticed that the diesel fuel tank, which was located on the port side of the engine room, was badly rusted on the bottom and diesel fuel was seeping out through a pin hole on the welded seam along the outboard edge of the tank. Luckily he did not point the leak out to the insurance company representative. He called Philippe, and Philippe gave us the bad news. *Nova Cura* needed a new fuel tank and it was not something that could be put off until spring. It was a do it as soon as possible item. Joy to the world, another big ticket item for Betty's nautical antique.

The weather gave us a break and most of the week was dry and partly sunny, although not exactly warm. CBV and H_2O completed almost all of the required work. Late Friday afternoon CBV reinstalled the propeller shaft and got the propeller on and, at sunset on Friday, one of H_2Os men finished applying the new coat of tar to the bottom. Final drive train alignment and engine testing would have to wait until Monday. During the week we did a little boat work, Betty sanded and painted all of the bollards and the cap rail, both sides, bow to stern. I partially disassembled the anchor winch;[83] wire brushed, sanded and painted it, and then reattached it with

---

83 *Nova Cura* had a big cable winch on the bow in lieu of a true anchor windless. The winch drum was large enough to hold fifty plus meters of thick steel cable and twenty-five meters of heavy chain. The winch was manually operated through a geared ratchet. Luckily I never really had to use it. I tested it once at dockside in shallow water and it worked; but in deeper water I doubt that I would have been strong enough to reel in all that cable and chain, and the fifty (I think) kilogram anchor on the end of it.

bolts and backing pads. Thursday we took the train to Dijon
and I saw the Ophthalmologist, who removed the, apparently
tiny, splinter from my left eye, assured me that there would be
no permanent damage and said I needed new glasses.[84]

It was a good thing that most of the work was done as
Friday night the weather reverted to its colder, wetter phase.
We spent most of the weekend reading aboard *Nova Cura*,
or in the gite, and hanging out in the chandlery and office at
H_2O. The office had a fine collection of boating magazines
and several shelves of books about canal boating and barging.
Few of our friends were still around, none of the boats and
small barges on D pontoon had anyone on board, and most of
the south bound transients were gone. Sunday, gray and hazy
with a light drizzle falling, we went to lunch at the Auberge
de la Marine, which was not crowded. On the Saone no boats
or barges were moving and the water looked gray and cold.
Over lunch we decided, even though it would be expensive,
to spend our last week in France this season in Paris. As nice
as St. Jean de Losne was, Paris sounded better than sitting
around on a cold barge in a rather lonely end of the season
marina.

After breakfast Monday, we checked out of the gite—
either the barge was floating, or the Auberge de la Marine
had some overnight guests. Mid-morning the last items on
the work list were done and CBV launched *Nova Cura*. One
of their mechanics was aboard with Betty and me. With the
barge in the water, but not actually afloat Betty started the
motor and let it warm up while the mechanic watched and

---

84 The visit to the Ophthalmologist was interesting. To me a splinter in the eye
was an emergency, with H_2Os help, I had called the hospital and made an appointment but it was still a week before I could see an Ophthalmologist. When we
arrived at the hospital, I filled out a couple of brief forms, waited two or three minutes, and then spent a long time with the doctor. The total bill was forty-one euros.

listened. The mechanic signaled to the railway operator who lowered the cradle the last little bit, and as *Nova Cura* floated free Betty put the engine in gear and drove us slowly away from the marine railway and out into the river. The mechanic from CBV had Betty drive up and down in the river while he checked everything and then we returned to the marina and D pontoon. After lunch we walked back to CBV, paid our part of the bill, retrieved the bicycles and went to the France Rail office where we bought tickets for the TGV—Dijon to Paris, Wednesday afternoon. The rest of the day was spent packing and getting ready to leave for Paris and home.

Early Tuesday I called Herrington Harbour North, told them when we would be back, and put in a work request to have the boat yard sand and paint *Walkabout's* bottom, the first time since buying the boat that I had not done that job myself. Having the boat yard do the bottom gave me a strange, almost guilty, feeling, as though I was failing my boat. We then talked to Philippe about having a new diesel fuel tank and an external diesel fuel cut off installed over the winter. The rest of the day was spent winterizing *Nova Cura*. During the afternoon a team from H_2O pumped the remaining diesel fuel out of our fuel tank, so that it would not leak before the new tank was ready. That night we had an end-of-the-season dinner at L'Amiral. During dinner I told the owner that this was our last dinner of the season, and he gave me a Bistro L'Amiral tee-shirt—the only one I ever saw that was not being worn by the staff at L'Amiral.

Wednesday, mentally done with this barging season and more than ready to go, we locked *Nova Cura*, turned the keys in at the office, said good-by, and took the town taxi to the train station. Arriving in Dijon with hours to spare, we stashed the luggage in a train station locker, lunched early at a sidewalk cafe across from the Ducal Palace, walked the streets and looked in the shops. In the late afternoon, when the TGV arrived in Paris, we took the Metro from the Gare de Lyon to Bonne Nouvelle and walked up to our hotel, the Tulip Inn Aida Opera. As soon as check-in was complete and our luggage in the room, it was off to Rue des Petits Champs, and Willi's Wine Bar, for a glass or two of wine and a good dinner—starting the week in Paris properly.

On previous visits to Paris we had always stayed near the Gare de Lyon, in the Marais or near the Louvre and the Palais Royal. This time we were near Boulevard Haussmann, Galeries Lafayette and the shopping district, and at the half way point between Montmartre and Sacre Coeur in one direction and the Louvre, the Palais Royal and the Ile de la Cite in the opposite direction—with a reasonable walk in either direction. Parts of New York, Washington, D.C., New Orleans, San Francisco and a few other cities in the United States are walkable and the central parts of many European cities are good for walking; but the two great walking cities that we have been to are London and Paris. In a most-walkable-city contest between the two, Paris would probably win. The whole of central Paris is a walking city and, and for all but one day of our week, we walked. Leave our hotel in the morning with no particular destination in mind. Stop mid-morning for a café au lait and a pastry. Stop anywhere that looked interesting. Do lunch in a good bistro. Be back at the hotel in time for a nap before dinner. It was a fine way to spend a week enjoying Paris.

The experience at the VNF's control lock on the Canal du Centre had made it clear that something needed to be done to regularize and clarify the barges documentation—flying beneath the bureaucratic radar was not going to work much longer. We went to the American Consulate, met with the Consul, discussed *Nova Cura*, gave the Consul copies of Betty's bill of sale and some other papers, and received in return a formal document titled "Certificate of American Ownership" which: described *Nova Cura*, stated that she was American owned, a historic Dutch built canal barge located in France, and the document carried Betty's Florida mailing address. Several American couples we knew who had barges or canal boats in France had similar letters, and they all said that the letter worked well in France and Belgium. One couple said it also worked in the United Kingdom. Germany and the Netherlands, more bureaucratic and rule focused, were an open question. Next season, the barge would be reasonably legal and would fly the American flag. No more the pirate's life of subterfuge, deception, stratagem and artifice for us. We were reformed.

The one day not spent in Paris, was spent in Conflans St. Honorine, a western suburb of Paris and a major barge center. The original name of the town was Conflans, from its site at the confluence of the River Oise[85] and Seine; St. Honorine was added in the thirteenth century in honor of Saint Honorina, whose relics were kept in a local church. The town, often called the inland waterways capital of France, is the site of the Musée de la Batellerie[86] (Barging Museum), the French National Inland Waterways Museum. The town is also the site of the Pardon National de la Batellerie (the National Pardon of the Barges) which is held every year on the last Sunday in June, and is a national version of the Blessing of the Fleet that

---

85 The Oise River is the primary navigable waterway coming down to the Seine and Paris from Belgium, the Netherlands and the English Channel. Both the Seine and the Oise are still active commercial waterways.

86 Musée de la Batellerie; Place Jules Gévelot, 787000 Conflans St. Honorine, France. Phone: 01 34 90 39 50

we watched in St. Jean de Losne. Along the Seine River quays in Conflans I counted more than forty barges. We did not walk up the Oise River quays; but as far as I could see up the river, barges lined both sides; often two or three deep and the barges and quays along the Oise looked actively commercial. After walking the quays, we opted for an early lunch at Au Bord de l'Eau, a classic French bistro with a great view of the Seine River quays.[87] The restaurant's walls were thickly hung with prints, paintings of barges and river scenes, barge name boards, and other artifacts of commercial barging on the Seine. By the time we finished lunch and moved on to the barge museum, the restaurant was jammed and there were people waiting outside. The Barge Museum held a nice collection of artwork, models and artifacts related to the inland waterways. It also had a research library with a large collection of historical canal documents, surveys and engineering drawings and a book and gift shop.

Tuesday, October third, the day before our flight, was our turn to enjoy one of the quintessential Paris travel experiences. One of the unions connected to the airport trains walked out over some trivial dispute, the other rail unions honored the strike, and rail service to Roissy-Charles de Gaulle ground to a halt. The desk clerk at our hotel told us not to worry, there was bus service to the airport from the combined airline ticket office at Place de Garnier, across Boulevard Haussmann from the Galeries Lafayette and, because the strike had been anticipated, extra buses were running. Sounded good. Wednesday morning after breakfast, towing our wheeled carry-on bags, we trundled up the boulevard toward the Place de Garnier.

---

87 Au Bord de l'Eau Restaurant; 15 Quai Martyrs de la Résistance, 78700 Conflans St. Honorine, France. Phone: 01 39 72 86 51. Red Book one couvert and very good.

From a block away we could see what looked like a lot of people with luggage. A few minutes later from in front of the Galeries Lafayette, still across the street from the Place, we could see a huge, disorganized crowd, with tons of luggage, milling around in front of the ticket office. What we did not see was buses. Not even one bus. No buses. Either the airlines had underestimated the number of passengers or the bus drivers had walked off the job in a show of solidarity with the rail workers. We executed an immediate change-of-plan and almost ran the three short blocks to the taxi stand at the Gare St. Lazare, and got to the taxis ahead of most of the mob. An expensive taxi ride later we were at the airport—with time to visit the duty free shops after clearing security.

The morning after our return *Walkabout* was launched and we moved to P dock, and stayed through October twenty-first, getting the boat ready to go south for the winter and dealing with two late season purchase offers. The day before we flew to France, I had listed *Walkabout* for sale. All through the summer there had been no action, not one purchase offer. Now, near the end of the sailing season on the Chesapeake Bay, there were two offers. Both were low, one extremely low. Apparently both of the couples who made the offers thought that after having the boat sit on the market for five months with no offers, we would take whatever low-ball end-of-the-season offer came in. I countered both offers but neither couple was willing to raise their initial offer by a meaningful amount. So thanks-but-no-thanks, and October twenty-second we sailed out of HHN bound south for the winter—looking forward to the clear, clean waters, white sand beaches and palm trees of the Florida Keys and The Bahamas.

The trip ended one week later in Oriental, North Carolina with a phone call from Dion Kennard, a friend and one of the salesmen at the Herrington Harbour yacht brokerage. Would I sell the boat to him, to be his personal boat? His offer was a little below what I had hoped to get, but it was better than either of the offers we had turned down. Considering that there would be no sales commission, because Dion was one of the salesmen in the listing brokerage, it was a marginally decent offer for an ageing cruising sailboat (*Walkabout* was twenty-two years old). I accepted. Dion scheduled a purchase survey for November twenty-second. I agreed to help him take the boat back to Herrington Harbour after the survey and that final settlement would take place there. Betty and I took the boat up the Neuse River to the lovely colonial town of New Bern to wait out the three weeks before the survey. In New Bern I fixed a couple of small things, just to be sure there were no survey issues. Although I had no doubts about that: I knew the buyer, and I knew and trusted the surveyor.

S/V Walkabout was sold...what now? Go to France and live on *Nova Cura*? *Nova Cura* was poorly insulated, had no real heat and was in Burgundy, where the winters are long and harsh. Go to St. Jean de Losne and stay in a gite for the winter? Get a short term lease on an apartment in Paris? Rent a furnished apartment in Florida for the winter, but that would mean buying a car and...forget that. Besides, we liked and were not ready to give up, our two boat cruising life style. I needed to buy another boat.

November twenty-first, the survey went well, except for moving her north and signing the papers—the damnable deed was done. Anticipating that outcome, Betty had purchased tickets for a round-trip flight to Texas; she would visit her family for a week while Dion and I took the boat back north. Dion and I left Oriental on the twenty-third and reached Norfolk, Virginia, on the twenty-sixth. The last day a cold front

caught us and the weather turned bitter cold, with a strong
north-northwest wind, sleet and freezing rain. We arrived in
Norfolk after sunset, freezing cold, ice beginning to form on
the rigging and a full gale blowing on the Chesapeake Bay.
After three days of waiting for the weather to improve, ignor-
ing common sense and the inconvenient fact that the weather
on the bay was still terrible, we tried to move further north.
In the open water of Hampton Roads, still several miles from
the Chesapeake Bay, the boat was plunging into a strong head
sea, the temperature was twenty-one degrees, Fahrenheit,
and the wind was north at twenty to twenty-five knots. We
turned back and went to a marina, the delivery trip was over.
Dion rented a car and drove home. Betty flew into Baltimore,
rented a car, drove to Norfolk where we packed our personal
belongings and everything that had not transferred with the
sailboat, such as my tools and our charts, and then drove to
our friends Mike and Brenda's house near Herrington Harbour North. On December third the sale of *S/V Walkabout* was
finalized. Signing the papers at the brokerage, and drinking
a bottle of champagne afterwards, everyone seemed happy...
except me.

From December fourth to early January 2003, we looked
for The Boat, and I finally settled for a small trawler type
yacht that we found on the Gulf coast near New Orleans. The
hull was twenty years old but the boat was newly painted,
a beautiful deep blue. The boat also had: a brand new John
Deere diesel (less than one hour on the engine hour meter),
a new generator, new water tanks, new fuel tanks, filters and
hoses, new batteries and cables, etc. It was basically a completely rebuilt boat. In mid-January we left New Orleans
aboard my new trawler—which I had named *Walkabout*—and
reached Jacksonville, Florida, in mid-April. The trip included

stops at several boatyards for a little work. At the Blue Water Marina in Apalachicola, Florida, I had the boat hauled so I could install a large bronze RF ground for my amateur radio. When the owner-manager of the marina saw the little trawler out of the water, he looked at me and said I would never be happy with that boat; it was not a cruising boat.

The boat and I spent a week in Jacksonville while Betty flew to Texas to visit her family, and I spent most of the week looking at boats for sale on the internet. The owner of the Blue Water Marina had been right; I had developed a deep dislike for the trawler and had taken to calling it "the bubble boat." It was top-heavy, had too little draft, an undersized rudder and the hydraulic steering system was soft and woefully inadequate.[88] On the Chesapeake Bay, during the final leg of the trip north, a twelve to eighteen knot southerly wind was sending short, steep seas (waves with a short time interval between each successive wave) up the bay. The waves came up from astern, hit the starboard quarter and the trawler would try to yaw (swing broadside to the waves). The boats shallow draft, small rudder and soft steering made keeping control very difficult. It wasn't actually dangerous, just sloppy, very uncomfortable and irritating—in the sailboat it would have been a broad reach and a fine sail. I finally realized that I had purchased a canal and river boat, not a coastal, or Bahamas, cruiser. That day on the bay was the last straw for the trawler. We reached Herrington Harbour on May twentieth and the

---

88 A good hydraulic steering system on a small yacht, or work boat, should feel firm and require approximately three full turns of the wheel, and never more than four or four and a half turns, from full right rudder to full left rudder. On that little trawler, the hydraulic steering was under sized and felt soft and mushy, full right rudder to full left rudder required twelve full turns of the wheel. The soft sloppy steering, shallow draft, an undersized rudder and a lot of windage made steering—basic boat control—difficult.

next morning I marched into the yacht brokerage and listed the thing for sale. I wanted a real boat, not a bathtub toy. The agent who listed it was Dion, and I found myself wishing that I didn't like him.

13. Bureaucracy, Heat & a Short Season

For a variety of reasons we lingered in Herrington Harbour for three weeks, finally flying from Baltimore-Washington International Airport to Paris on June twelfth. The flight to France was a harbinger of the things that have come to pass in the airline industry—the plane was packed, no empty seats, back in the cattle car section the seats were too close together, my knees were against the back of the seat in front of me, and the in-flight entertainment system did not work. Drinks, which had been free the previous fall, were five dollars apiece, and the one in-flight meal was more snack than meal. The flight left Baltimore-Washington International at the scheduled time but it was a late flight did not arrive in Paris until almost noon, and it was mid afternoon before we were through customs and immigration and had made it into Paris. Instead of continuing on to St. Jean de Losne, we checked into the Grand Hotel de France, on the Rue de Lyon near the train station, walked into the Village of St. Paul for what was either a very late lunch or an early dinner. In the morning France Rail delivered us to St. Jean de Losne well before lunch—looking forward to the new season.

In November, in an e-mail to Betty, H_2O had told her that the new diesel fuel tank and the emergency fuel cut-off were in. Then a second e-mail told her that *Nova Cura's* rebuilt wheelhouse had been badly damaged in a violent thunderstorm. The barge had been at the inside end of D pontoon, next to shore and a very strong wind gust during the thunderstorm had swung the stern into some low branches on a tree at the edge of the basin. Three of the eight roof panels had been torn completely off, as had one of the sliding doors and one of the starboard side panels. The door and one roof panel had gone in the water and there was considerable damage to all the parts that came off and to the attachment points on the rest of the wheelhouse. H_2O had filed an insurance claim, on Betty's behalf, for €4,500.

We left our luggage in the office at H_2O, retrieved our keys and went to lunch—at L'Amiral of course. After lunch we walked down to *Nova Cura* to see what was left of our wheelhouse. The wheelhouse had been propped up, more or less put back together, and covered with a tarp. Expecting the worst, we removed the tarp. Whoever tried to put the wheelhouse back together had not known how all the pieces fit. We took it apart, put it back together with everything in the right place and it, more or less, looked the way it should. There was clearly some damage but, at least initially, it didn't look like €4,500 worth. Closer inspection however, revealed a lot of damage: the wooden runners for the starboard sliding door were cracked, splintered and partly missing, screws and metal fittings were ripped out of most of the roof panels and half the side panels, three of the roof panels had splintered, broken corners, sections that were split apart and chunks of missing wood where screws had been ripped out.

Except for the damage to the wheelhouse, *Nova Cura* actually looked pretty good; just badly in need of a bath and some TLC. We put the bicycles ashore, retrieved our luggage, filled the water tanks, turned everything on and walked over to the Casino Supermarche for food, beer and wine. Home again. According to an English couple we knew casually, who had wintered over aboard their large barge, January and February had been unusually cold. Both the gare d'eau at St. Jean de Losne and the basins at St. Symphorien had frozen and had four or five inches of ice in mid-February. I went over the plumbing looking for winter damage and the previous fall, I apparently had not gotten all the water out of the fresh water system. The hoses, pipes, faucets, hot water heater, water pump and thru-hull fittings were fine, but the accumulator tank (which helps to regulate the water pressure), had frozen, cracked, and was dribbling and failing to regulate. An eighty-two euro replacement later and the water system was back to normal. The bilge must have also frozen because the outlet hose fitting on the bilge pump in the engine room had cracked, and come off—some epoxy and a pipe fitting and the bilge pump was back on the job. Three days after arriving in St. Jean de Losne, the normal daily routine of life aboard a barge had returned: the morning visit to the boulangerie for bread and to the presse for the paper, a little late morning boat work, and then a bike ride, a long walk, or nothing at all.

There were two noticeable differences between this year and the previous two. The first big difference was the euro. In 2001, the year Betty bought *Nova Cura* and the year France transitioned from the franc to the euro, a euro had been worth around eighty-five U.S. cents. In 2002, the euro and dollar had been near parity, with just a slight edge in the dollar's favor. When we arrived in France in 2003, one euro was worth one dollar and ten cents and the dollar fell, slowly but steadily, through the season. The change in the dollars to euros ratio had a definite impact on our day to day life. Over a two year period, the dollar had dropped twenty some percent in value relative to the euro and, from our point of view, everything had become noticeably more expensive. The second big difference was the weather. In 2001, we wore blue jeans, sweaters and sweat-shirts, and often jackets and/or rain gear, for most of the canal boating season and we complained constantly about the cold, wind and rain. 2002 was a nice and, we were told, very average year. This year was hot and dry. Very hot. Bahamas and Florida Keys boating, shorts, tee-shirts and no socks hot. In the afternoon the temperature inside *Nova Cura* was rising into the nineties every day. The lady on a Canadian owned barge across the pontoon from us told Betty that they had arrived in early April and the first two weeks they were aboard their barge had been characterized by thunderstorms almost every day. Since then the weather had been hot and there had been no rain at all. We learned later that she was the person who had run to the H_2O Chandlery, during the thunderstorm that damaged *Nova Cura's* wheelhouse, and alerted Jean-Paul, the harbormaster, to the problem. He had immediately gone down to D pontoon, secured the barge, and fished out the door and roof panel that had gone overboard.

Wednesday, June eighteenth, a disturbing e-mail from the office of a dermatologist I had visited in early June came in. I had gone to the dermatologist to have an odd looking mole on my chest and a crusty, brown, patch on my right hand checked. Both growths had been biopsied, the results were back from the pathologist, and both were abnormal. The e-mail implied that the mole might be a melanoma, a serious skin cancer, and said that it was potentially dangerous and would have to be cut out and that it should be removed soon. The brown, crusty growth was less serious and could be frozen off at my convenience. Betty and I discussed this problem and I booked a round-trip flight, Paris to Baltimore and return, on British Air (July fourth to July twenty-second). I would go back and have both items removed.[89]

---

89 "Cancer" is an attention grabbing word. A word that causes a tendency to overlook details. The e-mail from the dermatologist's office was

Between June eighteenth and July fourth *Nova Cura*, lived on D pontoon, in the spot closest to shore, next to the tree that damaged the wheelhouse. It turned out to be a choice spot and we became very fond of that tree. The tree became our good friend. The weather stayed hot and sunny, the tree was southeast of us and until past noon its limbs and leaves shaded the wheelhouse and a good part of the main cabin. The Herald Tribune, and CNN Europe, were frequently commenting on the unusual heat wave that was blanketing Europe from the United Kingdom to Poland and Greece and from Spain and Italy to the Baltic Sea. St. Jean de Losne's thirty-third "Pardon des Mariniers" (Blessing of the Fleet), was June twenty-first and twenty-second. Our first year in France the event took place on two cold, windy and rainy days. This year it was sunny and very hot. I bought a pair of shorts in a local shop, it was too hot for jeans or khaki slacks.

A week after the Pardon des Mariniers, a rather modest traveling circus came to town for three days: circus acts under the medium top, rides, food vendors, fireworks every night, one elderly camel, no elephants. At times during circus week, it felt like we were part of the circus—a floating side show. The circus was set up in a large parking area along the north side of the gare d'eau, not far from the pontoons, and in the evenings a bunch of circus goers felt that a stroll down a pontoon or two, and a good gawk at the boats and barges and the people on them, was part of the show. During circus week

---

full of caveats. It did not actually say the mole was a melanoma, nor did it say that it had to be removed immediately. I should have sent an e-mail to the dermatologist saying that I would see them when we returned in the fall. Even better, I should have just gone to the excellent hospital in Dijon and had the one cut off and the other frozen, it would have been easier, and quicker.

a tjalk, (Dutch sailing barge) with its lee boards[90] and a full
sailing rig, tied to the T-head of D pontoon. The couple on
the tjalk were American and we had met them in the Caribbean when they were sailing an Island Packet 35 named *Twist
of Fate*.

In June, 2001, when we were working on *Nova Cura*,
Philippe had shown us a generic requirements list of items
that a French marine surveyor would look for, and probably
require, on an old barge that was to be registered in France.
Since then the plan had been to eventually register *Nova Cura*
in France. French registration would solve most potential
French and European Union legal problems with regard to
the barge. The only remaining problem would be the necessity of a carte du séjour, or extended tourist visas, if we wished
to spend more than ninety days at a time on the barge. H_2O
was working on a Dutch barge that was being converted into
a small hotel or B&B barge, and they were now at the survey and certification stage. Toward the end of June, Philippe
brought a surveyor down for a quick look at *Nova Cura*. The
man came on board, said nothing, took a very brief look in
the engine room, looked forward, aft, up, down and around,
shrugged and left. We never heard what he thought or may
have said. Later, Philippe showed us an up-dated and revised
requirements list that that surveyor, the VNF, or someone
else, had given him. Basically, the rules had changed. Without
the sort of massive infusion of money, time and effort that we
were not interested in making, and, simply, could not begin
to afford, *Nova Cura* could not be brought into compliance

---

90 Lee boards are the large, generally oval or ovoid, boards attached to
the sides of shallow draft sailing barges and some other shallow draft
sailboats. When swung down into the water they function like a keel and
increase the vessels draft and decrease its drift to leeward (downwind).

with the revised requirements. This development left us disappointed and re-thinking some of our assumptions and plans.

The main problem was that *Nova Cura* did not have an actual engine room. The engine was in the space beneath the wheel house, and was accessed by raising one of the wheelhouse's plywood floor panels and climbing down a short ladder. The only thing separating the wheelhouse from the engine was the plywood floor. In addition, *Nova Cura's* diesel fuel tank was in the engine space (and close to the hot, dry, exhaust), and there was no automated fire suppression system. The revised requirements specified: a dedicated engine room with "outside and separate" access, fuel tanks located outside the engine room, and an automated fire suppression system in the engine room.

The revised requirements were a clarification of the older ones, the gray areas and ambiguities had been edited out. There was now a clear distinction between yachts and barges. The gray space between the requirements for yachts and the barge requirements, the space small private barges had lived in was no longer there. A purpose built yacht designed and built to look like a barge, even if as large or larger than a barge, was a yacht. A converted freight barge, regardless of size and age was a barge, and the barge requirements had been written for commercial vessels—for full size hotel and freight barges. Philippe thought he could find a surveyor who was flexible and willing to work with the owners of small private barges, and that the rules were still a work in progress and, over the next few years, would be changed, re-clarified, and adjusted several times, and, in the end would account for small, old, converted barges that were now, in reality, yachts. But, in the mean time...

On the thirtieth we went to the local VNF Office and purchased our annual cruising permit. When Betty filled out the purchase form she used our Florida mailing address and when she turned in the form she handed the agent the letter from the American Consul. While we waited, nervously, he read the letter, nodded, xeroxed it, accepted Betty's payment, handed her our annual permit and the barges window tag, and wished us a good year. From the VNF Office we pedaled out to Brazey en Plaine for lunch and saw two freight barges loading grain, an unusual sight. It was a hot day, back at *Nova Cura* after our ride the temperature in the main cabin was one hundred degrees, in-spite of the shade from our friend the tree. I went to H_2O's chandlery and bought another 12 volt fan, our third. We now had one in the main cabin, one in the wheelhouse and one in the aft cabin. They were turned on a lot over the summer.

Tuesday, July first, Bernard, the head carpenter, came by and, with Philippe helping with a little translation, showed us why the estimate to repair the wheel house was so high. Mostly four new roof panels. The original wheelhouse roof had been composed of six rectangular varnished plywood panels—thin poor quality plywood that was already in bad condition when Betty bought the barge. When the wheelhouse was rebuilt and extended at Chantier Fluvial de Migennes, two new roof panels were added and two of the original six were replaced. The four new panels were thick, high quality, marine grade plywood that had been soaked with epoxy, and they were undamaged except for a few pulled out screws. The four remaining old panels, three of which were the ones that had been ripped completely off, needed to be replaced. Beyond the roof panels, the wheelhouse needed new runners for the starboard (sliding) door and some other time consuming detail work. In the end the job came in below the original estimate, but was still expensive.

Friday, July fourth, Independence Day, my cancer removal trip began badly—entirely too early. I had a late morning flight from Paris to Baltimore and the TGV from Dijon direct to Roissy-Charles de Gaulle departed Dijon at 6:40 a.m. We had stayed up late the night before getting me ready to go and Friday morning were up at 4:00 a.m. to take the local to Dijon. Betty rode to Dijon with me, saw me off, and returned to St. Jean de Losne. In Baltimore I rented a car and drove to Mac and Nancy's in Annapolis. On July seventh, the mole and what seemed like an awful lot of surrounding skin and tissue was excised and the patch on my hand was frozen with liquid nitrogen. Until the stitches were removed I shuttled between my sister's house, Mac and Nancy's, and Herrington Harbour North. The trawler was still there, right where we left it, looking just the same, it hadn't improved any, and no one was showing much interest in buying the thing.

Monday the twenty-first I was so anxious to leave for France, Betty and *Nova Cura*, that I drove to the airport and turned in the rental car right after breakfast. My flight to Paris was at 9:05 p.m.—twelve hours after I turned in the rental car. I could have spent the whole day enjoying Baltimore. I could have had a great lunch at one of the many fine pubs or restaurants in Fell's Point or on Federal Hill. Instead, well... it was a really long day. The British Air counter did not open until 5:00 p.m.; I could not check my luggage. Baltimore-Washington International Airport was being expanded, there was a lot of construction in progress and, during the current phase of construction, all of the sources of food, drink and a newspaper were behind the security gates. There was nothing out front except the check-in counters, a couple of rest rooms and a water fountain. I had to check my luggage, I could not go through security with it, there was boat stuff in there that would be verboten in carry-on baggage. No lunch. No cold beer. No magazine or newspaper. As soon as the British Air check-in counter opened, I checked my luggage, got a boarding pass and marched through security into the international terminal. The one and only restaurant/bar in the international terminal was closed and the news stand was under construction. No problem. Back out through security and over to the domestic area, there was lots of stuff over there. Stuff was there...it was just not available to me. Because I had an international ticket, and boarding pass, security at the domestic terminals would not let me through. No lunch, no cold beer, no magazine or newspaper and no dinner. A guy could develop an attitude problem. When they called my flight I boarded and, like magic, everything improved. I briefly told a flight attendant about my day, and she brought me a sandwich and a cold beer. The in-flight dinner was excellent, with a good English ale, not Bud Light, and before landing in Paris the flight attendants served a good breakfast. God save the Queen and bless British Air. I caught the 4:44 p.m. TGV from the Gare de Lyon to Dijon—the train had a dining car and a bar—and arrived in St. Jean de Losne a little after 7:00 p.m., well fed and not one bit thirsty. Betty met me at the station and took me to L'Amiral for dinner...and a bottle of wine.

While I was off on my medical mission, Betty had completed all the necessary sanding, painting and cosmetic work, and had entertained friends from the States who had come over for a hire-boat trip and to look into buying a small Dutch barge. Betty had also been thinking. She was not, realistically, going to be able to register her barge in France. The dollar was falling against the euro, France was becoming expensive. She had decided to try out the market for small Dutch barges...lightly used...well cared for...in excellent condition. On July twenty-fourth, she filled out the necessary paperwork and Betty's barge was "A Vendre" (for sale). The asking price was €88,500. After the papers were signed, we bicycled over to St. Symphorien and Bourgogne Marine, where we enjoyed a glass of wine with George and Maggie Pringle on *Bengta*, and talked about a cruise to Epernay and Champagne that they were leaving on in a few days and about the purchase, transformation, and possible sale of *Nova Cura*.

Two days after Betty listed *Nova Cura* for sale, after a large early morning grocery run and filling the water tanks, we went to the fuel barge, bought two hundred liters of diesel, and cruised up the Saone eighteen kilometers and one lock, to Auxonne. It was the start of our last significant cruise on Betty's barge. Betty would keep Catherine at H_2O, the sales agent, informed about our location and if anyone expressed interest in the barge, they could come to wherever the barge was or wait until our return to St. Jean de Losne.

The Saone River from its source in the Vosges Mountains to its confluence with the Rhone at Lyon is approximately four hundred eighty kilometers long. Three hundred and eighty-one kilometers of the river, from Corre to Lyon has been made navigable. From St. Jean de Losne downstream to Lyon the Saone is an up-graded commercial waterway with large, one hundred and eighty-five meter long by twelve meter wide, industrial locks (there is an on-again, off-again plan to enlarge the Canal du Rhone au Rhine so that it can accommodate large Rhone and Rhine river barges). From St. Jean de Losne upstream to Corre, the Saone is often referred to as the "petit Saone" and the locks are the ubiquitous Freycinet gage. At Corre, the navigable Saone joins the Canal des Vosges. From

the French annexation of Burgundy following the death of
Charles the Bold, to the Sun King, Louis XIVs seizure and
annexation of the Franche-Comté, much of the Saone River
was the boundary, and an active military frontier, between the
Kingdom of France and the Holy Roman/Austrian Empires.
Today the Petit Saone runs down from the Vosges Mountains
peaceful, clear, clean and quite wild. The river still has some
commercial traffic, hotel barges and freight barges going
north or south to one or another of the feeder canals travel the
river and a few barges still load timber, sand, stone and grain
along the river. But the Petit Saone is primarily a pleasure
boat river, heavily used by private barges, yachts and hire-
boats...lots of hire-boats. In 2003 the Petit Saone had more
hire-boats during the summer vacation season than any other
river or canal in France.

Upstream from the Saone River Bridge, Auxonne had a
municipal halte de plaisance which had improved dockage,
power, water—and a mob of hire-boats. We tied up on the old
stepped granite quay downstream from the bridge and at the
foot of the modern ramparts. In France "modern" can be a relative term. The ramparts were designed and built by Vauban
(Sébastien le Prestre, Marquis de Vauban; 1633-1707), Louis
XIVs great military engineer. Remaining parts of the ancient
fortifications, the Dukes of Burgundy's medieval towers and
curtain wall, left in place by Vauban, loomed over the modern
ramparts. At night both the modern and ancient defensive
works were lit by colored floodlights. It was a pretty and
romantic setting and the sort of place that we most enjoyed in
France. The evening we arrived in Auxonne a cool breeze, the
first relief from the heat in many days, brought thunder, lightning and rain; the first real rain since our arrival in France. For
dinner we walked through the rain to a small, cozy bar in the

oldest part of town where we enjoyed an excellent pizza baked in a stone wood burning oven that looked, and may have been, centuries old. I washed my pizza down with a superb Belgian ale, Betty had champagne.

That really wonderful Belgian ale made me remember the shelves in the beer section in St. Jean de Losne's Casino Supermarche. On our first visit to the Casino this season I had noticed something new on the shelves, Bud Light®, Anheuser-Busch's tasteless, watery, swill. That's my opinion of it. I actually know people who drink it; a few of them even think its real beer. Apparently, although the shelves were crowded with better and less expensive beers and ales from Belgium, France, Germany, the U.K. and elsewhere, some people were willing to pay the high import premium for that stuff to show that they were trendy and with-it. It was a great illustration of modern advertising and marketing in action, successfully selling an inferior American product at a time when the United States was not all that popular with many Europeans. There were Bud-Light® commercials on television and in some of the French magazines and newspapers. One of the television commercials must have come straight from American television. It showed a California beach, the sun setting over the ocean, surf boards stuck in the sand and a group of good looking young people gathered around a bonfire while slurping that tasteless, watery ...

The next day was pleasantly cool, with occasional light rain; we stayed in Auxonne and went to a nice museum devoted to the cities most famous resident, a young Second Lieutenant of Artillery named Napoleon Bonaparte who was stationed at the Auxonne College of Artillery between 1788 and 1791. The building with the apartment that Napoleon occupied is still military housing. That night there

was a sound and light show in Vauban's Artillery Arsenal;
no fireworks, but repeated firing of several cannon and loud
martial music. Because northern France is so far north and the
summer days so long, the sound and light show started late.
Docked where we were, at the foot of the ramparts, there was
no escaping it, so we went and it was a nice show. Afterwards,
before turning in for the night, I checked our dock lines and
noticed that the river had risen a few inches. Two of our fenders were automobile tires and I lowered them down under
water between our hull and the quay, to protect the hull if
the river rose enough to raise our regular large balloon fenders above the lip of the lowest of the quays granite steps. It
didn't and in the morning, after a too short night's sleep, we
moved another eighteen kilometers and one lock upstream to
Pontailler Sur Saone, a pleasant enough little town where we
tied up for lunch and just stayed. In the late afternoon *Bengta*
came up the river, as they passed George and Maggie slowed
and exchanged a few pleasantries. We never again saw *Bengta*
or George and Maggie.

The next stop upstream was Mantoche, twenty-five kilometers and two locks from Pontailler-sur-Saone. Just above
Pontailler, we passed the entrance to the Canal de la Marne a
la Saone (built between 1881 and 1907), which links the Petit
Saone to the Canal Lateral a la Marne at Vitry le Francois.
The Petit Saone was becoming more serpentine and wilder,
the banks more vegetated and less inhabited. We saw cranes,
several varieties of herons, vultures and three beavers; I think
a mother and two kits. On the outside of many of the river's
bends there were small sandy beaches, often with hire-boats,
their bows up on the sand or with a line to shore, while the
people aboard sun-bathed and played in the water. It was a
peaceful, warm and very pleasant day on the river. Mantoche

was a small clean and attractive town with a chateau and all of the traditional amenities of a classic French village. It also had a good halte nautique that featured coin operated water taps—a one euro coin filled *Nova Cura's* tanks and rinsed off the decks.

From Mantoche upstream to the very old town of Gray was all of seven kilometers and one shallow lock that lifted us less than two meters. The lock was in Gray, right at the end of the day's trip. We left Mantoche early and could have eaten breakfast in Gray, the whole trip, quay to canal bank, took less than an hour and a half. Gray has two quays, both have coin operated electrical outlets and water taps. One of the quays is below the lock and on the left bank directly in front of the old town. The other is on the right bank above the lock. Both were full to past maximum capacity with hire-boats. So we ended up with another barge, several yachts and still more hire-boats on the right bank above the town. One of the yachts on the canal bank was an English sailboat on their way to the Mediterranean and they cheerfully informed us that there were an insane number of hire-boats all the way up the Petit Saone and the Canal des Vosges.

Our afternoon in Gray was spent walking the steep streets of the old town and visiting the Baron Martin Museum. The museum was a combination art and archeology/history museum built into a seventeenth century chateau. The rooms on the upper floors housed a collection of miscellaneous art dating from the seventeenth to the twentieth centuries. The basement and part of the ground floor housed a collection of local archeological and historical artifacts that ranged from Stone Age tools to Gallo-Roman stone work to relatively modern arms and armor. Lying on two big tables in the basement were several dozen late Bronze Age weapons and bits and pieces of armor that had been found in the Saone when the channel was dredged. Most of the pieces were Celtic but a largely intact helmet, two swords, a shin guard and several other pieces of armor were labeled as being of Greek origin. Relics of a late bronze age battle between Celts and Greeks in the valley of the Petit Saone? There was no explanation, no time line, no context, just small labels.

The chateau housing the museum was almost more interesting than the collections in the museum. The chateau had been built in the seventeenth century on the site of, and incorporating parts of, a fifteenth century fortress that had belonged to the Dukes of Burgundy. The Great Dukes fifteenth century fortress had been built on, and incorporated, an eleventh century castle that had been built in an old Merovingian town that had supplanted a Gallo-Roman town that developed around a Roman fort which was built on...and so on. The place was old. For that matter, in historical terms the valley of the Petit Saone is old. A trade route dating to the early Bronze Age and maybe earlier ran through it. Celtic and Germanic tribes travelled it. Rome's legions marched up it. Part of Attila's army of nomadic horseman is believed to have ridden down it on the way to a battle at Orleans and then defeat at Catalaunum (modern Chalons en Champagne).

We ate dinner in town, and as we were walking back to the barge there was thunder and distant lightning. Later in the night it rained but the night was warm and humid, our brief cool spell was passing. The last day of July we left Gray and moved upstream seven locks and fifty-seven river kilometers—although we travelled only fifty kilometers as a short tunnel (six hundred and forty meters long) cut off a wide seven kilometer long bend in the river. None of the small towns we passed looked particularly inviting and all their quays and docks were crowded with hire-boats. The day ended with *Nova Cura* moored to the canal bank a few hundred meters above lock number nine. The already pretty countryside was becoming hillier and prettier and our spot on the canal bank was very pleasant. In the morning I was up well before 6:00 a.m. and we were alone, the only boat, there was no noise, the sun was already up, the sky clear, a light humidity haze hung over the river and a small heron was perched on one of our mooring lines. After breakfast, as the day's heat began to build and the first hire-boats destroyed the serenity, we cast off and ascended the river to Port sur Saone. At Port sur Saone there was a long quay on the left bank in front of the town where mooring was free and on the right bank, across from the town there was a nice, full service, privately owned port de plaisance that had, in addition to dockage for hire-boats, a long riverside bulkhead with electricity and water that was reserved for barges and private yachts. We happily paid for two nights.

Port sur Saone is an old, and nice, town that is known to date to at least Gallo-Roman times, but there is nothing very remarkable in the way of architecture or ruins. Stone has been recycled. The tourist office pointed us to one house in the old part of town that had the capitals from three Gallo-Roman era columns incorporated into a side wall. History is relative. In the United States any house that pre-dates the Civil War is apt to have a bronze plaque declaring that it is on the National Register of Historic Homes, and in south Florida, any shack that pre-dates World War II is considered historic. In Port sur Saone a four hundred year old house incorporates stone taken from a seventeen or eighteen hundred year old building that may have been constructed on the site of, and used stone from, something that went back into the pre-Christian era. In

France, a two or three or four hundred year old house is just a house, somebody's home.

Our full day in Port sur Saone we did laundry, filled the water tanks and tried to do a little cosmetic boat work. By 9:00 a.m. it was too hot to paint and we ended up spending most of the day sitting in the shade with a Canadian couple off another barge, trying to stay cool, talking, reading and watching the hire-boat circus. *Nova Cura* was at the upstream end of the barge and yacht bulkhead next to the hire-boat dockage area. The hire-boats were supposed to med-moor—go stern first to the dock with a bow line to a mooring ball out in the river and two stern lines to shore. Med-mooring in a river, broadside to the current, is a tricky operation that takes some skill and generally requires line handlers on at both ends of the docking vessel. During the day we saw some strange and less than skillful boat handling techniques. One big hire-boat came slowly and carefully down the river, turned stern to the dock and, using frequent pulses on a bow thruster to keep the boat in line, started to back in. To that point all was well; the man on the wheel was doing a pretty good job. Unfortunately, the young lady on the bow with a boat hook, who was probably supposed to be ready to pick-up the mooring buoy line... didn't. She was lying down on the job, on a sunbathing mat, and realized they were docking when the bow thruster started going off. Startled, she jumped up, grabbed her boat hook and then realized that something had stayed on the sunbathing mat. Opting for modesty, she dropped the boat hook, retrieved the errant object and returned it to its rightful place. The river current did do what it was supposed to do, it took charge without a moments' hesitation and swung the bow of the docking boat downstream and into its neighbor. A minute or so of shouting, arm waving, flailing boat hooks and at least four people yelling instructions, and the situation was brought under control. There was no damage done, hire-boats are festooned with fenders and have thick heavy rubber bumpers screwed to their hulls. We sometimes referred to the hire-boats as "bumper-boats", and saw a few that were driven that way. When the excitement was over, our little group settled back down in our shady spot, opened another beer, resumed our conversation and waited for the next act.

Sunday, already hot an hour after sunrise, we left Port sur Saone early and moved upstream five locks and forty-two kilometers to Corre, passing the town of Conflandey and the Ile Cantin, an island in front of the town enroute. Two bridges carried a road across the island and there was a fortified chateau that looked as though it had been rebuilt on the island. None of our guides or tourist literature mentioned the island chateau. Just upstream of Conflandey there was an automated lock and a small river, the Lanterne, flowed into the Petit Saone. The chart carried the notation "courant fort á l'aval de l'écluse" (strong current below the lock). That notation was a bit of an understatement, enter that lock at speed or lose control. Most of the little towns along this stretch of the river had very small floating docks or quays and every one had a hire-boat, or two, or three, or...tied to it. We waited in the hot sun for over an hour downstream from the deep automated lock at Ormoy. First two loaded cargo barges had to clear the lock (as in the U.S., the rule is that commercial and official vessels go first at all locks and draw bridges) and then a hire-boat screwed up the automated system and we had to wait for the VNF to re-set it. The lock at Ormoy is Saone River lock number one, the last upstream lock on the Petit Saone. The next lock, at Corre, is the entrance to the Canal des Vosges and the head of navigation on the Petit Saone.

The large and well equipped port de plaisance at Corre is in the canal, just above the entrance lock. The port was managed by Locaboat Plaisance and was one of their largest bases. When we finally arrived, there was no room for an almost twenty meter long barge. There was a VNF tug and deck barge just outside the port and we rafted to the deck barge. It is technically illegal to tie to a VNF vessel, but a man whom I assumed was a VNF employee was aboard the tug, he watched us tie up, and said nothing. Once tied up, I went below to the refrigerator for a cold beer, the thermometer in the main cabin showed one hundred and two degrees (Fahrenheit). The air was still and humid, it felt like a mid-August day in New Orleans. We were hot, sticky and wearing tee-shirts, shorts and sandals. On August 3, 2001, at Pont Royal on the Burgundy canal (another Locaboat Plaisance base), we were both wearing jeans, sweaters, jackets and rain jackets—and complaining about the cold, wind and rain.

We thought about laying over for a day in Corre, but there was nothing very interesting to do or see and, except for the hire-boat base, which had a small cafe, nothing in town was open on Monday. I did not want to press our luck, and the VNF's patience, by lingering alongside their barge, so in the morning, as soon as the locks opened, we got underway and started up the canal. After the territorial loses of the Franco Prussian war, the French needed a new eastern canal to link the Meuse and Moselle Rivers and northern France to the Saone and Rhone Rivers and southern France. The solution was the Canal de l'Est, built between 1874 and 1884. The southern section of the Canal de l'Est, from Nancy via Epinal, to the Petit Saone at Corre is today's Canal des Vosges—still called the Canal de l'Est Branche Sud in some publications. If the Embranchement de Nancy is included, the Canal des

Vosges is one hundred and fifty-seven kilometers long and has one hundred and eighty-three locks, all of which are Freycinet gage. The locks-to-kilometer ratio is worse than the Burgundy Canal.

Twenty-one kilometers and eleven locks, up the canal we stopped at Fontenoy le Chateau, a pretty town with everything that could be hoped for in a small country village, even a good Tuesday morning market. The excellent port de plaisance was managed by, and was a major base for, Crown Blue Lines. There is a lock in the center of town and the port is in two sections, separated by the lock. In the section below the lock a long quay with full facilities was reserved for barges and yachts, the very large hire-boat base was above the lock. When we arrived, there were half a dozen barges and at least as many yachts, and one lone hire-boat, along the quay in the lower port. The flags of France, Belgium, Sweden, Germany, The U.K., Canada and, with our arrival, the United States, flew aboard the vessels along the quay. The quay was lined with plane trees and, in the hottest part of the afternoon they offered some relief. There were stone benches and tables in the shade under the trees and they were the coolest place around and the best place to sit and enjoy the view. It was too hot to cook on board so we ate both lunch and dinner at a small, and at best indifferent, restaurant by the port.

We spent the next day in Fontenoy, walking to the open air market in the first marginally cooler hours of the morning and then trying to do a little boat painting; but it was much too hot, so most of the day passed just sitting in the shade reading and conversing with some of the other barge people—most of whom were doing the same thing. In the early evening we took a hot bicycle ride around the town and spent an hour at the cleaned up and stabilized, although not restored, chateau. Large sections of what must have been an impressive and heavily fortified chateau had been pounded almost to rubble in a prolonged siege during the thirty years war.

That night we decided to turn around and start back to St. Jean de Losne.

From Fontenoy to Epinal was only thirty-three kilometers, but there were forty-nine locks in that short stretch and we just did not want to compete with the hire-boats through that many locks in the heat. From Epinal, if we carried on to Nancy, we would have a lot of kilometers and locks between us and St. Jean de Losne and there were, possibly apocryphal, rumors that the heat wave and drought were causing a shortage of water and that some of the canals might be closed, or be put on restricted operating schedules. We might find ourselves looking for somewhere in northern France to lay-up *Nova Cura* for the winter. In addition we were having a problem with our twelve-volt house batteries. *Nova Cura* had two electrical systems—barge and house. The barge system was twenty-four volt; the engine starter, engine instruments and running lights were on the barge system and it was fine, H_2O had installed new batteries in 2001. The water pump, bilge pumps, cabin lights, fans, twelve-volt electrical outlets (vital for the fans) and the refrigerator, when it was not on shore-power, were on the twelve-volt house system. During our second evening in Fontenoy, a minute in the engine room with the volt meter revealed a dead house battery. The house batteries were a pair of large, old (they were on the barge when we bought it), 8-D lead-acid batteries. I took the dead battery off-line, disconnected it, but left it where it was. I could barely move it, couldn't lift it out of the battery box, let alone up and out of the engine room. The remaining battery could not support our refrigerator for forty-eight hours. To keep anything cold (hot beer?), we would have to plug in to shore-power at night, which we could do back-tracking to St. Jean de Losne. St. Jean would also be a good place to deal with a pair of new jumbo sized batteries.

The canal by the port was wide and Wednesday morning we flipped *Nova Cura* end for end and started down the canal to Corre. The trip was slow; the heat was causing the automated locks to malfunction. To keep the locks working, the VNF was using a traveling lockkeeper system and was basically operating the locks manually. On the way up we had gotten to Corre on Sunday, change-over day for the hire-boats. Most of the charters were for one week and ran weekend to weekend, leave on Sunday and return on Saturday, so on the weekends the hire-boat bases were crowded. On a Wednesday, mid-week, there was room for us and *Nova Cura* wasn't even the only barge. A nice twenty-four meter Dutch barge named *Peke*, based in Belgium and owned by an English couple, David and Penny Warren, was already on the quay. We had encountered *Peke* on several occasions and seeing David and Penny again was nice. I plugged in the shore-power, to keep the refrigerator and all three fans running. It was again too hot to cook, so dinner was part of a baguette, some cheese and a small salad, eaten on deck after sunset—it was still over one hundred degrees in the cabin. Late that night CNN Europe reported that the temperature in London had set a new, all-time record high. When we finally went to bed, near midnight, I noticed that the family on the hire-boat in front of us was sleeping out on deck.

It did not cool off overnight and both of us were up early, tired and already hot, so we moved down the river to Baulay, where there was room on the quay for us. The cruising guide stated that Baulay "had all the basic shopping facilities", but it didn't. There was nothing left in the town, not even a boulangerie. Across the river, the equally tiny town of Fouché- court had a larger halte nautique, with better facilities and a small cafe, and we walked over there for lunch. The halte and the cafe were owned by a German couple who lived on a Luxemotor moored to the canal bank: lunch was good German food and good German beer. After lunch, in spite of the heat, we should have moved on down the river. We didn't, but we should have. Baulay, and therefore the town quay, was on the left bank, on the east side of the river, and in the afternoon *Nova Cura* lay broadside to and fully in the sun. The halte across the river at Fouchécourt, on the west side, was shaded by some large trees and looked cool, or at least cooler. It was also full of boats, no room for us. In the late afternoon the temperature in our main cabin reached one hundred and ten degrees. Betty's antique iron barge was one hot sardine can.

There was no electricity on the quay at Baulay. In the morning the refrigerator had cut off and the fans were run- ning slow, the remaining house battery was not doing well. We moved on down to Port sur Saone and plugged in. I hoped that our battery would recover. From Port sur Saone, a long hot day with too many hire-boats on the river and clogging the locks brought us to Gray. The only place we could find to tie up had no facilities, no electricity. Again in the morning, the refrigerator had stopped and the fans were barely turning, the poor old battery could not hold a charge. Another long hot day brought us back to Auxonne, where we could plug in, save the contents of the refrigerator and run our fans at high speed. In the evening the cabin temperature was again well over one hundred degrees and dinner was again eaten out. On CNN Europe's late night news there was a story about a number of the nuclear power plants in France being forced to cut their power output, which was causing brownouts and rotating power outages. France gets a large percentage of its electrical power from nuclear plants and the river water used to cool some of them was too warm and in other cases, because of the low water levels, the rivers could not provide enough cooling water; the plants were running hot and had to cut their output.

Monday, August eleventh, before leaving Auxonne I called H_2O and asked where to Park *Nova Cura*—there would be a place for us on A pontoon, with the other small barges and boats that were for sale. When Betty and I were looking at barges, they had been scattered all over the marina, since then H_2O had consolidated most of the small barges and boats that were for sale on A pontoon. When we arrived the one open slot on A pontoon was an easy, straight in spot. As soon as the barge was secure we walked up to the chandlery for the check-in formalities, and bought two new batteries (to be installed by H_2O). On the bulletin board by the chandlery there were a number of interesting notices posted, the rumors of canal restrictions and closings that we had heard in Fontenoy le Chateau had not been apocryphal after all. All or parts of several canals were on a restricted operating schedule and a few would be closing early. It was a beastly hot day, too hot to stay on the barge, so lunch was at the usual place, L'Amiral. The proprietor had covered most of the terrace with a tent, for shade, and had set up several large fans. The fans helped a little, but not much. August 11, 2001, in Montbard, seemed like an impossible dream, the temperature had been fifty-two degrees. That evening I received an e-mail from Dion at the yacht brokerage in Herrington Harbour North; there was a good purchase offer on the bubble boat. Here we go, all over again.

Betty's sister Kerry and her companion Berry were due to arrive in St. Jean de Losne on the first of September, to spend a week on the barge with us. From our return to H$_2$O through to Kerry and Berry's arrival, *Nova Cura* sat on A pontoon, a For Sale sign hanging on her nose. In the mornings, before the heat became intolerable, we, mostly Betty, would do a little cosmetic painting or other boat work, mostly just trying to keep the old barge, clean and shiny so it would catch the eye of any possible buyers. Until late August the heat, if anything got worse and except for a few widely scattered thunderstorms, there was no rain. An article in the Herald Tribune reported that an estimated three thousand (mostly elderly or poor) people had died of heat related causes in Paris alone. Around St. Jean de Losne the apples were falling from the trees, small green and withered, and the sunflower, corn, summer wheat and soy bean crops had largely failed and were being plowed under, the tractors and gang plows raising huge clouds of brown dust. In the wine areas the grapes were ripening too early and had too much sugar, the reverse of the normal problem in France. The dollar continued to fluctuate around $1.10-$1.12 to the euro and the news reports indicated that tourism was way down. A pair of hotel barges came into St. Jean de Losne and were laid-up, the crews sent home. There were also few people looking at barges and no one was buying. *Colvert*, a nice barge on A pontoon near *Nova Cura* had been on the market for over a year, the asking price dropping: €140,000 €120,000 €95,000.

A week before Kerry and Berry were to arrive, I received an e-mail from the yacht brokerage advising me that the bubble boat would be surveyed and sea-trialed on September tenth. Convinced, without cause or anything approaching a rational reason, that the bubble boat was going to sell and that for some mystical reason my presence was essential, I changed my return flight to the U.S. from October first to September seventh. I wanted to be there to sign the papers and get our stuff off that boat.

The night of August twenty-sixth we had lightning and thunder to the west. There was no rain but by morning the sky was overcast and there was a light westerly breeze, and that afternoon and evening the heat wave broke. It didn't just break; it ended, almost as though someone at France Meteo (the Meteorological Office) had flipped the rain switch. From aperitif time to after midnight we had one thunderstorm after another, and by sunrise there was intermittent rain and a westerly breeze cool enough that blue jeans, socks and a light jacket felt good. Everyone was smiling: the people on the streets, the proprietor of the presse, and the ladies in the boulangerie.

Saturday the thirtieth was overcast and cool, with a few scattered showers. For no particular reason Betty decided it was a good day for a train ride out to Beaune. We re-visited the Hotel Dieu, had a memorable lunch, and paid a repeat visit to the wine museum. The high point of the day was lunch. The entrance to the wine museum is off Rue Paradis, a narrow, medieval, cobblestone street in the oldest part of the old city. Down from the wine museum, around a bend the already narrow street becomes little more than an alley. There, in an ancient stone building on the narrowest part is the Restaurant Le P'Tit Paradis (one couvert in the Red Book). Le P'Tit Paradis was...perfection—tiny, just twenty-two seats, a staff of three (a chef, a helper, and an elegantly dressed lady who took care of everything else), the days menu hand written on a blackboard by the door, the wine list short, every entry a top quality Burgundy. As we entered, a rain shower started.

It was early for lunch and there were only two other couples, well spaced in the restaurant, we were seated at the window table. Sitting by that window enjoying the day's superb offerings from a gifted chef, drinking a bottle of wine far better than the stuff that normally graced our table, while watching and listening to the rain on the old gray stones of that medieval alley was unforgettable. Some of the small panes in the leaded window appeared new, but most were, perhaps, centuries old poured glass of uneven thickness, with small bubbles, ripples and distortions that even on a gray and rainy day split the light coming through into pastel segments of the rainbow. My always overactive imagination conjured up the ghosts of armored Burgundian Knights on horseback and peasants in wool hats, short cloaks and wooden sabots. It was the last great and memorable meal that Betty and I enjoyed, by ourselves, in France. Walking back to the train station in the late afternoon, we stopped at one of the better wine merchants and bought a half dozen bottles of very good wine, but not as good as the wine we had enjoyed at Le P'Tit Paradis—a welcome to *Nova Cura* for Kerry and Berry.

September first, Monday, Betty and I rode our bikes out to the train station four times, meeting every train until; at last, the right one arrived. Returning to the barge, Betty showed Kerry and Berry their cabin, the aft cabin, while I opened one of the fine wines we had lugged back from Beaune. Then we let them get settled and enjoy a glass or two, before taking them to dinner at L'Amiral—followed by a long evening walk through town. The next morning, we backed *Nova Cura* out of her spot on A pontoon, went to the fuel barge for another two hundred liters of diesel and started up the Burgundy canal to Dijon. The week passed quickly: a day and a half driving up the canal to Dijon, another day and a half of sightseeing in

Dijon, a dinner at the place we seemed to take all our guests to—Le Gril Laure, not the greatest restaurant in Dijon, but near the port, in an old and picturesque part of the city, with food that was consistently good, and a great atmosphere. Friday morning we started back down the canal and spent the night moored to the canal bank near Brazey en Plaine. Saturday *Nova Cura* was back in her spot on A pontoon—For Sale sign in place—in time for a good lunch. That night our guests took us to dinner at the Auberge de la Marine, we stayed too late and had way too much wine. Sunday morning Kerry and Berry left for the south of France, and Betty and I spent the rest of the day cleaning up and getting me ready to leave.

All through the week that our guests were aboard the weather had been nearly perfect: partly sunny, cool but not cold, and no rain. Monday, September eighth, at 5:30 a.m., in a cold driving rain we, and enough luggage to overload a large, healthy donkey, were waiting under the balcony at H_2O for St. Jean de Losne's taxi to come and take me and that heap of stuff to the train station in Dijon. It was appropriate weather for the occasion. This season was drawing to a premature and unsatisfying close and our adventure in France with Betty's antique Dutch canal barge was winding down.

Epilogue

I took the early TGV from Dijon direct to Roissy-Charles de Gaulle and a U.S. Air flight to Philadelphia, where I spent the night with my sister and left most of that heap of luggage. I brought back a lot of stuff that we wanted to keep, that we did not want on the barge if it sold over the winter: my annual journals (the source for most of this book), our charts and books, a few things that we had purchased in France, and some clothing. From Philadelphia I took the train to the Baltimore-Washington airport, rented a car for a week and drove to Herrington Harbour North—to be present for the trawler's survey and sea-trial, sign the sale papers and pack our belongings and the equipment that would not transfer with the boat. Betty planned to stay in St. Jean de Losne, living aboard *Nova Cura*, until our originally scheduled October first return date. She would keep the old barge in as close to pristine condition as possible and talk to any prospective buyers that seemed interested.

The afternoon before the bubble boat was to be surveyed; I got to the boatyard, moved aboard, gave it a bath and started getting it ready for the big day. Wednesday, September tenth, I got up very early and listened to the marine weather while I ate breakfast. It was the usual late summer/early fall stuff: a tropical depression in the Gulf of Mexico and a hurricane named "Isabel" way out in the Atlantic. After breakfast I gave the boat a serious scrubbing. Then I moved most of my tools, the charts and books, our foul weather gear, and some other loose items, to the trunk of the car or to the brokerage office, getting as much stuff as possible off the boat so that it would not be in the way during the survey. Late in the morning the couple who had made the offer and their surveyor arrived, the boat was picked up and moved to the launch area and the out-of-the-water part of the survey began. I sat on a block of wood under a near-by boat and waited, in case anyone had any questions. There were no questions and, after a break for lunch, the boat was launched and sea trialed. Conditions on the Chesapeake Bay were ideal for sea-trialing that little cork of a boat—flat calm, not a ripple, not a breath of wind, just perfect. I was on board for the sea-trial and thought it went as well as could be expected. After a very pleasant hour and a half long boat ride, we returned to the dock and, leaving me to tie-up, hose off and tidy up, the buyers, their surveyor and Dion (the brokerage sales agent) got off, held a brief confer-ence, too far away for me to eves-drop, and went their separate ways.

Late that afternoon, over a beer in the brokerage office, Dion said he felt that things had gone well, that the bubble boat was a sold boat. I wasn't so sure. As the buyers and their surveyor were leaving, the male half of the couple was smiling and talking animatedly with the surveyor while his wife, or girl friend, marched along staring straight ahead with a stony expression, tight-lipped and saying nothing. I bet Dion a case of good beer that they would turn down the boat. Three days later, I won my bet. It was a him and her thing, he loved the boat and was all for buying it, she didn't and wasn't, half the money was his, half hers—no sale. I should have saved myself a lot of money and effort and stayed in France...let the boat brokerage handle everything, that's why they get a commis-sion. That evening Betty sent me an e-mail and said she had moved her return flight up ten days, she had an early flight on September twenty-first, direct to Baltimore—she was tired of France and would be barge buyers. *Nova Cura* would remain on A pontoon, with the barges that were for sale, and H_2O would winterize her.

The morning of Monday, September fifteenth, two days after the sale officially fell through, I moved the boat to a slip on G dock, home until Betty got back and we again went south for the winter. In the afternoon I returned the rental car. That evenings marine weather up-date had hurricane Isabel coming ashore somewhere on the southeast coast. Wednesday morning's forecast put the impact point south of Cape Hatteras and said landfall would be Thursday afternoon. I spent that day and Thursday preparing the little trawler for possible hurricane conditions. Thursday night Isabel moved up the Chesapeake Bay as a strong category one hurricane. By sunrise Friday, Isabel had past. Trees and power lines were down, the water was still four feet above the docks and there was a lot of damage along the shores of the Chesapeake Bay. At Herrington Harbour North alone, more than fifty boats were destroyed and many more damaged. The little trawler survived with minimal, easily repaired, cosmetic damage.

September twenty-first Mac and Nancy came down to Herrington Harbour North, picked me up and we went to the Baltimore-Washington airport to meet Betty. Three weeks later, repairs made, Betty and I set out yet again on the long trek down the Intracoastal Waterway to Miami and the Florida Keys—still the owners of a canal barge in France and that trawler. Moving on to the next adventure was proving difficult.

BETTY'S BARGE

The little blue trawler sold on March 13, 2004.

Betty signed a sales contract for *Nova Cura* on May 7, 2004.
The sale fell through when the buyers, who were
French, realized how difficult, and expensive, it
would be to register the barge in France.

Betty's Barge finally sold on September 8, 2004.
The buyers were British and the barge went
back on to the Small Ships Register.

In early 2010 we learned, via an e-mail from Catherine
Rault at H_2O, that *Nova Cura* had left St. Jean de Losne,
cruised down the Saone and the Rhone to the Canal du Midi
and Bordeaux, and from there, by sea, to Rennes on the
south coast of Brittany. It was nice to know that
Betty's Barge is still chugging around.

Addendum

Author's Note

Betty owned her barge for three and a half years and I kept detailed journals with an entry for every day that we were aboard or working on the barge. The entries included: kilometers travelled, locks transited, weather notations, activities, expenditures, maintenance, restoration work, notes on the people and boats/barges met and sometimes extensive notes on the towns and places visited. In addition the journals became, to some extent, scrap books. Taped or pasted in, or just stuck between the pages or inside the covers are: museum and tourist site tickets, train and bus ticket stubs, wine and beer labels (sometimes annotated for date, place and quality), business cards, a few restaurant menus, and a wide variety of other stuff. Both of us sent a lot of e-mail home to our friends and families and my sister, Jane Hutchinson, printed and saved, chronologically in a loose leaf binder, every e-mail we sent to, or copied, her on—she must have thought I would eventually want to write a book or something. My journals and that thick binder of e-mails, supplemented by my memory, are the basis for more than ninety-eight percent of the material in this book. The remainder comes from our canal cruising charts, a stack of tourist office brochures and handouts, and a few other (credited) sources. Anytime memory is involved error is possible and my memory is not perfect. I am sure that canal cruisers with more experience than we have who may read this book, will find some errors and omissions, hopefully minor.

Measurements

In a book focused on and set in France that is written primarily for an American audience, the problem of metric vs. American standard measurements comes up. In general, when writing about *Nova Cura* and the French canals I have used metric measurements and in the short sections of the book that deal with events in the United States, I have used American standard measurements.

Basic Metric Measurements:

1 kilometer = 1,000 meters = 0.62 of a statute mile

1 statute mile = 1.609 kilometers

1 meter = 39.37 inches

1 centimeter = 0.01 of a meter = 0.3937 of an inch

1 liter = 1.06 liquid quarts (4 quarts = 1 U.S. Gallon)

1 kilogram = 1,000 grams = 2.2 pounds

Metric Prefixes:

kilo = 1000, hecto = 100 and deca = 10

for example: 1 hectoliter = 100 liters

deci = 0.1, centi = 0.01 and milli = 0.001

For example: 1 deciliter is 0.1 liter or one tenth part of a liter and 1 centimeter is 0.01 meters or one one-hundredth part of a meter

Knots and the Nautical Mile:

A knot is a measure of speed equal to one nautical mile per hour. Speed through the water and wind speed are generally given in knots per hour. An International nautical mile = 1,852 meters = 1.15 statute miles = 6,076.115 feet. A vessel moving through the water at 7 knots is traveling at 12.95 kilometers per hour or 8.05 statute miles per hour.

Suggested Reading

This is not a comprehensive reading list on or about the French canals—it is just a list of some of the books and guides that we read, enjoyed and learned from.

The Canals of France, Michel-Paul Simon, 1997, Editions du Chene, ISBN: 84277.071.4. The book is primarily lovely photos of the French canals.

Code Vagnon Fluvial; Rivieres et Lacs, Henri Vagnon, Les Editions du Plaisancier, ISBN: 2-85725-274-9. The rules, regulations and requirements for inland boating in France, heavily illustrated and frequently up-dated; when we went through a check lock in 2002, having a copy of this volume met the VNF's requirement that barges have a copy of the Inland Rules of Navigation on board.

A Culinary Journey in Gascony, Recipes and Stories from my French Canal Boat, Kate Ratliffe, 1995, Ten Speed Press, ISBN: 0-89815-753-6

Cruising French Waterways, Hugh McKnight, 1999 (3rd Edition), Sheridan House Inc., ISBN: 1-57409-087-9. In places a bit dated, but still The Essential Guide to the inland waterways of France.

The English Channel, Nigel Calder, 1986, Penguin Books, ISBN: 0-1401-0131-4

The European Waterways, a Manual for First Time Users, Marian Martin, 1997, Adlard Coles Nautical, ISBN: 0-7136-4356-0. A clear, clean, complete and well written book.

Profession? Marinier, Annie Lorenzo, Editions Ch. Massin, ISBN: 2-7072-0103-0. An annotated photo book about the life of commercial mariners on the canals and rivers of France, the text is French. The photos are superb.

The Secret Life of The Seine, Mort Rosenblum, 1994, Da Capo Press, ISBN: 0-306-81074-3

Through Europe at Four Knots, Les Horn, 2000, International Marine/McGraw-Hill, ISBN: 0-07-136137-5

Watersteps Through France, to the Camargue by Canal, Bill and Laurel Cooper, 1996 (2nd Edition), Adlard Coles Nautical, ISBN: 0-7136-4391-9

Watersteps Round Europe, From Greece to England by Barge, Bill and Laurel Cooper, 1996, Sheridan House, ISBN: 1-57409-016-X

In addition, numerous books, brochures, guides, DVDs and Videos, often frequently up-dated, are available from The Dutch Barge Association (DBA), and from Tam and Di Murrell.

Made in the USA
Monee, IL
15 September 2020